CHICKEN SOUP FOR THE MOTHER'S SOUL

101 Stories to Open the Hearts and Rekindle the Spirits of Mothers

Jack Canfield
Mark Victor Hansen
Jennifer Read Hawthorne
Marci Shimoff

Health Communications, Inc.
Deerfield Beach, Florida

www.hci-online.com

We would like to acknowledge the many publishers and individuals who granted us permission to reprint the cited material. (Note: The stories that were penned anonymously, that are in the public domain, or, that were written by Jack Canfield, Mark Victor Hansen, Jennifer Read Hawthorne and Marci Shimoff are not included in this listing.)

After an exhaustive search, we were unable to find the authors or copyright holders of the following stories that we have included in the book:

To My Children

Joy to the World, by W. Shirley Nunes

The Day We Flew Kites, by Frances Fowler

How Santa Knew, by Fay Porter

What's a Grandmother?

If you are, or if you know, the authors or copyright holders, please contact us and we will properly credit you and reimburse you for your contribution.

(Continued on page 349)

Library of Congress Cataloging-in-Publication Data

Chicken soup for the mother's soul: 101 stories to open the hearts and rekindle the spirits of mothers/Jack Canfield . . . [et al.].

p. cm.

ISBN 1-55874-504-1 (hardcover)—ISBN 1-55874-460-6 (trade paperback)

1. Mothers—Literary collections. I. Canfield, Jack, date.

PN6071.M7C48 1997 97-17783

810.8'03520431—dc21 CIP

ISBN 1-55874-460-6 (trade paper)—ISBN 1-55874504-1 (hardcover)

Publisher: Health Communications, Inc.
3201 S.W. 15th Street
Deerfield Beach, FL 33442-8190

Cover re-design by Andrea Perrine Brower
Cover photo by George and Felicity Foster, Foster & Foster, Inc.

What People Are Saying About *Chicken Soup for the Mother's Soul*...

"As 'The Mommies' we know that the biggest gift you can receive is to know that you're not alone! *Chicken Soup for the Mother's Soul* does just that by touching you at the core and bringing you tenderly back to the true meaning and reverence of motherhood."

Marilyn Kentz and Caryl Kristensen
"The Mommies"

"It's a warm, touching book that will make you laugh and cry as we celebrate being women together."

Kim Alexis
model/spokesperson

"Thank you, *Chicken Soup for the Mother's Soul,* for the stories that express the exquisite beauty of the love between mother and child. Your perspective reminds us of what is really important in life."

Susan N. Hickenlooper
national executive director, *American Mothers, Inc.*
official sponsor, *Mother's Day* and *Mother of the Year®*

"Sitting down to read *Chicken Soup for the Mother's Soul* is a treat! The stories are powerful, heartwarming and full of life. Every story speaks to me of the depth and power of the love between mother and child."

Alison Schwandt
planner, *Gymboree*

"*Chicken Soup for the Mother's Soul* will make you laugh, cry and warm your heart like no other book because it is about the most precious of relationships . . . that between mother and child."

Anne Jordan
president, *Children & Families, Inc.*

"No matter what I do in life, my most important accomplishment will be mothering my two daughters and two sons. Each time I read the stories in *Chicken Soup for the Mother's Soul* I laugh and cry and snuggle up to warm, wonderful motherly memories that fill my heart until it's nearly bursting."

Patricia Lorenz
inspirational writer, speaker
author of *Stuff That Matters for Single Parents,*
and *Parents, 365 Down-to-Earth Daily Devotions*

"*Chicken Soup for the Mother's Soul* is a moving reminder of the joys and sacrifices of motherhood, as well as the tremendous blessings that loving mothers everywhere bestow upon our world."

Reverend Melissa Bowers

"The tender, deep attunement between mother and child that starts before birth and continues throughout life is beautifully expressed in the stories of *Chicken Soup for the Mother's Soul.*"

Dr. Melanie Brown
president and founder, *My Baby U., Inc.*

"Grandmothers, too, will find *Chicken Soup for the Mother's Soul* a true celebration of their lifelong role. Here is inspiration for all who are mothers or who have ever had one."

Dr. Lillian Carson
author, *The Essential Grandparent:*
A Guide to Making a Difference

"*Chicken Soup for the Mother's Soul* is an affirmation of the most precious and powerful force on earth—the love between a mother and her children. These tender stories tickle the heart and warm the soul like only a mother can."

Karan Ihrer
certified childbirth educator

A Tribute to Mothers

Your gentle guidance has immeasurably influenced all that I have done, all that I do, and all that I will ever do.
Your sweet spirit is indelibly imprinted on all that I have been, all that I am, and all that I will ever be.
Thus, you are a part of all that I accomplish and all that I become.

And so it is that when I help my neighbor, your helping hand is there also.
When I ease the pain of a friend, she owes a debt to you.
When I show a child a better way, either by word or by example,
You are the teacher once removed.

Because everything I do reflects values learned from you,
any wrong that I right, any heart I may brighten,
any gift that I share, or burden I may lighten,
is in its own small way a tribute to you.

Because you gave me life, and more importantly, lessons in how to live, you are the wellspring from which flows all good I may
achieve in my time on earth.

For all that you are and all that I am, thank you, Mom.

David L. Weatherford

With love we dedicate this book to
our mothers, Ellen Taylor, Una Hansen, Maureen Read
and Louise Shimoff, whose love and guidance
have been the foundation for our lives.

We also dedicate this book to all mothers everywhere,
whose loving hands and hearts have touched,
healed and nurtured us all.

Reprinted by permission of Dave Carpenter.

Contents

3. A MOTHER'S COURAGE

4. ON MOTHERHOOD

5. BECOMING A MOTHER

6. SPECIAL MOMENTS

7. MIRACLES

Acknowledgments

Chicken Soup for the Mother's Soul has taken more than a year to write, compile and edit. It has been a true labor of love for all of us. One of the greatest joys of creating this book was working with people who gave this project not just their time and attention, but their hearts and souls as well. We would like to thank the following people for their dedication and contributions, without which this book could not have been created:

Our families, who have given us love and support throughout this project, and who have been chicken soup for *our* souls!

Georgia Noble, for her love, her graciousness, and for being a great example of Mother to all of us.

Christopher Noble Canfield, for sharing his innocence, his art, his singing, his acting, his great hugs and his irrepressible love for life with us.

Patty Hansen for being the most supportive, loving, life-enhancing marital and business partner in the world, as well as an extraordinary mother.

Elisabeth Day Hansen for her wisdom, love, joy and zest for life and learning.

Melanie Dawn Hansen for her radiant countenance, irrepressible spirit, exuberance and bliss in being fully alive and present-time available.

Dan Hawthorne, whose commitment to truth uplifts us and keeps us on track. Thank you for your ever-present sense of humor, and for reminding us of what's important in life.

Amy and William Hawthorne, for their infinite patience and for being "like, really cool kids."

Maureen H. Read, for being the embodiment of the unconditional love of mothers.

Louise and Marcus Shimoff, for their eternal support and love—and for being two of the best parents on earth.

Jeanette Lisefski, who is the epitome of motherhood. She is not only an extraordinary wife and mother of three children, but also an invaluable support in our lives. She has blessed us and this project with her dedication, steadfastness, creativity and love. We thank you for always being there—we couldn't have done it without you.

Elinor Hall, who did an extraordinary job in helping us read and research stories for *Chicken Soup for the Mother's Soul.* We deeply appreciate your support, your love and your friendship.

Carol Kline, for her wonderful contributions in researching, writing and editing stories for this book. We are grateful for the excellence you brought to this project, and for your loyal friendship.

Amsheva Miller, for her clarity, her light and her loving attention to this project and to us. We are so grateful for your care and guidance.

Peter Vegso and Gary Seidler at Health Communications, Inc., for recognizing the value of this book from the beginning, and for getting it into the hands of millions of readers. Thank you, Peter and Gary!

Patty Aubery, who was always there when we needed guidance and advice on anything from story leads to how to get the computer to work, as well as for keeping the whole *Chicken Soup for the Soul* central office up and running in the middle of what always feels like a tornado of activity. Thank you, Patty, from the bottom of our hearts.

Nancy Mitchell, for her invaluable feedback as well as the outstanding job she always does in getting permissions for all of the stories, poems and cartoons—especially the hard-to-track-down ones. Thanks, Nancy, for hanging in there!

Heather McNamara, senior editor of the *Chicken Soup for the Soul* series, for coordinating all of the readers' evaluations, for her Internet research, and for her impeccable and insightful editing and masterful preparation of the final manuscript. You are definitely a pro and a joy to work with!

Kimberly Kirberger, managing editor of the *Chicken Soup for the Soul* series, for her important feedback, for submitting stories and cartoons, and for taking care of things so that we could concentrate all of our efforts on completing this book. We also thank you for your emotional support.

Veronica Romero and Leslie Forbes, for helping to ensure that Jack's office ran smoothly during the production of this book.

Rosalie Miller, who kept all of the communication flowing efficiently throughout this project. Your smiling face and never-ending encouragement have lightened our hearts.

Teresa Esparza, who brilliantly coordinated all of Jack's travel, and speaking, radio and television appearances during this time.

Christine Belleris, Matthew Diener and Allison Janse, our editors at Health Communications, Inc., for their generous efforts in bringing this book to its high state of excellence.

Randee Goldsmith, *Chicken Soup for the Soul* manager at Health Communications, Inc., for her masterful coordination and support of all the *Chicken Soup* projects.

Terry Burke, Kelly Johnson Maragni, Karen Baliff Ornstein, Kim Weiss and Ronni O'Brien at Health Communications, Inc., for their incredible publicity and marketing efforts.

Andrea Perrine Brower at Health Communications, Inc., for working with us so patiently and cooperatively on the cover design of this book.

Arielle Ford, Peg Clark, Laura Booth and everyone at The Ford Group for an outstanding public relations job, setting up national book signings and radio, television and print interviews.

Sharon Linnéa and Eileen Lawrence, for their marvelous job of editing numerous stories. Your editor's touch captured the essence of *Chicken Soup.*

We also want to thank the following people who completed the monumental task of reading the preliminary manuscript of the book, helped us make the final selections, and made invaluable comments on how to improve the book: Patty Aubery, Diana Chapman, Linda DeGraaff, Teresa Esparza, Leslie Forbes, Kelly Foreman, Mary Gagnon, Randee Goldsmith, Elinor Hall, Ciel Halperin, Jean Hammond, Melba Hawthorne, Kimberly Kirberger, Carol Kline, Robin Kotok, Nancy Leahy, Laverne Lingler, Jeanette Lisefski, Barbara McLoughlin, Heather McNamara, Barbara McQuaid, Rosalie Miller, Nancy Mitchell, Holly Moore, Sue Penberthy, Maureen H. Read, Wendy Read, Carol Richter, Loren Rose, Heather Sanders, Marcus and Louise Shimoff, Karen Spilchuk and Carolyn Strickland.

Diana Chapman, Patricia Lorenz and Jean Brody, for their enthusiastic support of this book.

Joanne Cox, for an outstanding job typing and preparing our initial manuscripts. Thank you for your great attention to detail and your loyalty to this project.

Fairfield Printing (Fairfield, Iowa), especially Stephanie

Harward, for their enthusiastic support of the book and their willingness to put *Chicken Soup for the Mother's Soul* ahead of almost any other printing project and at any time.

Felicity and George Foster, for their artistic input and invaluable ideas on cover design.

Jerry Teplitz, for his inventive approach to testing manuscript and cover design.

Clay Aloysius White, who nourished our bodies and our souls with his exquisite food in the final weeks of the project.

Terry Johnson, Bill Levacy and Blaine Watson, for their astute guidance on aspects of this project.

M., for the gifts of wisdom and knowledge.

The following people, who supported and encouraged us during this project: Ron Hall, Rusty Hoffman, Belinda Hoole, Pamela Kaye, Robert Kenyon, Sue Penberthy and Lynn Robertson.

We also wish to acknowledge the hundreds of people who sent us stories, poems and quotes for possible inclusion in *Chicken Soup for the Mother's Soul.* While we were not able to use everything you sent in, we were deeply touched by your heartfelt intention to share yourselves and your stories with us and our readers. Thank you!

Because of the size of this project, we may have left out the names of some people who helped us along the way. If so, we are sorry—please know that we really do appreciate all of you very deeply.

We are truly grateful for the many hands and hearts that have made this book possible. We love you all!

Introduction

This book is our gift to you, the mothers of the world. In writing this book, we wanted to honor mothers everywhere, but how can you thank a mother for the gift of life? As we read the thousands of stories that we considered for *Chicken Soup for the Mother's Soul,* we were deeply moved by the depth of feeling people expressed for their mothers.

Many people talked about the sacrifices their mothers had made; others, how courageous their mothers were. Still others shared the inspiration and encouragement they had received from their mothers. But no theme was more widely expressed than that of the eternal nature of a mother's love.

One piece we came across beautifully captures the essence of this theme:

> One calm, bright, sweet, sunshiny day, an angel stole out of heaven and came down to this old world, and roamed field and forest, city and hamlet. Just as the sun went down he spread his wings and said: "Now my visit is out, and I must go back to the world of light. But before I go, I must gather some mementos of my visit here."
>
> He looked into a beautiful flower garden and said, "How lovely and fragrant these flowers are." He plucked

the rarest roses and made a bouquet and said, "I see nothing more beautiful and fragrant than these; I will take them with me."

But he looked a little further and saw a bright-eyed, rosy-cheeked baby, smiling into its mother's face. And he said, "Oh, that baby's smile is prettier than this bouquet; I will take that, too."

Then he looked just beyond the cradle and there was a mother's love pouring out like the gush of a river toward the cradle and the baby. And he said, "Oh, that mother's love is the prettiest thing I have seen on earth; I will carry that, too."

With the three treasures he winged his way to the pearly gates, and lit just on the outside and said, "Before I go in, I will examine my mementos." And he looked at the flowers and they had withered. He looked at the baby's smile and it had faded. He looked at the mother's love and there it was, in all its pristine beauty.

He threw aside the withered flowers and faded smile, and winged his way through the gates and led all the hosts of heaven together and said, "Here is the only thing I found on earth that would keep its beauty all the way to heaven—it is a mother's love."

So with love in our hearts, we offer you *Chicken Soup for the Mother's Soul.* May you experience the miracles of love, joy and inspiration when you read this book. May it touch your heart and move your spirit.

Jack Canfield, Mark Victor Hansen,
Jennifer Read Hawthorne and Marci Shimoff

1

ON LOVE

Love is a fruit in season at all times, and within reach of every hand.

Mother Teresa

THE FAMILY CIRCUS® By Bil Keane

"I must have TWO hearts, Mommy, 'cause I love you so much."

Reprinted with special permission of King Feature Syndicate.

The Choice

Forgiveness is the final form of love.

Reinhold Niebuhr

I slid impatiently into the small car next to my fiancé, Greg. Mama was standing on the sidewalk outside the Brooklyn apartment where she'd raised me, smiling hopefully.

"Good-bye, Mama," I said offhandedly. When she leaned toward my rolled-down car window to kiss me good-bye, I moved my cheek slightly away—I didn't want her to kiss me.

I'd hoped Greg couldn't see how hurt Mama looked, but his light-blue eyes were glancing curiously at me as we drove away. I sat beside him silently, my back rigid against the vinyl seat, my own dark eyes fixed stubbornly on the shadows that flickered across the windshield.

"Linda," Greg finally said, "I know it was all my idea to meet your mother . . . "

I stared stonily ahead.

"And I'm glad I did. She seems very nice."

I still gave no response.

He sighed. "Well, frankly, I've never seen you act this way. You were so cold. I don't know what's gone on between you and your mother, but I do know that there must be a reason for the tension I just saw."

A reason! How dare he judge me? I had years of reasons, lists of reasons! But when I turned to glare at him, I saw that his face held no judgment, only quiet concern. His hand left the steering wheel and tentatively covered mine. And slowly, I began to tell him about Mama—and Daddy . . .

In the 1950s, when I was growing up, my father was a very troubled man. While other children's fathers came back from work in a stream of gray flannel suits, my father sat on the stoop in front of our apartment building, wearing torn blue jeans and a white T-shirt. He never held a job. He'd just be sitting there, staring into space, his hands cupping a lighted cigarette.

Sometimes I would see the little girl who lived next door running to greet her father as he walked up the block with his shiny leather briefcase, and I would run into our apartment to hide my embarrassment. All my childish prayers revolved around my father: "Please, God, just let Daddy get better."

Mama's frustration grew with each unpaid bill she added to the pile on the kitchen shelf. Sunday mornings were the worst. While Daddy slept through the morning, Mama would throw a coat over her nightgown and run out to buy the *New York Times*. Then her red pen would come out. She'd sit at the white Formica table with its pattern of tiny boomerangs, furiously circling ad after ad under "Help Wanted—Men." When she had covered the newsprint with bright red circles, she'd take them to Daddy.

"Here are some jobs you could do!"

Daddy would only burrow more deeply under the old brown blanket. "I can't," he'd whisper. "Not this week."

One time Mama grabbed him by the shoulders. "We have no milk, no bread!" she pleaded.

Daddy stared at her helplessly. "Do you think I want to be like this?"

I believed he didn't. But Mama was too desperate to be sympathetic. Her lips pressed together in a thin line. The next Sunday, when she opened the *Times,* it was to "Help Wanted—Women."

But in the 1950s, it was considered a gamble to hire a woman with small children. One night, from the hushed darkness of the tiny room I shared with my sister, I heard her praying. When Mama had a problem, she wouldn't use fancy words; she'd just say it straight out to God, like she was talking to a friend who hadn't ever let her down. "I'm a hard-working woman, God," she was saying. "Please don't let us go on welfare. I'll take any job I can get, even if it's for a tiny paycheck. I'll be the best worker they ever hired."

Eventually a friend of a friend gave Mama a secretarial job—and a warning: "I'm taking a chance on you. But if you plan on taking time off for every runny nose and blister your kids get, you can plan on finding another job."

Mama never took one day off. Even when my sister and I were miserably ill with the measles, she made it in to work. When we needed special care, we were trundled off to a neighbor's. I would lie feverishly on a couch there and hear her whisper loudly into her pink telephone, "What kind of mother goes off and leaves her children?" I didn't like this neighbor, but her attitude made me wonder about my mother.

Daddy grew worse and worse. Without Mama there to care for him, he became increasingly disoriented. I'd come home to find the apartment filled with smoke from cooking pots he'd left forgotten on the stove. I'd run around flinging windows open, terrified of what Mama might do if she found out.

One day I came home and found Mama there alone.

"Where's Daddy?"

"You could have been killed," she said reproachfully. "He could have set the house on fire."

"Where's Daddy?" I demanded.

"I sent him to the city hospital."

I raced to the door, as if he would still be there, but of course he wasn't.

"He was very sick, Linda. I had no choice. I can't look after all of you." She was, I suppose, trying to comfort me, but I ran away from her, inconsolable. The next day she was back at work, and Daddy had been placed in the psychiatric unit.

When my father was released from the hospital, he didn't bother even trying to come home. His emotional problems and chronic depression made it impossible for him to face the pressures of family life. He lived alone, supporting himself with odd jobs. I blamed Mama for locking him out of our lives.

"You've got to forget the past," Mama would say when she noticed me looking particularly unhappy. But I couldn't forget. And I couldn't forgive her for sending my father away. Not a day went by when I didn't think, *If only she'd tried harder to help him . . .*

Greg had almost reached my apartment now, and my voice was hoarse. "Has your mother forgiven your father?" he asked.

"No!" I launched into a diatribe on how Mama still spoke against Daddy. "She can't forget the past. She still blames him for things he couldn't help. She can't forgive, she won't forgive—"

"Well," Greg interrupted gently, "can you?"

"Of course I can! I *have* forgiven. I know my father couldn't help the way he was. He never meant to hurt us. He—"

"I meant," Greg said patiently, "can you forgive your mother?"

For many seconds the only sound was the noise of the traffic outside the car windows. *Me? Forgive my mother?*

"You know, Linda," Greg said, breaking into my thoughts, "I've learned that times come in life when you have to make a really tough decision, a choice that is actually brutal. That's what happened to your mother. The situation got down to no food on the table, and was she going to take care of her husband or her kids? So she made that brutal choice. She had to choose between your father and you and your sister. She chose her children. She chose *you*."

I turned to look at Greg. What was he saying? *Mama chose me.* I had begun a silent review of all the hurts, but now, unexpectedly, those thoughts faded, and a different sort of memory crept into my mind.

It was a morning long ago. I was sitting on our worn green sofa, sulkily watching Mama rush around getting ready for work.

"You're never home," I said accusingly. "You're never here. You don't do anything for us like a *real* mother. Robin's mother bakes jelly cookies for her lunch box."

"Linda," she said wearily, "I go to work so you can *have* a lunch. I'm tired when I come home. I have no time for baking."

"You have no time for anything!"

"Would you rather see us go on welfare?" she asked quietly.

I wasn't sure exactly what that meant. "Yes!"

Mama grew pale. "Oh, honey, you think welfare's fun? My mama and I were on welfare once. We never had enough food, or clothes, or money for doctors. I just want you and your sister to have it a little easier. But I can't be everything. I get tired, too."

"Well, in real families," I said spitefully, "the mommy stays home."

She winced, but said lightly, "In this family I'll get fired if I'm late again," and she ran out to catch the train.

The following week I found three large homemade jelly cookies in my lunch box. But I never thanked Mama, never even mentioned that I'd seen the cookies. How many times, I wondered, had I ignored Mama's efforts to please me?

Now all the little things she'd done came flying to me. Mama staying up late to restitch my worn-out seams, Mama teaching me how to braid my long dark hair, Mama stepping in when my sister and I had an argument. As badly as I had treated her, it was still Mama who had always been there for me. Why hadn't I been able to see this before?

Right there in the car I did what I had seen Mama do so many times—I bowed my head and prayed, silently. My prayer was for forgiveness—but this time for myself. *And please, God, help me to get rid of my bitterness.*

"Greg, I know this is going to sound crazy, but—"

"You want to go back to your mother's," he finished. He was already smiling, turning the car around.

Later, sitting in Mama's familiar, cozy kitchen, I gave silent thanks. I had watched Mama move about this kitchen a thousand times, but I had always been too angry to feel the strength of her love, the steady warmth of her support.

"Mama?" I said hesitantly, not sure how to begin. "Do you think sometime you could show me your recipe for jelly cookies?"

For a moment I thought she wasn't going to answer, but then I realized she was nodding, and in a voice so low I could hardly hear, she whispered, "You remember those cookies after all these years?"

"Yes, Mama," I said, "I remember."

Linda Brown

Baby-Lift

A mother's love perceives no impossibilities.

Paddock

As my friend Carol Dey and I rode through the dusty streets of Saigon in a creaky VW bug on April 26, 1975, I was sure we looked exactly like what we were: a couple of Iowa homemakers. Three months earlier, when Carol and I had each agreed to escort three Vietnamese orphans to their American families, the trip seemed exciting but safe. My husband, Mark, and I had applied to adopt an orphan ourselves, in the future. We all wanted somehow to make a difference. How were Carol and I to know we would arrive just as Saigon was under siege?

Bombs were falling less than three miles from the city, and even now citizens streamed past our car, their worldly possessions tied onto pushcarts or onto their backs. But our driver, Cheri Clark, the overseas director of Friends of the Children of Vietnam (FCVN), seemed more excited than scared. From the moment we landed, she had pelted us with unexpected news.

"Did you hear President Ford okayed a giant baby-lift

as a last resort to save these children? Instead of taking out six orphans, you'll be taking home 200!" Carol and I looked at each other in amazement.

"We were able to get a planeload of children out yesterday," Cheri continued. "At the last minute, the Vietnamese government refused to let it go, but the plane was already cleared for takeoff—so it just left! That's 150 children safe in San Francisco!"

Even our years as nurses hadn't prepared us for what we found at the FCVN Center. Every inch of every floor of the stately French mansion was covered with blankets or mats—each of which was covered with babies—hundreds of crying, cooing infants, each orphaned or abandoned.

Although jet lag threatened to overwhelm us, Carol and I were determined to help prepare the children for the next day's airlift. Ours was scheduled to be the first airlift out. Each child needed clothes and diapers, a check-up and a legal name. The devoted volunteers—Vietnamese and American—worked around the clock.

The next morning we learned that, in retaliation for the earlier unauthorized takeoff, our agency would not be on the first flight out after all. We would be allowed to leave only when—and if—the Vietnamese government permitted.

"There's nothing we can do but wait and pray," Cheri said calmly. We all knew that time was running out for the Americans and orphans in Saigon.

In the meantime, Carol and I joined other volunteers hastily preparing children for another flight that had been cleared, this one going to Australia.

In scorching heat, we loaded babies into a VW van from which the middle seat had been removed. I sat on a bench seat with 21 infants packed around my feet; the others did likewise.

We arrived at the airport to find traffic at a standstill. An enormous black cloud billowed into the sky in front of us. As we passed through the gate, we heard a terrible rumor: The first planeload of orphans—the plane we had begged to be on—had crashed after takeoff.

It couldn't be true. We chose not to believe it. We had no time to worry as we went about the task of loading fussing, dehydrating babies onto the flight to freedom. Carol and I stood together holding hands while the plane took off. Once they were gone, we danced on the tarmac. One planeload was free!

Our joy was short-lived. We returned to find the adults at the center in stunned grief. Cheri haltingly confirmed what we'd refused to believe. Hundreds of babies and escorts had been killed when their plane blew apart after takeoff. No one knew if it had been shot down or bombed.

Relief workers and babies! Who could do such a thing? And would they do it again? Overcome, I sank onto a rattan couch and sobbed uncontrollably. The plane we fought to be on had crashed, and so had my faith. I had the terrible feeling I'd never see my husband and daughters again.

That evening, Cheri beckoned me. Even in a world of drastic surprises, I was unprepared for her words: "In the satchel of papers you brought over were your adoption papers. Instead of waiting to be assigned a son, why don't you go and choose one?"

It seemed my worst fears and deepest desires came true on the same day. Wouldn't our daughters be thrilled if I came home with their new brother! But . . . how could I choose a child? With a prayer on my lips, I entered the next room.

As I meandered through the sea of babies, a child crawled over to me wearing only a diaper. When I lifted him to me, he nestled his head into my shoulder and seemed to hug me back. I carried him around the room, looking at and touching each baby. Upstairs, the hall was carpeted with more infants. The little one in my arms seemed to cuddle closer as I whispered a prayer for the decision I was about to make. I felt his shallow breath as he embraced my neck and settled into my heart.

"Hello, Mitchell," I whispered to him. "I'm your mom."

The next day we got the thrilling news that our flight had been cleared to leave that afternoon. Together, all the volunteers packed up the 150 children still remaining.

Babies were placed three or four to a seat on an unused city bus for the first of several trips to the airport; Carol and I rode along. Again, a disaster. We arrived at the airport to find that Vietnamese President Thieu had canceled our flight. Trying not to panic, Carol and I helped unload the babies into filthy Quonset huts in the stifling heat. Would we never get out? Would we all die in the siege of Saigon?

Finally Ross, an FCVN worker, burst in. "President Thieu is allowing only one flight, and it's got to leave immediately. Let's get these babies loaded on—and you, too!" he said to Carol and me. Our chance to leave!

"No," I said. "I left my son back at the center for a later bus. I've got to go back and get him."

"LeAnn," Ross said, "you see how things are. Leave while you can. I promise we'll try to get your son out to you."

Yes, I saw how things were. "I won't leave without Mitchell!"

"Hurry, then," Ross said. "I'll hold the plane as long as I can, but we can't ruin these other children's chances."

I ran to the bus. The driver screeched recklessly through the chaotic city and delivered me a mile from the center. The strap of my sandal broke and the shoe flapped wildly against my ankle. I took it off while still running. My side ached fiercely as I raced up the stairs to the center.

"The plane . . ." I gasped as Cheri eased me into a chair.

"I know. I just got off the phone with the airport."

"And?"

Cheri grinned. "The plane will wait for you!"

I beamed a smile while gasping for breath.

"Not only that—we can take more babies for this flight—and a second flight has been approved, as well!"

Tears streaming down my face, I found Mitchell and held him close. I made a silent vow never to leave him again.

A few hours later, I felt my heart pound as I boarded a gutted cargo plane. Twenty cardboard boxes formed a row down the center, with two to three infants per box. Toddlers and older children sat belted on the long side benches, bewilderment on their faces.

The doors were closed; the engine's roar was deafening. I couldn't remove the image of the black cloud from the downed plane from my mind. A panic came over me and I gripped Mitchell closer. I prayed the Lord's Prayer as the plane taxied down the runway. Then . . . we were airborne. If we could only live through the next five minutes, I knew we'd make it home.

Finally the captain spoke. "We're out of artillery range. We're safe. We're going home!" Shouts of joy filled the plane.

As I thought of the chaos of war, I prayed for those we'd left behind. And then I uttered a prayer of thanks that Carol and I had been allowed to make a difference, in a bigger way than we'd ever dreamed. We were all headed for lives filled with new hope—including the son I hadn't known I had.

LeAnn Thieman
As told to Sharon Linnéa

A Surprise Gift for Mother

On Christmas Day, all the joys of close family relationships were seen and felt throughout our parents' home. The smells of roasted turkey, Southern-baked ham and homemade bread hung in the air. Tables and chairs were set up everywhere to accommodate toddlers, teenagers, parents and grandparents. Every room was lavishly decorated. No family member had ever missed Christmas Day with our mother and father.

Only this year, things were different. Our father had passed away November 26, and this was our first Christmas without him. Mother was doing her best to be the gracious hostess, but I could tell this was especially hard for her. I felt a catch in my throat, and again I wondered if I should give her my planned Christmas gift, or if it had become inappropriate in my father's absence.

A few months earlier I had been putting the finishing touches on portraits I had painted of each of my parents. I'd planned to give them as Christmas gifts. This would be a surprise for everyone, as I had not studied art or tried serious painting. There was an undeniable urge within that pushed me relentlessly to do this. The portraits did look like them, but I was still unsure of my painting techniques.

While painting one day, I was surprised by a doorbell ring. Quickly putting all my painting materials out of sight, I opened the door. To my astonishment, my father ambled in alone—never before having visited me without my mother. Grinning, he said, "I've missed our early morning talks. You know, the ones we had before you decided to leave me for another man!" I hadn't been married long. Also, I was the only girl and the baby of the family.

Immediately I wanted to show him the paintings, but I was reluctant to ruin his Christmas surprise. Yet something urged me to share this moment with him. After swearing him to secrecy, I insisted he keep his eyes closed until I had the portraits set on easels. "Okay, Daddy. Now you can look!"

He appeared dazed but said nothing. Getting up, he walked closer to inspect them. Then he withdrew to eye them at a distance. I tried to control my stomach flip-flops. Finally, with a tear escaping down one cheek, he mumbled, "I don't believe it. The eyes are so real that they follow you everywhere—and look how beautiful your mother is. Will you let me have them framed?"

Thrilled with his response, I happily volunteered to drop them off the next day at the frame shop.

Several weeks passed. Then one night in November the phone rang, and a cold chill numbed my body. I picked up the receiver to hear my husband, a doctor, say, "I'm in the emergency room. Your father has had a stroke. It's bad, but he is still alive."

Daddy lingered in a coma for several days. I went to see him in the hospital the day before he died. I slipped my hand in his and asked, "Do you know who I am, Daddy?" He surprised everyone when he whispered, "You're my darling daughter." He died the next day, and it seemed all joy was drained from the lives of my mother and me.

I finally remembered to call about the portrait framing

and thanked God my father had gotten a chance to see the pictures before he died. I was surprised when the shopkeeper told me my father had visited the shop, paid for the framing and had them gift-wrapped. In all our grief, I had no longer planned to give the portraits to my mother.

Even though we had lost the patriarch of our family, everyone was assembled on Christmas Day—making an effort to be cheerful. As I looked into my mother's sad eyes and unsmiling face, I decided to give her Daddy's and my gift. As she stripped the paper from the box, I saw her heart wasn't in it. There was a small card inside attached to the pictures.

After looking at the portraits and reading the card, her entire demeanor changed. She bounced out of her chair, handed the card to me and commissioned my brothers to hang the paintings facing each other over the fireplace. She stepped back and looked for a long while. With sparkling, tear-filled eyes and a wide smile, she quickly turned and said, "I knew Daddy would be with us on Christmas Day!"

I glanced at the gift card scrawled in my father's handwriting. "Mother—Our daughter reminded me why I am so blessed. I'll be looking at you always—Daddy."

Sarah A. Rivers

Mother's Day

It's been 26 years since my Army buddy Dan and I loaded his metallic blue 427 Corvette with ice coolers, cutoffs and T-shirts, and drove past the somber-faced military police at Fort McClellan's main gate. Armed with weekend passes and pockets full of crisp, new dollars from our first week's pay at our Army Reserve summer camp, we were on our way to Florida—and the Army was the last thing on our minds. Blessed by not finding our names on the weekend duty roster, we had decided a weekend at the beach would be just the thing we needed to recover from four days of C-rations and mosquitoes in the hills of eastern Alabama.

Our camp that year was early. The May weather had been delightful, and with the top down and stereo up, we cruised into Birmingham and decided to stop to phone our mothers and wish them happy Mother's Day before resuming our journey south on I-65.

Reaching my mother at home, I learned she had just returned from grocery shopping. I could tell by the tone in her voice that she was disappointed I wouldn't be spending her special day with the family. "Have a nice trip and be careful. We'll miss you," she said.

When I got back into the car, I could tell by Dan's face that he was suffering from the same guilty conscience that was haunting me. Then we had the brainstorm. Send flowers, of course.

Pulling into the parking lot of a southside Birmingham florist, we each scribbled a note to go with the flowers that would absolve us of the guilt of spending our only free weekend on the beach rather than with dear old Mom.

We waited while the clerk assisted a little boy who was selecting a floral arrangement, obviously for his mother. Fidgeting by now, we were anxious to pay for our flowers and be on our way.

The little boy beamed with pride as he turned to me and held up his selection while the clerk rang up his order. "I'm sure my mama would love these," he said. "These are carnations. Mama always loved carnations."

"I'm going to put them with some flowers from our yard," he added, "before I take them to the cemetery."

I looked up at the clerk, who was turning away and reaching for a handkerchief. Then I looked at Dan. We watched the little boy leave the store with his prized bouquet and crawl into the back seat of his dad's car.

"Have you fellas made a selection?" asked the clerk, barely able to speak.

"I guess we have," answered Dan. We dropped our notes in the trash and walked to his car in silence.

"I'll pick you up Sunday evening about five," said Dan, as he pulled up in front of my parents' house.

"I'll be ready," I answered, as I wrestled my duffel bag out of the back of the car.

Florida would have to wait.

Niki Sepsas

"We're off to the bait shop to get you your Mother's Day present."

Reprinted by permission of Bill Canty.

All Those Years

My friend Debbie's two daughters were in high school when she experienced severe flu-like symptoms. Debbie visited her family doctor, who told her the flu bug had passed her by. Instead, she had been touched by the "love bug" and was now pregnant.

The birth of Tommy, a healthy, beautiful son, was an event for celebration, and as time went by, it seemed as though every day brought another reason to celebrate the gift of Tommy's life. He was sweet, thoughtful, fun-loving and a joy to be around.

One day when Tommy was about five years old, he and Debbie were driving to the neighborhood mall. As is the way with children, out of nowhere, Tommy asked, "Mom, how old were you when I was born?"

"Thirty-six, Tommy. Why?" Debbie asked, wondering what his little mind was contemplating.

"What a shame!" Tommy responded.

"What do you mean?" Debbie inquired, more than a little puzzled. Looking at her with love-filled eyes, Tommy said, "Just think of all those years we didn't know each other."

Alice Collins

The Bobby Pins

When I was seven years old, I overheard my mother tell one of her friends that the following day was to be her 30th birthday. Two things occurred to me when I heard that: one, I had never before realized that my mother had a birthday; and two, I could not recall her ever getting a birthday present.

Well, I could do something about that. I went into my bedroom, opened my piggy bank and took out all the money that was inside: five nickels. That represented five weeks' worth of my allowance. Then I walked to the little store around the comer from my house, and I told the proprietor, Mr. Sawyer, that I wanted to buy a birthday present for my mother.

He showed me everything in his store that could be had for a quarter. There were several ceramic figurines. My mother would have loved those, but she already had a house full of them and I was the one who had to dust them once a week. They definitely would not do. There were also some small boxes of candy. My mother was diabetic, so I knew they would not be appropriate.

The last thing Mr. Sawyer showed me was a package of bobby pins. My mother had beautiful long black hair, and twice a week she washed and pincurled it. When she took the pincurls down the next day, she looked just like a movie star with those long, dark curls cascading around her shoulders. So I decided those bobby pins would be the perfect gift for my mother. I gave Mr. Sawyer my five nickels, and he gave me the bobby pins.

I took the bobby pins home and wrapped them in a colorful sheet from the Sunday comics (there was no money left for wrapping paper). The next morning, while my family was seated at the breakfast table, I walked up to my mother and handed her that package and said, "Happy birthday, Momma!"

My mother sat there for a moment in stunned silence. Then, with tears in her eyes, she tore at that comic-strip wrapping. By the time she got to the bobby pins, she was sobbing.

"I'm sorry, Momma!" I apologized. "I didn't mean to make you cry. I just wanted you to have a happy birthday."

"Oh, honey, I am happy!" she told me. And I looked into her eyes, and I could see that she was smiling through her tears. "Why, do you know that this is the first birthday present that I have ever received in my entire life?" she exclaimed.

Then she kissed me on the cheek and said, "Thank you, honey." And she turned to my sister and said, "Lookee here! Linda got me a birthday present!" And she turned to my brothers and said, "Lookee here! Linda got me a birthday present!" And she turned to my father and said, *"Lookee here! Linda got me a birthday present!"*

And then she went into the bathroom to wash her hair and pincurl it with her new bobby pins.

After she left the room, my father looked at me and said, "Linda, when I was growing up, back on the frontier (my daddy always called his childhood home in the mountains of Virginia *the frontier*), we didn't set much store by giving birthday presents to adults. That was something done just for small young 'uns. And your momma's family, they were so poor, they didn't even do that much. But seeing how happy you've made your momma today has made me rethink this whole birthday issue. What I'm trying to say, Linda, is I believe you have set a precedent here."

And I did set a precedent. After that, my mother was showered with birthday presents every year: from my sister, from my brothers, from my father and from me. And, of course, the older we children got, the more money we made, and the nicer presents she received. By the time I was 25, I had given her a stereo, a color television and a microwave oven (which she traded in for a vacuum cleaner).

For my mother's 50th birthday, my brothers and my sister and I pooled our resources and got her something spectacular: a ring set with a pearl surrounded by a cluster of diamonds. And when my oldest brother handed that ring to her at the party that was given in her honor, she opened up the velvet gift box and peered at the ring inside. Then she smiled and turned the box around so that her guests could see her special gift, and she said, "Don't I have wonderful children?" Then she passed the ring around the room, and it was thrilling to hear the collective sigh that rippled through that room as the ring was passed from hand to hand.

After the guests were gone, I stayed to help clean up. I was doing the dishes in the kitchen when I overheard a conversation between my mother and father in the next room. "Well, Pauline," my father said, "that's a mighty pretty ring you've got there. I reckon that's about the best birthday present you've ever had."

My own eyes filled with tears when I heard her reply. "Ted," she said softly, "that's a mighty pretty ring and that's a fact. But the best birthday present I ever got? Well, that was a package of bobby pins."

Linda Goodman

Squeeze My Hand and I'll Tell You That I Love You

Remember when you were a child and you fell and hurt yourself? Do you remember what your mother did to ease the pain? My mother, Grace Rose, would pick me up, carry me to her bed, sit me down and kiss my "owwie." Then she'd sit on the bed beside me, take my hand in hers and say, "When it hurts, squeeze my hand and I'll tell you that I love you." Over and over I'd squeeze her hand, and each time, without fail, I heard the words, "Mary, I love you."

Sometimes, I'd find myself pretending I'd been hurt just to have that ritual with her. As I grew up, the ritual changed, but she always found a way to ease the pain and increase the joy I felt in any area of my life. On difficult days during high school, she'd offer her favorite Hershey chocolate almond bar when I returned home. During my 20s, Mom often called to suggest a spontaneous picnic lunch at Estabrook Park just to celebrate a warm, sunny day in Wisconsin. A handwritten thank-you note arrived in the mail after every single visit she and my father made to my home, reminding me of how special I was to her.

But the most memorable ritual remained her holding my hand when I was a child and saying, "When it hurts, squeeze my hand and I'll tell you that I love you."

One morning, when I was in my late 30s, following a visit by my parents the night before, my father phoned me at work. He was always commanding and clear in his directions, but I heard confusion and panic in his voice. "Mary, something's wrong with your mother and I don't know what to do. Please come over as quickly as you can."

The 10-minute drive to my parents' home filled me with dread, wondering what was happening to my mother. When I arrived, I found Dad pacing in the kitchen and Mom lying on their bed. Her eyes were closed and her hands rested on her stomach. I called to her, trying to keep my voice as calm as possible. "Mom, I'm here."

"Mary?"

"Yes, Mom."

"Mary, is that you?"

"Yes, Mom, it's me."

I wasn't prepared for the next question, and when I heard it, I froze, not knowing what to say.

"Mary, am I going to die?"

Tears welled up inside me as I looked at my loving mother lying there so helpless.

My thoughts raced, until this question crossed my mind: *What would Mom say?*

I paused for a moment that seemed like a million years, waiting for the words to come. "Mom, I don't know if you're going to die, but if you need to, it's okay. I love you."

She cried out, "Mary, I hurt so much."

Again, I wondered what to say. I sat down beside her on the bed, picked up her hand and heard myself say, "Mom, when it hurts, squeeze my hand and I'll tell you that I love you."

She squeezed my hand.

"Mom, I love you."

Many hand squeezes and "I love you's" passed between my mother and me during the next two years, until she passed away from ovarian cancer. We never know when our moments of truth will come, but I do know now that when they do, whomever I'm with, I will offer my mother's sweet ritual of love every time. "When it hurts, squeeze my hand and I'll tell you that I love you."

Mary Marcdante

In the Genes

A young woman named Mary gave birth to her first child, and because her husband was on military duty, she spent a couple of weeks after the birth at the home of her parents.

One day Mary mentioned to her mother that she was surprised the baby's hair was reddish, when both she and her husband were blonde.

"Well, Mary," said her mother, "you must remember, your daddy's hair is red."

"But Mamma," said Mary, "that doesn't make any difference because I'm adopted."

With a little smile, Mamma said the loveliest words that her daughter had ever heard: "I always forget."

The Best of Bits & Pieces

A Child Is Born

One Sunday near Thanksgiving, Angus McDonnell, a member of my congregation, told me of the birth of his grandson, "little Angus Larry," and asked me to perform the baptism. Our church board was reluctant because the child's family lived in another state; the church takes very seriously its commitment to support one who is baptized.

But the will of Angus McDonnell prevailed and the following Sunday, little Angus Larry was baptized, with his parents, Larry and Sherry, Grandpa Angus and Grandma Minnie and many other family members present.

Our congregation has a baptism custom: The pastor asks, "Who stands with this child?" and then the whole extended family of the little one rises and remains standing for the ceremony. So with Angus Larry in my arms, I asked the question, and up stood all the relatives.

After church, everybody rushed home to turkey leftovers, and I went back into the sanctuary to turn off the lights. A middle-aged woman was sitting in the front pew. She seemed at a loss for words and was hesitant about looking at me for very long. Finally, she said her name was Mildred Cory, and she commented on how lovely the baptism had been. After another long pause, she added, "My daughter, Tina, just had a baby, and, well, the baby ought to be baptized, shouldn't it?"

I suggested that Tina and her husband call me and we would discuss it. Mildred hesitated again, and then, catching and holding my eyes for the first time, she said, "Tina's got no husband. She's just 18, and she was confirmed in this church four years ago. She used to come out for the Senior High Fellowship, but then she started to see this boy who was out of school . . ."

Now the story tumbled out fearlessly: ". . . and then she got pregnant and decided to keep the baby and she wants to have it baptized here in her own church, but she's nervous to come and talk to you, Reverend. She's named the baby James—Jimmy."

I said that I would take the request to the church board for approval.

When the matter came up at the next meeting, I explained what everybody already knew—namely, that Tina was a member of the church and an unwed mother and that I didn't know who the father was. They all knew who the father was, of course; this is a small town.

A few questions were asked as to whether or not we could be certain that Tina would stick to the commitment she was making in having her child baptized. I remarked that she and little Jimmy were, after all, right here in town where we could give them support.

The real problem was the picture we all had in our heads: Tina, teenage spots and all, little Jimmy in her arms; the father no longer around; and Mildred Cory the only one who would stand when the question was asked. It hurt each of us to think about it. But the board approved the baptism. It was scheduled for the last Sunday in Advent.

The church was full that day, as it always is the Sunday before Christmas. Down the aisle came Tina, nervously, briskly, smiling at me only, shaking slightly, holding month-old Jimmy.

This young mother was so alone. It would be a hard life for this pair.

I read the opening part of the service and then, looking for Mildred Cory, I asked my question: "Who stands with this child?" I nodded at Mildred slightly, to coax her to her feet. She rose slowly, looking to either side, and then returned my smile.

My eyes went back to my service book. I was just about to ask Tina the parent's questions when I became aware of movement in the pews.

Angus McDonnell had stood up, Minnie beside him. Then a couple of other elders stood. Then the sixth-grade Sunday school teacher, then a new young couple in church, and soon, before my incredulous eyes, the whole church was standing up with little Jimmy.

Tina was crying. Mildred Cory held on to the pew as though she were standing on the deck of a rocking ship, which, in a way, she was.

The Scripture reading that morning was a few verses from John:

> *See what love the Father has given us that we should be called children of God. . . . No one has ever seen God; if we love one another, God abides in us and his love is perfected in us. . . . There is no fear in love, but perfect love casts out fear.*

In that baptism, those old words came alive; they were clothed in flesh, and everybody felt it.

Reverend Michael Lindvall

A Perfect Child

The only genuine love worthy of the name is unconditional . . .

John Powell

Quite unexpectedly one day, a close friend surprised me by announcing her plans to go to Lourdes to bathe her young handicapped son in the curative waters. Marie was a Catholic and, to many Catholics, the French city of Lourdes is a place for miraculous cures. She saved up for the trip for a solid year.

Marie and I had helped each other through our late 30s. Her Billy and my David were born brain-damaged. They were both the fourth of five children, and a unique source of joy and grief. Marie and I had been through many trials together.

It would be a difficult trip for her alone, with an unpredictable seven-year-old; in addition, she'd never been out of the country and didn't speak a word of French. But even if there was only a slim chance that the waters of Lourdes would miraculously help Billy and transform him into a normal child, she must have felt she owed it to him to try.

We didn't discuss it much before she left. When I asked if I could help with her other children, she said everything was taken care of. Then Marie and Billy were gone.

Almost before I had time to miss her, Marie returned. She came back with a spring in her step and a new vitality in running her teeming household. She was more patient. There was a peace about her.

Billy, on the other hand, seemed exactly the same.

I was puzzled. As the weeks went by, I kept expecting Marie to tell me what had happened at Lourdes. But I didn't dare ask. The trip had obviously been a private experience. She didn't have to come out and tell me of her inner struggle. I knew.

I loved my David, but I wanted him to be like other kids. How often had I thought, *Wouldn't it be wonderful if David were a normal child? A completely different child?* Other parents might wish their sons were better students or more athletic, their daughters less moody or more ambitious. Those weren't monumental changes, like what I wanted for David. What I wanted for my son would take a miracle.

Then one day while I was visiting Marie, she went up to her room and came back carrying a small plastic bottle. "Here, Kathy," she said. "I brought you some Lourdes water."

I held the container tightly in my palm and searched Marie's eyes. Maybe she was ready to talk. "Do you think it worked for Billy?" I asked.

Marie looked away.

Suddenly I felt terrible; of course it hadn't worked for Billy. How could I be so cruel?

"You don't understand," Marie said slowly, "I didn't dip him in the waters."

"You *didn't*?"

"I couldn't," she said. "When it came time to do it, I just couldn't."

Mental pictures of Marie dropping coins and one-dollar bills into a mayonnaise jar, week after week, to save up for the trip; the 10-hour plane ride, plus hours on the train; the stress on her family; her expectations—all passed through my mind. How could she have refused such an opportunity if she truly believed that a miracle might take place?

The word came out in a whisper. "Why?"

"Because I love him the way he is."

All at once, I understood. I recognized the source of the peace Marie had discovered.

"Even if he'll never be the way I dreamed he'd be," Marie said, "I still love my son."

A healing *had* taken place at Lourdes. And now it touched me. My child was from God. If someday, by some miracle, David were different, or "normal," I would praise God for his healing. And I'd love David—but no more than I love him at this very moment.

Kathleen Lukens

Most Kids Are Born Only Once

Before you were conceived I wanted you
Before you were born I loved you
Before you were here an hour I would die for you
This is the miracle of love.

Maureen Hawkins

Mother is always there when you need her. She helps, protects, listens, advises and nurtures physically and morally. She makes sure that her family is loved 24 hours a day, seven days a week, 52 weeks a year. At least that's how I remember my mother, for the few precious years I was blessed to have her. But no words can describe the sacrifice she made out of love for me, her young son.

I was 19 years old, and I was being taken to a concentration camp with a large group of other Jews. It was clear that we were destined to die. Suddenly my mother stepped in and traded places with me. And although it was more than 50 years ago, I will never forget her last words to me and her good-bye look.

"I have lived long enough. You have to survive because you are so young," she said.

Most kids are born only once. I was given birth twice—by the same mother.

Joseph C. Rosenbaum

Room for Another

When I awoke that morning in late June, I still couldn't believe what my husband, Mark*, had suggested the night before. *Take in Jason, a 12-year-old from his Little League baseball team, as a foster son?* I knew Mark was a dedicated coach, but this was beyond dedication!

I was already juggling life with four children, ages three months to 13, and all their activities. I had just finished my teaching year, and our summer was already filling up with camps, lessons and lots of baseball. Mark had coached our son's team to a perfect 14-0 season. Now he was priming the team for the Tournament of Champions.

The players were at our home all day long, either practicing or trading cards—especially Jason, who lived on the block behind our house. In fact, Jason often acted as our summer wake-up call, as he was doing that June morning.

"Is Coach here?" he asked, as I peered out the door, fastening my robe.

I stared at him. Approaching 13, Jason looked me eye-to-eye even though he was standing a step down. His thick blond hair stuck out from under his backward baseball

---

* Names have been changed to protect their identities.

hat. He was the ecumenical dresser: Giants cap, A's shirt, Dodgers shorts. This was typical Jason, the people-pleaser.

He fidgeted with his glove. "I wondered if Coach would want to throw me some grounders."

It wasn't the first time a boy had come to our door asking for my husband. Mark often hit flies or grounders or shot hoops with a bunch of them—boys with absent or uninterested dads.

I stifled a yawn. "Jason, it's 7:00 A.M. It's Saturday. We're just getting up." He shuffled and mumbled something, but I caught his expression the moment before he turned. In spite of his wanting-to-appear-cool stance, his face echoed pain and I knew why.

His parents were separated and his dad lived only an hour away but never called, never wrote, never visited. Jason was a troublemaker at school and had learning disabilities. Nonetheless, he was a gifted athlete. But he often missed practice, and on some days, even when his body was present, his mind didn't seem in the game at all.

The night before, his mom had called Mark to say that Jason might not be able to fulfill his commitment to the team. She had pleaded guilty to a welfare-fraud charge and was going to prison for an evaluation that could take as long as 90 days. She could then be sentenced for up to three years. She said she wanted to place Jason in a good home before county authorities took him away.

I closed the door. *Lord, I don't think I can handle another child. We don't have room in this house. And . . . I guess I just don't have room in my heart for someone else's child.*

As I closed the door I heard our three-month-old's first stirrings. It wasn't that I didn't like kids. In fact, my life was surrounded by them—as a mom, elementary school teacher and junior church leader. But late-night feedings had drained me physically and I needed my summer recharge.

My mind was made up as I nursed the baby. We had only a three-bedroom house. The baby's crib was squished into a corner of my small office. This baby had been a later-in-life surprise that was wonderful . . . but a fifth child in our home? No way.

An hour later Mark and I sat quietly at the tile-topped kitchen counter for breakfast. The kids were still sleeping and the baby was napping. My husband pushed scrambled eggs around on his plate. I crumbled my toast.

"There's something I've never told you," he said. "When I was about Jason's age, my dad got into trouble and I was put into a foster home."

I hadn't known. He paused, swallowing. His father had been falsely accused of a crime and the authorities broke up the family.

"They just came and picked us all up," Mark continued. "The girls were put with families. We boys were put in a children's home. It was the worst two weeks of my life until Dad was cleared, and we all got to be home again together."

"Why didn't you ever tell me about this?" I asked.

"There are some things you just don't want to remember, much less talk about. I felt humiliated that people said such terrible things about my father. But worse was the fear that I'd never see my mom or dad again."

He stopped fiddling with his fork and looked up at me. His eyes were brimming with tears. And suddenly I could see him as a young boy—crew-cut hair, skinny, painfully shy—being led away by people he did not know to a place he'd never seen. I saw the hurt and embarrassment he'd held inside all those years. It was the same anguish I had seen earlier in Jason's eyes.

I imagined Mark standing on a neighbor's front porch wanting to ask if they'd take him in. Wanting to ask, but never getting the words out. Shuffling his feet, mumbling something, never getting to the point. And some nice lady saying it was too early in the morning and closing the door.

I put my hand on Mark's. It sometimes wasn't necessary to talk after 20 years of marriage; we just knew what the other was thinking. He wouldn't ask me again to take in Jason, wouldn't push me, make me do something I didn't feel I could do.

But I knew then that Jason was an opportunity for Mark—and for me—to redeem the pain that Mark experienced as a boy. It was not just "doing unto others." Anything we could do to help Jason would somehow help ease the hurt in Mark's own past.

Okay, Lord, I'm willing to find a spot in my home—and my heart—for another, if that's what you want. Please release in me the same love for Jason that Mark already feels.

"I've been wondering," I said, picking at crumbs on the counter. "Do you think the attic room could be a bedroom?"

He smiled and nodded. "I think it would work out fine."

Jason lived with us for about three months. He brought many things with him—his computer, his sports posters, his mother's plants. But he also brought his willingness to do dishes and vacuum, his enthusiasm, and even better, his wild sense of humor, entertaining us many nights with his stand-up comedy routines.

His mom came home in September, two days before his 13th birthday. I was glad that they could be together again. But his leaving left a void in my heart.

Or maybe it's not a void. Maybe it's just room for another.

Maxine Roberts

The Unlocked Door

When you were small
And just a touch away,
I covered you with blankets
Against the cool night air.
But now that you are tall
And out of reach,
I fold my hands
And cover you with prayer.

Dona Maddux Cooper

In Glasgow, Scotland, a young lady, like a lot of teens today, got tired of home and the restraints of her parents. The daughter rejected her family's religious lifestyle and said, "I don't want your God. I give up. I'm leaving!"

She left home, deciding to become a woman of the world. Before long, however, she was dejected and unable to find a job, so she took to the streets to sell her body as a prostitute. The years passed by, her father died, her mother grew older, and the daughter became more and more entrenched in her way of life.

No contact was made between mother and daughter during these years. The mother, having heard of her daughter's whereabouts, made her way to the skid-row section of the city in search of her daughter. She stopped at each of the rescue missions with a simple request. "Would you allow me to put up this picture?" It was a picture of the smiling, gray-haired mother with a handwritten message at the bottom: "I love you still . . . come home!"

Some more months went by, and nothing happened. Then one day the daughter wandered into a rescue mission for a needed meal. She sat absent-mindedly listening to the service, all the while letting her eyes wander over to the bulletin board. There she saw the picture and thought, *Could that be my mother?*

She couldn't wait until the service was over. She stood and went to look. It was her mother, and there were those words, "I love you still . . . come home!" As she stood in front of the picture, she wept. It was too good to be true.

By this time it was night, but she was so touched by the message that she started walking home. By the time she arrived it was early in the morning. She was afraid and made her way timidly, not really knowing what to do. As she knocked, the door flew open on its own. She thought someone must have broken into the house. Concerned for her mother's safety, the young woman ran to the bedroom and found her still sleeping. She shook her mother awake and said, "It's me! It's me! I'm home!"

The mother couldn't believe her eyes. She wiped her tears and they fell into each other's arms. The daughter said, "I was so worried! The door was open and I thought someone had broken in!"

The mother replied gently, "No dear. From the day you left, that door has never been locked."

Robert Strand

Mom for a Day

As a mother of three beautiful children, I have many special memories to share. But one of my most special moments as a mom was actually with someone else's child. It is a moment that I will always cherish.

Michael came to our self-esteem-building camp last summer, referred to us by a boys' home where he was currently residing. Michael was 12 years old, and his life had been a difficult one. His father had brought him to the U.S. from a war-torn country after his mother's death, so that he could have "a better life." Unfortunately, he was left to the care of his aunt, who emotionally and physically abused him. He had become one tough little boy, with very little trust and a belief that he was not lovable.

He hung out with a few other boys who were likewise negative, angry and tough. The "gang" was a challenge to the counselors, but we hung in with them and continued to accept and love them for who they were. We recognized all their exterior behavior as a reflection of how deeply they had been hurt.

Around the fifth night of our seven-day experience, we treated the kids to an overnight camp-out under the stars. When Michael heard of this event, he said it was "stupid" and he wasn't going. We avoided getting into a power struggle with him and went on with the evening.

As the moon shone brightly and the evening waned, the kids began arranging their sleeping bags for the evening on a huge deck near the lake.

I noticed Michael walking around by himself with his head down. He saw me and quickly walked toward me. I thought I would avert his whining and said, "Come on, Michael, let's get your sleeping bag and find a good spot for you with your friends."

"I don't have a sleeping bag," he muttered in a low voice.

"Oh well, that's no problem," I exclaimed. "We'll just open up several bags and get you some blankets for covers."

Figuring I had solved his dilemma, I began to walk off. Michael tugged at my shirt and pulled me away from the crowd of kids.

"Anne," he said, "I need to tell you something." I saw that tough big boy's face melting with embarrassment and shame at what he had to tell me. In a barely audible whisper, he said, "You see, I have this problem. I . . . I . . . I'm a bed wetter and I wet the sheets every night." I was so glad he whispered into my ear and couldn't see the look of astonishment on my face. I hadn't even considered this as a reason for his negative attitude. I thanked him for letting me in on his "problem" and told him I understood why he was upset about the evening. We decided together that he could sleep in his cabin alone and just slip out quietly from the group.

I left with him and on the long walk back to the cabin, I asked him if he was afraid to sleep alone. He assured me that it was not a problem and that he had faced much scarier things before in his life. As we put his last set of fresh sheets on his bed, we talked about how difficult his first 12 years had been, and he told me how much he wanted the future to be different. I told him how he had all the power he needed to make his life the best it could be. He looked so vulnerable and sweet and real for the first time that week.

He hopped under the covers and I asked if I could tuck him in. "What does 'tuck in' mean?" he asked with curiosity. With tears in my eyes, I covered him up, tucked them under his chin and kissed him on the forehead.

"Goodnight, Michael, I think you are awesome!" I mumbled.

"G'night and uh, uh, thanks for being kinda like a mom to me, okay?" he said earnestly.

"My pleasure, sweetheart," I said with a hug. As I turned to go, three sets of dirty sheets under my arms and tears rolling down my cheeks, I thanked God for the love that can happen between a mom and her son, even if only for a day.

Anne Jordan

Daddy's Little Girl

I took my month-old son to my parents' house for a visit. During the first night back in my childhood bedroom, I heard my father get up and start down the hall. Then I listened to my mother say to him, "It's cold. Make sure the baby is covered."

Pretending to be asleep so I could observe the new grandfather in action, I soon learned that I would always be Daddy's little girl. When he came in the room, he didn't go near the baby's crib. But he made sure I was tucked in before he shuffled back down the hall.

Contributed by Brenda Collins Blume
Reader's Digest

2

A MOTHER'S GUIDING HAND

God cannot be everywhere, so he made mothers.

Arab Proverb

To Read When You're Alone

I was 13 years old. My family had moved to Southern California from North Florida a year before. I hit adolescence with a vengeance. I was angry and rebellious, with little regard for anything my parents had to say, particularly if it had to do with me. Like so many teenagers, I struggled to escape from anything that didn't agree with my picture of the world. A "brilliant without need of guidance" kid, I rejected any overt offering of love. In fact, I got angry at the mention of the word love.

One night, after a particularly difficult day, I stormed into my room, shut the door and got into bed. As I lay down in the privacy of my bed, my hands slipped under my pillow. There was an envelope. I pulled it out and on the envelope it said, "To read when you're alone."

Since I was alone, no one would know whether I read it or not, so I opened it. It said "Mike, I know life is hard right now, I know you are frustrated and I know we don't do everything right. I also know that I love you completely and nothing you do or say will ever change that. I am here for you if you ever need to talk, and if you don't, that's okay. Just know that no matter where you go or what you do in your life, I will always love you and be proud that you are my son. I'm here for you and I love you—that will never change. Love, Mom.

That was the first of several "To read when you're alone" letters. They were never mentioned until I was an adult.

Today I travel the world helping people. I was in Sarasota, Florida, teaching a seminar when, at the end of the day, a lady came up to me and shared the difficulty she was having with her son. We walked out to the beach, and I told her of my mom's undying love and about the "To read when you're alone" letters. Several weeks later, I got a card that said she had written her first letter and left it for her son.

That night as I went to bed, I put my hands under my pillow and remembered the relief I felt every time I got a letter. In the midst of my turbulent teen years, the letters were the calm assurance that I could be loved in spite of me, not because of me. Just before I fell asleep I thanked God that my mom knew what I, an angry teenager, needed. Today when the seas of life get stormy, I know that just under my pillow there is that calm assurance that love—consistent, abiding, unconditional love—changes lives.

Mike Staver

With a Little Help from Mama

To dream of the person you would like to be is to waste the person you are.

Unknown

It was a beautiful spring morning when Mama and I set off from our ranch in Oklahoma for Nashville, Tennessee, where I was going to audition for a recording contract. I was 20 years old, well-prepared vocally, and ready to take a chance on the dream of a lifetime.

But as the hillsides rolled by, resplendent with the whites and pinks of dogwood and redbud blossoms, I felt a creeping uneasiness. The closer we got to the country music capital, the more I tried to prolong the trip, making Mama detour for some sightseeing, then for a snack, then for anything I could think of. Finally, I yelled "Stop!" and Mama pulled the big blue Ford into a Dairy Queen on the side of the highway, and we went inside.

As I toyed with my mountain of ice cream, I didn't have to explain I was scared. Mama knew me too well. "Reba Nell," she said, adding the Nell for gentle emphasis, "we can turn around right now and go on back home if that's what you want, and I'll understand. The music business is not for everyone."

I looked at Mama across the melting swirl of my sundae. She wasn't pushing me. But when she was my age, Mama would have given just about anything to have had the opportunity I was getting a chance at now. I wondered if that was what was confusing me.

We'd always had a special bond. Maybe it was because of my singing. Music had gone way back in Mama's life. But right out of high school she had to take a teaching job, working in a two-room schoolhouse. Then she married, worked as an assistant to the school superintendent, and did all the bookkeeping on our ranch while raising four kids.

Mama and I were middle kids, both the third of four children. Being a middle kid, I was always looking for attention. I was a tomboy, doing everything my older brother, Pake, did. "Anything you can do I can do better!" was our sibling motto. Whether it was throwing rocks and doing chin-ups, or riding horses and roping, I was out to be the best, to get the attention. Then I learned to sing.

I remember in the second grade my music teacher, pretty Mrs. Kanton, helped me learn "My Favorite Things" from *The Sound of Music.* When I went home and sang it for Mama, her eyes met mine and just sort of glowed. It tickled me to think I could make Mama react like that, and to hear adults say I was gifted.

That's what my grandmother—Mama's mother and my namesake—used to say when I was growing up. But she called it a special gift, a gift from God. I was almost as close to her as I was to Mama. Grandma used to take me fishing at a pond on her place. We never did catch much, but we liked to throw in our lines and sit on the pond dam while Grandma told stories, mostly from the Bible. She told me about David, Moses and Daniel, and the special gifts that God had given them, like courage and leadership and prophecy. In fact, David was a songwriter.

I probably learned as much of my Bible going fishing with Grandma as I did in Sunday school. She taught me gospel songs and hymns so I could sing to her. "Reba," she'd say, "God gives us all our own special gifts, and he's given you yours for a reason. Now you have to learn to use it."

The cherry was sliding down the whipped cream peak on my sundae. I looked outside at the glowing Dairy Queen cone rotating slowly, almost as if it were sitting on a record turntable. Mama was nursing a cup of coffee and watching the traffic flash by. She was not about to rush me.

We'd spent many an hour on the road together. Grandpap and Daddy were champion steer ropers. Summers, we'd all go with Daddy on the rodeo circuit. We had a two-horse trailer that was so heavy, all four of us kids had to stand on the back of it so Daddy could pull the nose up and hitch it to the Ford. Then we'd pile into the back seat and take off for rodeos in Wyoming and Colorado. We'd play road games, like counting mile markers or Volkswagens. We'd see who could spot the most out-of-state license plates.

Then someone would strike up a song and everybody joined in. Mama coached. She kept us on pitch and taught us how to harmonize. If the lyrics got lost in the jumble, she announced, "Okay, stop. Reba Nell, *enunciate.* Now go ahead." One word would do it. That was the schoolteacher coming out in her.

When we got older, Pake, my younger sister, Susie, and I formed a country-and-western band at Kiowa High School. We called ourselves the Singing McEntires. We practiced in the living room while Mama was in the kitchen frying potatoes. I remember one day we were singing harmonies and things got a little messed up. I was on Susie's part or Susie was on Pake's—we couldn't tell—but Pake got really aggravated and started bossing us around. Quick enough, Mama marched in, spatula in hand. "All right," she said, "sing it."

We sang it.

"Susie, you're on Reba's part," she said, pointing with her spatula. "Now, just sing the song." We sang it.

"That sounds better. Sing it again." We sang it again.

"That's perfect. Now do it once more." Then she walked back into the kitchen. That was Mama.

After my voice had matured into a real singer's instrument, I started performing at rodeos. I loved singing to the big crowds. I'd listen to my favorite country music stars, like Loretta Lynn and Dolly Parton, and go out there and try to sound just like them and get all that attention. Then one day Mama took me aside for a quiet talk that would turn out to be one of the most important conversations we ever had.

"Reba Nell," she said, "you have a beautiful voice all your own. If people want to hear Dolly or Loretta sing, they'll buy their albums. But now you've got to find your own style. Sing what you feel, sing from your own heart, and you'll discover the voice God intended for you. That's what people will really come to hear."

She was right. After our talk, people in the music business started taking a real look at me, and that's why we were now sitting here in this Dairy Queen outside Nashville.

Across the Formica tabletop I caught Mama glancing at her watch. I couldn't stall much longer. My ice cream had turned to soup.

I looked up at Mama. She was fishing in her purse for the keys to the Ford.

"Reba," she said, pulling them out, "I'm serious about turning back. But if you get that record deal, I'll be very proud of you. If you don't—I'll be just as proud." Then she reached over and gave me a tight hug, and suddenly I remembered the glow in her eyes when I sang "My Favorite Things."

I knew what that glow had meant. All Mama wanted—all any mother wants for her child—was for me to be myself. And she'd seen what I could be. She didn't have to say that if I signed a record deal she'd be living out her dreams a little bit through me. I understood that now and I was proud. Suddenly I wanted to get to Nashville as quick as we could.

And I've been making records ever since, using those gifts that Grandma talked about and Mama helped me find. The gifts God provides to make each of us unique.

Reba McEntire

My Mother Says . . .

Mother love is the fuel that enables a normal human being to do the impossible.

Marion C. Garretty

After graduating from West Point and gaining a commission in the United States Army, I spent several weeks of summer on leave at my family's farm in Mystic, Connecticut. One day at dinner I spoke to my parents about my desire to go to Ranger School that coming winter.

I described Ranger School to my parents. The Army sends only its best soldiers to undergo the grueling course. There the men receive just one meal a day, sleep two to three hours a night, and carry rucksacks full of personal and squad equipment on 30-kilometer patrols. They learn to survive behind enemy lines and to conduct raids, ambushes and reconnaissance missions. Usually only one out of three ranger students graduates.

My mother's reaction to my intentions surprised me. Instead of giving me her immediate support and encouragement, she hesitated. She wanted to know what the possibility was that I would be injured. She asked me to explain again why I wanted to go so much. My mother knew that soldiers had died during ranger training in the past.

I explained that I didn't have to go to Ranger School. It wasn't important or necessary for my career as an Army officer. I wanted to go to see if I could do it. Did I have what it took? My mother listened quietly. She didn't ask me any more questions. I knew how she felt. Or so I thought.

Shortly after that conversation, I left home to attend the Engineer Officer Basic Course (EOBC) at Fort Leonard Wood, Missouri. After that course I would go on to a construction battalion in Germany. During the second week of EOBC, I attended a briefing on Ranger School. At the conclusion of our briefing, the officer-in-charge broke some news to us that made the odds of becoming rangers seem insurmountable. Out of the 60 second-lieutenants in the room, only six of us would be allowed to attend Ranger School. Over the next three months we would compete in five areas: physical fitness, land navigation, knot tying, swimming and academics. At the end, the top six soldiers would go on to Ranger School.

I called my parents that night. "There's only a slight chance that I'll be able to go to Ranger School," I said, explaining further about the number of people who wanted to go and how many slots were available. I was sure the news would come as a relief to my mother. But it didn't. In my mother's eyes, something much more dangerous than Ranger School was now facing me. My dream was getting out of my reach. She moved instinctively to put it back within my grasp.

"You can do it," she told me. "I know how badly you want to go to Ranger School, and I know you'll go. You'll make it. And you'll graduate." Her words pushed away my doubts and filled me with strength and resolution.

Over the next three months, the 60 of us "ranger wannabes" competed aggressively. I filled my parents in on my progress as the weeks passed. My mother's steadfast encouragement continued. She was unmoved by the odds. She kept saying she knew I would make it.

In late October, I was boarding the bus that was taking our class back from a training area. I was running a bit late, so I was the last one to get on. As I climbed the steps, someone from the back shouted, "Hey Whittle, did you get the word?"

I paused at the front of the bus. A crowd of second lieutenants was staring back at me. Somehow I knew it was bad news. And I knew it was about Ranger School. "What?" I asked.

"The commander says that nobody who's going to a construction battalion will be going to Ranger School," came the reply. I was crushed. All that work, and now I wasn't going to go.

I kept my head up and faced the bus, which was completely silent. Everyone was watching to see my reaction. The first thing that came to my mind was Mom's words. With a grin, I spoke the truth. "Well I guess the commander hasn't talked to *my mother* yet, 'cause *my mother* says *I'm* going to *Ranger School.*" Everyone on the bus burst into laughter.

Word of my unlikely comment quickly spread through the rest of the staff and faculty. A week later, the commander reversed his decision. Evidently he didn't want to mess with my mother.

The officer-in-charge announced the results of the competition. I had placed sixth. My mother was right. On November 30, 1990, I started Ranger School, and on March 19, 1991, I graduated.

Robert F. Whittle Jr.

The Inspection

The scouts were in camp. In an inspection, the director found an umbrella neatly rolled inside the bedroll of a small scout. As an umbrella was not listed as a necessary item, the director asked the boy to explain.

"Sir," answered the young man with a weary sigh, "did you ever have a mother?"

Author Unknown
Submitted by Glenn Van Ekeren

"Mother, please!"

What Color Is a Hug?

One touch is worth ten thousand words.

Harold Bloomfield

When my youngest daughter, Bernadette, was 10 years old, I found myself very worried about her. The last four years had been difficult ones for our family. Bernadette was especially close to her grandparents, who doted on her. One by one, they had died, in a short period of time.

A relentless series of losses like that is hard on anyone, especially a child. But it was particularly hard on Bernadette because of her sensitive and loving nature. By the time she was 10, she was immersed in what I could only call depression. For nearly a year, she rarely smiled. She seemed to just go through the motions of living. Her trademark sparkle dimmed drastically.

I didn't know what to do. Bernadette could tell I was worried about her, and that seemed to increase the burden she carried. One day after she'd left for school, I sat in the family room in an overstuffed chair. Our family had been big on hugs. As a child, my parents, grandparents, aunts and uncles were all quick to pull us kids into a warm embrace. Ever since I'd left home, whenever problems weighed on me, I visualized myself in my dad's lap, settling into his embrace. "Oh, Dad," I murmured to my missing parent, "what can I do to help Bernadette?"

I almost laughed out loud when it struck me. Recently, I'd been reading about the therapeutic effects of hugs. Could it be that "hug therapy" would do my daughter some good?

Not knowing what else to try, I resolved to hug her as often as I could, without making it seem premeditated.

Slowly, over the next weeks, Bernadette grew more cheerful and relaxed. Smiles appeared with increasing frequency—the genuine kind that animated her eyes as well as her mouth. She worked and played with heightened enthusiasm. Within a few months, the frequent, heartfelt hugs had conquered the gloom.

I never told Bernadette about my strategy. But she clearly recognized how important the hugs had been. Whenever she felt troubled, uncertain or just a little "down," she asked me for a hug. Or when she noticed that I was sad or tense, she would say, "You look like you could use a hug." The darned things turned out to be habit-forming!

The years passed. Hugging for us had become such an easy comfort that I never expected it to become a problem. But at some time during her months of college selection, she and I both realized that we were certainly facing a period of withdrawal—especially since her college choice was 1,700 miles away.

We celebrated my birthday a week before Bernadette was to leave for college. A week earlier, she had told me excitedly that she'd thought of a great idea for a gift. She embarked on mysterious shopping expeditions and periodically disappeared into her bedroom to work on her creation.

On the day itself, she presented me with a beautifully wrapped package. Somewhat nervously, she said she hoped I didn't think it was silly.

I opened the accompanying envelope and found a photocopy of a story, which she told me to read aloud. "The Hugging Judge" had appeared in the original *Chicken Soup for the Soul.* Bernadette listened as I read about Lee Shapiro, a retired judge who offered hugs to everyone who seemed to need one—a harried bus driver, a harassed meter maid. He created a Hugger Kit containing little stick-on hearts that he could offer strangers in exchange for a hug. Ultimately, he faced a personal test when a friend took him to a home for the disabled, where he found people in desperate need of hugs. At the end of that sobering day, he was faced with an unfortunate man who could do nothing but sit and drool. After the judge forced himself to embrace this solitary person, the patient smiled for the first time in 23 years. The story ended with "How simple it is to make a difference in the life of others."

Deeply moved, I tore the wrapping paper from the gift itself. Tears coursed down my cheeks. Inside was a tall, clear canister decorated with the glittering label "Hugs," and packed with miniature, hand-sewn, heart-shaped pillows.

Bernadette is far away now, but every time I look at that canister of hearts, I feel as if she's just hugged me again.

Some families leave future generations a legacy of wealth or fame. But I remember the importance of my own father's hugs, and I feel that if I can pass along to future generations this simple act of love and acceptance, our family will be blessed indeed.

Loretta Hall

"This is my favorite place—inside your hug."

Garlic Tales

When I remember my mother, I picture her in the kitchen concocting some potent remedy. She couldn't read or write, but her head was crammed with a thousand years of folk wisdom from the old country. In her eyes, *Mala-ha-muvis,* the angel of death, was always trying to strike us kids with childhood diseases. She was in a constant struggle with the evil one. There was no way he could win against my mother and her potions. The only trouble for us was that all her remedies smelled of garlic!

"Here, gargle with this and swallow it."

"But Ma," I'd yell, "it's garlic and junk. My breath will smell."

"So? You have a sore throat. Gargle! Mala-ha-muvis can't stand the smell either."

Of course, the next day the symptoms were gone. It was always that way. Crushed garlic compresses for a fever. Poultices of garlic, cloves and pepper for a runny nose or a toothache. Some families smelled like Lifebuoy soap, but not us. We always smelled like goulash.

With each dose of her homemade antibiotics, Mama muttered secret chants to ward off the evil eye, while we listened to the mystical sounds and tried to guess what they meant. While this may sound overly superstitious, lots of families in our neighborhood were this way, only with a different ethnic twist. My pal Ricci had tea bags, loaded with Italian herbal "medicine," sewn into his shirts—what a whiff! And my Greek friend, Steve, had Bull Durham tobacco bags stashed all over his body. "Lucky amulets," he called them.

Long before the miracles of modern medicine, all the members of our melting pot had their own cures. Can you imagine 35 ripe kids crammed into a classroom, with those curative aromas wafting through the air? God, what a smell! It drove our fifth-grade teacher, Miss Harrison, up the wall. Tears often welled up in her eyes—from the odors or from frustration, I never knew.

"Tell your mothers to stop rubbing you down with garlic," she would shout at us, dabbing her nose daintily with a lace handkerchief. "I can't stand the smell! Do you understand?"

Apparently, Miss Harrison didn't belong to an ethnic group that subscribed to folk medicine. *We* smelled nothing to get excited about.

But when polio struck, and my mother met her enemy Mala-ha-muvis head-on, even I couldn't stand the smell of her new secret weapons. Each of us got three linen bags, stuffed with garlic, camphor and God-knows-what, on a rope around the neck. This time, Miss Harrison called a truce with her smelly kids and just opened the windows a little wider. And sure enough, Mama beat the evil one to the draw; none of us came down with the dreaded disease.

Only once in her life did Mama's artillery fail her. My brother Harry was stricken with diphtheria, and this time the garlic cure didn't work. So she had to pull a different kind of trick from up her sleeve. Harry was gasping for breath, when all of a sudden my mother told us to pray very loudly for *David's* life.

"Who's David, Ma?" we asked.

"That's David lying in the bed."

"No, Ma, that's Harry." We thought she had lost her mind.

She grabbed us and said in a loud voice, *"That's David, understand?"* Then, in hushed tones, she explained, "We'll fool the Mala-ha-muvis. If he thinks it's David, he'll leave our Harry alone. Speak very loudly when I tell you to."

We listened intently as she spoke to the evil one, the angel of death.

"Mala-ha-muvis," she said, "listen to me. You have the wrong little boy. That's David in the bed. We have no Harry in this house. Go away! Leave David alone! You have made a mistake!"

Then she motioned to us, and we all started to shout together, "Mala-ha-muvis, it's true! It's true! We have no brother Harry. This is our brother David. *It's David, Mala-ha-muvis!"*

As we pleaded for our brother's life, Mama chanted in a combination of Yiddish and all the other languages that she remembered from her past. Over and over, she repeated her chants. All through the night, we three frightened little souls stayed awake, pleading a case of wrong identity to the angel of death.

David lived. That's right—I said *David.* From that day on, the name Harry disappeared forever from our little universe. Superstitious? Why take a chance?

Over the years, we all grew up, left the tenements, and educated ourselves. Mama more or less stopped practicing medicine. Then, when I was 47, I was struck with a heart attack. What a look of relief on the nurse's face when Mama's first visit ended and she left my hospital room.

"What a smell! Is it garlic?" the nurse asked. I, of course, smelled nothing. But when I felt under the pillow, there they were, sure enough. Three linen bags on a rope, filled with garlic, camphor and some other stuff.

Mike Lipstock

The Tooth Fairy

As parents, we always hope to develop character traits in our children that will enhance their success in life. When our daughter Meegan, the eldest of five children, lost her front tooth at the age of six, we found the following note wrapped around the tiny tooth:

Der Tooth Fary. Pleze leve me yor majik wand. I can help. I want to be a tooth fary too.

Luv Meegan

Recognizing potential leadership skills, precious opportunity and the teachable moment, the "Tooth Fary" left the following note for little Meegan:

Dear Meegan,

I have worked hard to be a good Tooth Fairy and I love my job. You are too young for the job just now, so I cannot give you my wand. But there are some things that you can start to do to prepare yourself for the job:

1) Always do your best in every job that you do.
2) Treat all people as you wish to be treated.
3) Be kind and helpful to others.

4) Always listen carefully whenever people speak to you.

I will interview you one day when you are older and ready for the job.

Good Luck, Meegan!
The Tooth Fairy

Meegan was thrilled at the response from the Tooth Fairy. She took the message to heart and carefully followed the instructions, always working to improve as she grew. Her character, her strength and her leadership skills grew right along with her.

After graduating *magna cum laude* from college, Meegan accepted a challenging management position. She excelled, and by age 27, she was the top manager of the company.

One day Meegan and I were talking about her success. She told me that the company president had once asked her what influences had motivated her toward success.

"What did you tell him?" I asked.

She replied, "My parents, my teacher and my friends. And, of course, the Tooth Fairy!"

Suzanne Moustakas

"It's the tooth fairy. She says if I FedEx her my tooth, she'll electronically transfer money into my bank account."

Love Notes

From the time each of my children started school, I packed their lunches. And in each lunch I packed, I included a note. Often written on a napkin, the note might be a thank-you for a special moment, a reminder of something we were happily anticipating, or a bit of encouragement for an upcoming test or sporting event.

In early grade school they loved their notes—they commented on them after school, and when I went back to teaching, they even put notes in my lunches. But as kids grow older they become self-conscious, and by the time he reached high school, my older son, Marc, informed me he no longer needed my daily missives. Informing him that they had been written as much for me as for him, and that he no longer needed to read them but I still needed to write them, I continued the tradition until the day he graduated.

Six years after high school graduation, Marc called and asked if he could move home for a couple of months. He had spent those years well, graduating Phi Beta Kappa *magna cum laude* from college, completing two congressional internships in Washington, D.C., winning the Jesse Marvin Unruh Fellowship to the California State

Legislature, and finally, becoming a legislative assistant in Sacramento. Other than short vacation visits, however, he had lived away from home. With his younger sister leaving for college, I was especially thrilled to have Marc coming home.

A couple weeks after Marc arrived home to rest, regroup and write for a while, he was back at work—he had been recruited to do campaign work. Since I was still making lunch every day for his younger brother, I packed one for Marc, too. Imagine my surprise when I got a call from my 24-year-old son, complaining about his lunch.

"Did I do something wrong? Aren't I still your kid? Don't you love me any more, Mom?" were just a few of the queries he threw at me as I laughingly asked him what was wrong.

"My note, Mom," he answered. "Where's my note?"

This year my youngest son will be a senior in high school. He, too, has now announced that he is too old for notes. But like his older brother and sister before him, he will receive those notes till the day he graduates—and in whatever lunches I pack for him afterwards.

Antoinette Kuritz

"Call when you get there!"

Saved by the Belt

As a mother, I have been blessed. I have a nice, smart, good-looking son who has given me much pleasure over the years. In the months leading up to Alan's 16th birthday, there was a lot of excitement and commotion about his upcoming rite of passage—the driver's license.

About a month before his birthday, there was an assembly about seat-belt safety presented at his high school. One of the presenters in this program, Kathy Hezlep, had lost her son in a horrible car crash the year before. When Kathy was first asked to speak at this assembly, she was reluctant. Her son's death had been extremely hard on her. She often felt helpless and discouraged, and she wasn't sure how she could make a difference by speaking with this group.

But the school had convinced her to talk to the students. Kathy spoke about how hard it had been since the loss of her son. There were days when it was an effort just to get out of bed. She spoke directly from her heart and my son took her words straight into his heart. I remember Alan coming home that day and the two of us talking about the crash. We thought it was interesting that she was a single mother (like me) and that her son, Ryan, was her only child (like Alan).

Well, the big day finally arrived. The state of Florida, in its infinite wisdom, granted my "child" a license to take a loaded weapon and drive it! At the time, I thought the worst feeling I could possibly experience was watching my only child drive off *alone* in my car. I was wrong.

Alan had his license exactly one week when the call that is every parent's worst nightmare came. The police told me my son had been driving down a curving road, lost control of the car and, because he was an inexperienced driver, didn't know how to come out of the spin. He managed to miss a lake and a traffic sign that were in his path, but went full force into a light pole. Thank God he wasn't going faster, because if he had hit the pole any harder, he and his two passengers could have been electrocuted.

When I was taken to the scene of the accident and saw the wrecked car, I felt physically sick. I couldn't believe three kids had walked away from that car alive. I thought, *My son must have a guardian angel.* I was right.

When I got to the hospital, I talked to Alan about the accident. He told me that none of the kids had been wearing their seat belts when he started the car. But Kathy Hezlep's words, spoken so sincerely and eloquently about her terrible loss, had impressed him so deeply that he insisted that everyone put on their shoulder and lap belts before he would leave. That is what had saved their lives.

My family is one of the lucky ones. We still have what we consider most precious—each other. I have unending admiration, respect and love for Kathy Hezlep. She is not a celebrity but an everyday person; a mother who, despite her immeasurable loss, had the courage to speak out and make a difference that saved three lives. To me, Kathy is a superstar.

Randee Goldsmith

Red-Letter Failure Day

Failure is delay but not defeat.
It is a temporary detour, not a dead-end street.

William Arthur Ward

Whenever I need help being a mother, I remember my mother and grandmother, women who planted seeds of wisdom in my soul, like a secret garden, to flower even in the bitterest cold.

On one particularly bleak day, I came home to find a "not so polite" second notice on my gas bill, and all three of my children almost down for the count.

Tommy, 11, suffered from a bad haircut. "My teacher took my ball cap away 'cuz gentlemen don't wear hats in the building." He'd endured remarks like "baldy" and "skin head" all day, he told me, as he hid his head with both hands.

Lisa had made the finals of her second-grade spelling bee, only to lose out on the word *afraid.* The irony was not lost on me.

Jenni, in first grade, had been chastised for her nervous giggle at the reading table and snickered at for stumbling over a sentence.

"Well, kids, what we have here is a Red-Letter Failure Day. Let's go celebrate!" Shocked out of their gloom, they watched me closely. "My Grandma Towse always used to say, 'We learn more from our failures than from our successes. The more a stone is weathered by troubles, the farther it will skip.' Let's go to McDonald's for our first Failure Party."

That led to many great failure parties, and we learned to look for what we could celebrate from our tragedies, rather than agonize over what we suffered. I hope I've planted seeds in my children's souls, gathered from the wisdom of the women before me, to be scattered in their own gardens someday.

Judith Towse-Roberts

"It's called a Happy Meal because *I* didn't have to fix it."

The Midnight Caller

I grew up in a rural hamlet in the days when the telephone was a wonder and automobiles were impractical, and unable to traverse muddy country roads. Those were the days before the Depression became a proper noun, when there was barely enough to go around, when neighbors had little to depend on but each other. I recall one fateful night:

The early October storm and darkened night pressed against our windows, wind and rain blending in shrieking turbulence. The rumbling filled our little frame house in deep, rural Arkansas. Inside, the storm even seemed to dim the kerosene lamp on the living room table.

A restless, nine-year-old girl, I was sure the house would blow away any minute. Daddy had gone north, looking for work, and I felt more vulnerable than I admitted, even to myself. But somehow Mama sat, quietly and peacefully, mending her clothes "to do another winter."

"Oh, Mama, you need new clothes," I said, trying to make conversation. On a night like this, I needed the comfort of a calm human voice.

She put her arms around me. "You need better clothes because you go to school."

"But you don't even have a coat for winter."

"God promises to supply our needs. He'll keep his promise, not on demand, but in his own time. I'll be all right."

I envied her stubborn, come-what-may faith. Especially on nights like this. One stormy gust even swept down the chimney and scattered the coals on the hearth.

"Can we lock the doors tonight?" I asked.

Mama smiled as she took the little black hearth shovel and spread ashes over the red coals of fire. "Edith, we can't lock out this storm. And you know we don't lock our doors—neither do our neighbors—especially on nights like this, when someone might need to come in out of the storm."

She picked up the lamp off the table and started for her bedroom. I followed her, crowding her steps.

She tucked me in, but before she could take off her crazy-quilt robe, the sudden crash of the front door opening to a charging wind brought in the smell of rain and the sound of objects being blown around the living room. Just as suddenly, the door slammed shut.

"Not all that noise was wind and thunder." Mama grasped the lamp and started back to the living room. I was afraid to go with her. I was more afraid not to.

At first, all we could see were the scattered contents of Mama's sewing basket. Then our eyes followed muddy boot prints across the bare pine floor, from the door to the overstuffed chair facing the fireplace.

A very wet, disheveled man, short and stout, wearing a dark, mud-spattered suit, sat slumped in that chair. His breath reeked offensively. His left hand still loosely held a gnarled can. "Mama—it's Mr. Hall!"

Mama merely nodded as she shoveled up buried coals from the fireplace, shook off the loose ashes, carried the coals to the wood-burning stove in the kitchen, and covered them with our rich morning kindling of pine. She instructed, "I'll make coffee. You build the fire to help our guest get warm and dry."

"But Mama, he's drunk!"

"Yes, so drunk he wandered into our home, probably thinking it was his."

"But that's a quarter-mile down the road."

"Young lady, Mr. Hall is not a drunkard. What happened tonight, I don't know. But he's a fine man."

I knew that Mr. Hall met someone at the highway each Monday morning and rode to his little tailor shop in Little Rock, where he worked long hours all week. Each Saturday afternoon he came trudging home, leaning on his cane.

As if she read my thoughts, Mama whispered, "He must get very lonely from time to time."

Standing in the kitchen doorway, I was struck by a vagrant thought. "Oh, Mama, what will people say about Mr. Hall—getting drunk?"

"*People* must never know. Do you understand me?"

"Yes, Mama."

As the storm raged, Mama brought Mr. Hall a mug of steaming hot, black coffee. She lifted his head, persuading him to swallow the coffee, a sip at a time. The mug was almost empty when he opened his eyes enough to recognize us. "Miz Un'wood."

"Yes, Mr. Hall, you're going to be just fine."

When Mama took the mug back to the kitchen, Mr. Hall managed to lean on his cane, leave the quilt half-folded across the chair and stagger out into the dying storm. We watched him walk none too steadily toward the front gate, leftover flashes of lightning showing him the way.

"It seems our guest can make it on his own now."

"Mama, why do you call him our guest?" I asked. "He's only our neighbor. We didn't invite him in."

"A guest is anyone who comes under our roof in peace. As for being our neighbor, do you remember who the neighbor is in the story of the Good Samaritan?"

"The man who helped the stranger."

"You see, by being our guest, even unintentionally, we were given the opportunity to be Mr. Hall's neighbor."

A few weeks later, we came home from church to find a brown paper bag on the table labeled, "Mrs. Underwood."

"Probably that dress pattern Mrs. Chiles said she'd loan me. She has a daughter about your size. Open it if you want to," Mama said, as she went to change her clothes.

I reached inside the crinkling bag. "Oh, no, Mama!" I called. "It's a coat for you and it's beautiful!"

Mama came back to look at the garment I held up. Almost tentatively, she turned and slipped her right arm, then her left, into the sleeves. At the time I didn't know I was learning the true meaning of neighborliness. All I knew was that when Mama tried on that winter coat, it fit perfectly.

Edith Dean

3

A MOTHER'S COURAGE

In the depths of winter, I finally learned that there was in me an invincible summer.

Albert Camus

My Son, Ryan

As a mother, my job is to take care of what is possible and trust God with the impossible.

Ruth Bell Graham

It has been seven years since my son, Ryan White, died. Ryan had hemophilia, and he contracted AIDS from a blood product that hemophiliacs take to help their blood clot properly. This was before anyone really knew very much about AIDS. He was only 13 years old when he was diagnosed. The doctors told us then that Ryan would be lucky if he lived another six months.

Ryan lived six more years and was "the kid who put a face to the AIDS disease and helped to educate the nation." President Clinton said that about my Ryan on the day that he signed the reauthorization of the Ryan White CARE Act. The Act provides medical and support services, medicine, home nursing and outpatient care to hundreds of thousands of people in America living with HIV. I know Ryan would be so happy that his life, and his death, have helped so many people.

In the beginning, when we first found out that Ryan

had a fatal disease, I was totally and utterly devastated. I was a single mother of two kids who meant everything to me, and my son, my first-born, was going to die. I didn't think I could go on. Then, on top of that nightmare, we had to deal with the ignorance, fear and hatred that surrounded AIDS at that time. Ryan wanted to go back to school but the school wouldn't allow him to return. Parents were afraid their children could catch AIDS from being in the same room with Ryan. We fought for him to go to school and we won, but the community hostility and pressure were too much for our family. We decided to move to another town.

At Ryan's new high school, it was a completely different story. The students actually went out of their way to welcome him: They organized AIDS education classes and arranged counseling to conquer any fear that still remained in any student. Educating the public about this disease became Ryan's life, his career. Ryan became an international spokesperson for AIDS, appearing on television and in magazines and newspapers around the world. This helped to give meaning to what had happened to our family and ease some of our pain.

We learned to live with AIDS. The nightmare of the disease is that it brings you one powerful infection after another. I thought every cough, every fever might be his last. With AIDS, you never know whether a symptom is serious or mild. The patient is sick and then gets well, and no sooner does he get well than he gets sick again.

Ryan was almost always in a good mood. Even when he had to go to the hospital, he'd try to give me a smile when I walked in the door. However, sometimes if he couldn't do something—go to a particular concert, or meet some exciting people, or travel to an interesting place because he was too sick or too tied up with school—he'd get pouty and upset. Then I might scold him. He'd feel contrite and apologize right away. Maybe write me a note or send me a card.

A sick person would have to be downright saintly never to give in to crankiness. And if you're the one giving care, you can't ever take an angry outburst personally—because it's really the illness spreading or the medication speaking and not the true, loving heart inside.

One day Ryan just grabbed my hand and started swinging it.

"Now, Ryan, when you do something as nice as this, you must want something."

"I don't want anything. Can't a son hold his mother's hand?"

"Come on now, Ryan . . ."

"No, really, Mom. I want to thank you for all you've done for me. Standing by me like you've done."

No one can ever take those words away from me. No one can ever take away what I felt that day as a mother.

I remember someone once asked me, "How do you live, Jeanne, day to day, knowing that your son is going to die?"

I answered, "We don't think about death. We don't have time for it. If you allow it into your life, it will eat you up. You have to go on with your life, making the most of every day and every hour."

Finally the time came when Ryan's body couldn't keep going. When Ryan was dying, the hospital staff must have thought we were insane. Here's this comatose kid, on life support, with a half-crazy mother calling his name, talking to him while he slept. He probably couldn't hear a thing, but we brought him music. He couldn't see a thing, but we stood precariously on chairs, hanging decorative posters and banners on the walls above the screens and the wires and the bleeping monitors. We didn't want to give up on him.

Yet as I stood there watching Ryan's thin little body, I knew there was nothing more anybody could do. Before he drifted into unconsciousness, Ryan had told me, "If you think there's a chance, Mom, go for it." We did. Until the last second, we went for everything we could.

I leaned down close to him and whispered, "It's okay, son. You can let go."

Then he died. They revived him for a few minutes. Momentarily he would die again: I knew that perfectly well. I knew there was no chance. But still, to have to call the battle lost . . . it was a moment of inexpressible sorrow for me and my family.

"If you want, you can tell them no more," a close friend said. "It's up to you, Jeanne."

I talked to my parents, and to Ryan's sister, Andrea. Then I told the doctors, "No more."

Dr. Marty Kleiman, who had taken care of Ryan from the beginning, who helped him live for almost six years when other physicians predicted that he would die in six months, went out and made the announcement that my boy had passed away in his sleep, without pain.

The sparkle was gone.

Now, seven years later, the sparkle is slowly returning. My state of mind is like the dawn these days. I look forward to everything. I love being married. My new husband, Roy, has made my life fun again. My daughter, Andrea, has grown into a strong, smart, beautiful person. I look forward to everything our life has in store for us—adventures, travels, grandchildren. On the edge of the sky just beyond a cloud, I think I really see the end of the plague of AIDS. Every day, people whose lives once seemed to be finished are bursting with new health. The cure is coming. It's almost here. I feel that I will live to see it. What greater gift can anyone receive than this sense of happy anticipation?

The garden has been my therapy. Here among the flowers and the bright fruit, when the light is brand new and everything is fresh and wet and the leaves are beaded up with dewdrops, I work in the household of nature and refresh my spirit. It seems to me that every weed I pull is a bit of grief I am learning to set aside, a tear I've weeded out so that good cheer can grow again.

I see in the faces of the flowers all the friends I have lost: I see my son's face. They are beautiful in the new morning, opening like smiles and shining with hope.

Thank you, Lord, for another day.

Jeanne White

Awright, Mom?

I was deep in thought, working on an important report, when the phone rang. *Why now?* I thought in frustration, as the baby-sitter told me my two-year-old son wasn't feeling well. "Jordan's just not acting like himself," she said. "He's not running a fever, but he's very lethargic."

During the long drive home, I calmed down and my thoughts turned to Jordan. I remembered how surprised I was when I learned I was pregnant with him. Growing up, I was convinced I would never want kids. But back then, I didn't plan on falling in love with a single father of two young daughters.

After five years of marriage, I had grown to love being a stepmom. It was a role that suited me, much to my new daughters' credit. But I remember worrying about how they would react to the news about the baby, since the girls were finally at a point where they felt secure. Recalling their response, I laughed out loud. The girls had taken me into the bathroom, away from their father, and expressed their only concern: "Does this mean you and Dad had sex?"

Seven months later, after 22 hours of hard labor, we were finally able to take our first look at Jordan. With a last name of Perez, we weren't expecting a little redhead, but that's what we got. A gorgeous, healthy little boy with eyes so dark they were almost black.

"He's a part of all of us," said Val, our oldest daughter, as she gazed lovingly at her new baby brother. "He brings us all together."

My reverie was broken as I pulled into the driveway and ran into the house. Jordan was sleeping, but his breathing was labored and he was damp with sweat. I picked him up, strapped him into his car seat and headed for the doctor's office.

As I drove, I divided my time between watching the road and watching Jordan. The baby-sitter was right, he wasn't acting like himself. He was awake now, staring at me with sad, tired eyes.

Several blocks from the doctor's office, I turned to take another look. I saw Jordan's lips start to quiver, slowly at first, then faster and faster. Soon after, I was terrified to see foam coming from his mouth. His entire body was shaking uncontrollably, and his eyes rolled back into his head. Then, just as suddenly as his seizure had started, it stopped, and Jordan slumped in his seat.

In panic, I ran two red lights and sped into the parking lot. When I lifted him out of the car, Jordan was completely limp. His lifeless eyes stared off into space. It was then I realized he wasn't breathing.

"Something is terribly wrong!" I wailed, as I ran into the building. The doctor, alerted by my screams, met me in the waiting room and pulled Jordan from my arms. He felt Jordan's neck for a pulse, then asked a nurse to call the paramedics while he started CPR. Another nurse held me in the hallway, where I listened helplessly as they tried to revive my son.

"Come on, baby," someone pleaded. "Come back to us."

"I can't get a line!" said another frantic voice.

I couldn't believe what was happening. I was so confused and terrified of losing my little boy. I wanted to be with Jordan. I wanted to hold his hand and kiss his cheek and tell him everything would be okay. I felt so frightened, so out of control.

By the time the paramedics arrived, Jordan still wasn't breathing. They worked on him for several minutes, then hurriedly wheeled him out on a stretcher.

"We have him on life support," explained a paramedic, as he led me to the ambulance. "Your son's not able to breathe on his own right now, so we're going to do it for him."

My husband met me in a private waiting room at the hospital. As he knelt on the floor and sobbed into my lap, I realized I had never seen him cry before. A nurse entered the room and gently asked if we wanted her to call our pastor. "No!" cried my husband in anguish. "He's going to be all right!"

An hour later, we were finally allowed to see Jordan. My indomitable toddler looked so small and fragile, hooked up to countless tubes and still shaking. The seizure had started again, immediately after he had been revived.

The emergency room doctor was clearly frustrated. "All I can tell you is that Jordan's a very sick little boy," he said. "We've given him the maximum amount of phenobarbital, but he's still seizing."

Another hour dragged by. Jordan was stabilized and transported to a pediatric hospital. He was still on life support, but the seizure had finally stopped.

The CAT scans showed nothing unusual. The spinal tap was normal. There was still no explanation for Jordan's severe seizure, and nothing to tell us whether the lack of oxygen had damaged his brain.

My husband and I were able to stay with Jordan in the intensive care unit. I held Jordan's hand and kissed his cheek and told him that everything would be okay. Late in the evening, while our pastor and family members prayed in the waiting area, Jordan coughed out his breathing tube and took his first unassisted breath since the seizure began.

The next morning when Jordan finally opened his eyes, my husband and I didn't know what to expect. Brain damage was a possibility, but we were convinced we could deal with anything. Losing him was the one thing we couldn't bear.

Still feeling the effects of the medication, Jordan tried to focus his eyes. I knew if he recognized us, everything would be okay. Slowly, he looked at my husband and me. When he reached for us and weakly whispered, "Momma. Daddy," I broke down and cried.

Seeing my tears, Jordan groggily asked, "Awright, Mom?"

I was overwhelmed by his concern. After spending the better part of the last 24 hours fighting for his life, my precious little two-year-old was worried about *me.*

"Oh yes, my darling boy," I answered, as I gently stroked his cheek. "I'm very all right."

Six months have passed since then, and Jordan has completely recovered. I've stopped sleeping on his bedroom floor at night and no longer feel a need to monitor his every move. We've never learned what caused the seizure. It may have been a viral infection, or perhaps a sudden change in body temperature. Because of this uncertainty, Jordan will take antiseizure medication for at least two years.

Last night I watched Jordan play soccer with his sisters and dad in the back yard, and I thought as I often do about how close we came to losing him. The ball bounced over to where I was sitting, and Jordan ran after it. As I handed him the ball, Jordan noticed the tears in my eyes. He put his tiny hand on my knee and asked, "Awright, Mom?"

"Oh yes, my darling boy," I answered, as I smiled and hugged him close. "I'm very all right."

Christine Perez

Moving Mountains

There were two warring tribes in the Andes, one that lived in the lowlands and the other high in the mountains. The mountain people invaded the lowlanders one day, and as part of their plundering of the people, they kidnapped a baby of one of the lowlander families and took the infant with them back up into the mountains.

The lowlanders didn't know how to climb the mountain. They didn't know any of the trails that the mountain people used, and they didn't know where to find the mountain people or how to track them in the steep terrain.

Even so, they sent out their best party of fighting men to climb the mountain and bring the baby home.

The men tried first one method of climbing and then another. They tried one trail and then another. After several days of effort, however, they had climbed only a couple of hundred feet.

Feeling hopeless and helpless, the lowlander men decided that the cause was lost, and they prepared to return to their village below.

As they were packing their gear for the descent, they saw the baby's mother walking toward them. They realized that she was coming down the mountain that they hadn't figured out how to climb.

And then they saw that she had the baby strapped to her back. *How could that be?*

One man greeted her and said, "We couldn't climb this mountain. How did you do this when we, the strongest and most able men in the village, couldn't do it?"

She shrugged her shoulders and said, "It wasn't your baby."

Jim Stovall
Bits & Pieces

Hearts Across the World

Clattering along in the hot Indian sun, our train neared the southern city of Nagpur, India. Beside me this Thanksgiving Day sat my husband and our two adopted Indian sons. We were traveling to Nagpur to meet the small Indian girl we were adopting to complete our family. Sadly, because the foreign adoption process takes a long time, we would not be able to take our daughter home to the United States right away. But at least we could visit her for a few hours.

Three years earlier, I had come to India from our home in Maryland and established a second residence in Hyderabad, near the orphanage where I was adopting my sons. Now I was staying in Hyderabad again, and my husband was visiting briefly from Maryland, where his job supported our efforts to adopt this little girl. The duration of my stay would be determined by the slow-moving Indian adoption court, a system over which we had no control. But at least for a few hours on this hot day, we could be a family.

Shortly after lunch, a bicycle rickshaw carried us the last miles to the overcrowded orphanage where we were greeted by a hundred eager faces, each hoping to belong to us. The sight was heartbreaking. And yet the people in charge seemed genuinely to care for the children, and the conditions, though humble, were orderly.

We waited, fidgeting in our seats, until a small, delicate girl was escorted into the room. Immediately, I recognized the child my heart had been praying for daily for almost a year. Ghita, our daughter! We hugged and kissed her in our joy, creating in that moment a bond that would last a lifetime.

Ghita could not speak a word of English, but it didn't matter. She was our daughter, and at last our family would be complete. We shared some ice cream and looked at picture books, then parted with tear-stained smiles, knowing that in a month we could be together for good.

My husband returned to his job in the States, and I settled in with my sons in Hyderabad, almost 300 miles from the Nagpur orphanage, anxiously awaiting notification that Ghita's papers were processed. I often lay awake at night, imagining myself holding her in my arms and protecting her from harm in the crowded orphanage. She was so delicate, so trusting.

Finally the news arrived that I could proceed to Nagpur immediately to take custody of my daughter. Wasting no time, I arranged to travel by air, so that I would not have to leave my boys overnight. Then it happened—the Hindu temple at Ayodhya in the north was bombed by Muslims. Although we were thousands of miles away, Hyderabad was a heavily Muslim city. All flights were canceled for fear of terrorism, and the entire city was placed under curfew.

Undaunted, I decided to travel to Nagpur by train instead, making arrangements for my sons to stay with friends. But our hired driver, himself a devout Muslim, advised against it. "Madam, you would not come home alive!" He explained that an American woman traveling alone would be a prime target for random violence. My close Hindu friends gave me the same advice and urged me to abandon my plans.

Then I hit on the idea of driving to Nagpur. After all, I reasoned, my driver was Muslim and I knew I could trust him. He had even helped us secure food during curfew, allowing the children and me to stay safely at home. But again he discouraged me. "Madam," he said, "I am only one man. What can I do against a gang of robbers? Be safe—remain at home!" I had to remember my responsibility to the children I already had, so I sadly surrendered to the reality that there was nothing to do but wait.

As the days turned into weeks and weeks into months, I prayed daily for my little daughter in the orphanage. *What did she think? Did she even know why I hadn't come?* My sons grew more agitated and harder to handle. I desperately needed support, but my husband and friends were 10,000 miles away. As the challenges I faced grew more severe, I realized that I alone had to meet them, through my own inner strength. *Keep cool. Try to act normal. God, please give me the strength I need to get through this.*

Gradually the tension between the Hindus and Muslims dissolved, curfew was lifted, and life in the city normalized. It was now March, four months since that sunny Thanksgiving Day when we met Ghita. My husband came to visit again, and I felt I had passed an enormous test. I could take a deep breath now and feel some lightness in my heart—and there in my heart was Ghita.

Then the miracle—the news that flights to Nagpur had resumed! We acted like lightning and within a few hours were holding tickets for the next day's flight.

The bicycle rickshaw to the orphanage seemed to move in slow motion. I could hardly contain myself. Then, finally, the moment we had waited for arrived. Out of the crowd of eager faces, I saw only one—one shining little face that stepped forward and said, "Mommy!" It was her first English word, spoken with eyes as big as the universe and enough love to last a lifetime.

Amsheva Miller

Real Vision

My friend Michelle is blind, but you'd never know it. She makes such good use of her other senses, including her "sixth sense" of intuition, that she rarely gives the impression she's missed anything.

Michelle parents her children pretty much like the rest of us, except that she doesn't sweat the small stuff. Her daughter, Sarah, six, and her son, Aaron, nine, really benefit from Michelle's relaxed attitude. Once, Michelle told me that it sometimes bothered her that her children probably weren't dressed according to her taste. You see, she relies on her husband and her friends to choose clothes for them. But since friends and Daddy don't presume to know what the kids like, Sarah and Aaron often get to pick out their own clothes. But Michelle avoids any battles. As long as the clothes are clean and weather-appropriate, she doesn't make it an issue. And she trusts that, at six and nine, her children can tell if they are too hot or too cold.

Another area where Michelle rarely argues with her kids is in keeping the house clean. It isn't that Michelle doesn't know when there's a mess. She knows it's time to clean when she steps on crumbs or toys that have been left out. But in Michelle's house, the kids have learned to put their things away because it wouldn't just annoy their mother to have a mess, it could be dangerous for her. Indeed, Michelle moves around her house so fast that often guests don't realize she's blind.

I realized this the first time my six-year-old, Kayla, went to play there. When Kayla came home, she was very excited about her day. She told me they had baked cookies, played games and done art projects. But she was especially excited about her finger-painting project.

"Mom, guess what?" said Kayla, all smiles. "I learned how to mix colors today! Blue and red make purple, and yellow and blue make green! Isn't that neat? And Michelle painted with us. She said she liked the way the paint feels squishing through her fingers."

Something about my child's excitement caught my attention, and I realized that I had never finger-painted with Kayla. I didn't like the mess. As a result, my child had learned about color from a blind friend. The irony made me sit down and take a look at my child and at myself.

Then Kayla said, "Michelle told me my picture showed joy, pride and a sense of accomplishment. She really saw what I was doing!" Kayla said she had never felt how good finger paints felt until Michelle showed her how to paint without looking at her paper.

That's when I realized Kayla didn't know that Michelle was blind. It had just never come up in conversation.

When I told her, she was quiet for a moment. At first, she didn't believe me. "But Mommy, Michelle understood exactly what was in my picture!" Kayla insisted. And I knew my child was right because Michelle had listened to Kayla describe her artwork. Michelle had also heard Kayla's pride in her work, her wonder at her discovery of the way colors blend, and her delight in the texture of the medium.

We were silent for a minute. Then Kayla said slowly, "You know, Mommy, Michelle really did 'see' my picture. She just used my eyes."

I've never heard anyone refer to Michelle as handicapped. She isn't. Hers is a special type of "vision" that all mothers could use.

Marsha Arons

Every Morning Is a Gift

I can't shake the images in my mind of the night before it all started. I can see myself at the dinner table, lifting my glass to toast my daughter and her fiancé.

Family and friends were all around me, smiling faces in the candlelight. My husband, Steve, leaned over and kissed me.

Those joyous hours would be the last before the fear set in. That night, as I lay in bed, my life changed forever.

I'd had discomfort for weeks, but I thought it was a backache. When I awoke in the middle of the night feeling as if someone was standing on my chest, I knew it was my heart. "Get me to the hospital," I gasped to Steve.

"You'll be okay," he said over and over. *He's so scared,* I wept. *And oh, God, I am too.*

At the hospital, I tearfully recalled another hospital long ago, and me—just 10 years old—standing over my father's hospital bed after his first heart attack.

My mother had died years before while giving birth to my sister, and Daddy was my world. Then, when I was 12, he had another heart attack—at work. I never had the chance to say good-bye, and the grief that set in on me felt endless. Now I was the one in the hospital. *Please,* I prayed, *don't let me die without saying good-bye to my children. Jeffrey's only 13 . . . Jason's 15—he's becoming such a young man—and Tricia's getting married! She needs me now.*

Steve went to get the kids as I underwent an angiogram to find out where the blockage was. "Three of the four major arteries are blocked," the doctors said.

"But I'm only 39!" I wept.

My doctor explained that I'd inherited heart disease from my dad. "You need bypass surgery," he said. "But your heart is so damaged, any procedure may . . ."

Kill me. I trembled with fear. But it wasn't fear of dying. More than anything, I couldn't accept leaving my loved ones to endure the grief I'd known as a child.

"I may not live . . ." I told the kids as their tears and mine fell.

In the days before the surgery, Steve visited as often as he could, trying to smile. But I saw the fear in his eyes.

Steve and I had been married only a year. "We waited for each other. We have a lot left to do," he whispered. I nodded wistfully.

Tricia talked about the flowers for her wedding. I smiled. Jeffrey and Jason talked about school.

"When you come home . . ." they'd say. They were all trying to be brave. But we were all so scared.

The morning of my surgery, I watched the sun rise over the lake. There was a sailboat gliding past. I tried to imagine the peaceful feeling of being on it. But as surgery neared, that feeling was replaced by terror. After kissing Steve and the kids and feeling their tear-streaked cheeks, I frantically wanted to live.

God, I prayed before I was anesthetized, *if you let me live to see my kids grown, I won't waste a minute . . .*

The next thing I knew, surgery was over, and I was holding Steve's hand and looking at my children. *How gentle his touch, how beautiful their smiles. And now I have all the time in the world to enjoy them,* I thought.

But two days later, my doctor explained that my arteries would probably clog up again. And my heart could not withstand another operation.

"The surgery might buy you another six years," he said. "I'm sorry." *Six years—that's the blink of an eye!* My throat tightened and I couldn't catch my breath.

Then I remembered: Six years was what I'd prayed for. My youngest child would be 18—grown. I'd have more time with Steve. Yes, God was keeping his end of the bargain. Now, I vowed, I'll keep mine—and make the most of my time.

So I celebrated life—as I watched my daughter walk down the aisle, as I counseled my boys through girl troubles, as I shared weekends in Steve's arms, as I baked birthday cakes.

Every single moment, from greeting the mailman to cradling my grandchildren, had a special magic.

Then, as I neared the six-year mark, the pain started. "There's nothing more we can do," doctors said. And that familiar fear swept over me. One day, Jeffrey laid his head on my chest and sobbed. Another day, Tricia tearfully said, "Mom, I need you. My kids need their grandma!"

"I'll be there as long as I can," I said soothingly to each of them. Why did I think my family would be more ready to say good-bye now? Six years, 10 . . . 20! Is it ever enough?

Fight for your life, Bev! I screamed inside. So I started reading books on diet and on positive thinking. *I will live!* I vowed.

Maybe it was God's gift. Maybe it was my strength. But now, two years later, I'm doing better than I ever hoped.

I continue to cherish each new morning. And snuggling up with Steve at night, I give thanks for all the simple, wonderful—even frustrating—things that happened that day.

I know the day may come when the sun rises without me. And I weep to think I could miss my granddaughter's curtsy at the close of her first school play, or her little brother's first ball game. But God has already given me more than I asked for. And I've learned how precious each moment is.

Bev Shortt
As told to Deborah Bebb

A Love Without Limits

This is courage . . . to bear unflinchingly what heaven sends.

Euripides

One of my favorite things to do is watch my son Andrew play at the park near our Baltimore home. Andrew is not as fast or as talkative as other children his age, but he's just as sweet and beautiful as they are. And I know that in his own way, he has just as much to give to the world as they do.

But there was a time when I wasn't sure I was ready to be a mother at all—let alone be Andrew's mother. I was 17 years old when I became pregnant. My high school sweetheart, Jim, and I had been married right after graduation, and although we both wanted children, we worried about becoming parents too soon. But we loved this baby from the moment we learned I was pregnant.

So as my stomach grew bigger, we imagined cheering our child on at Little League games and watching him toss his cap in the air at his high school graduation. Like most parents, we dreamed our child would be the smartest, strongest, best-looking kid on the block.

Then, in my eighth month, I suddenly started bleeding, and Jim rushed me to the hospital.

Doctors gave me drugs to stop my labor, but then a sonogram showed my baby was unusually small. "It could be Down's syndrome," they told me gently.

Jim and I cried and prayed. "God, please make our baby all right." Tests showed our baby not only had Down's syndrome, but he also had a blockage in his intestinal tract that required immediate surgery. Even if he survived the stressful birth, he easily might die on the operating table.

I lay in my hospital bed hugging my belly. From the way doctors described Down's syndrome, I knew my baby would never play Little League, go to a regular school or have a family of his own. He'd always be different, slower, unable to do all the things we had dreamed of for him.

Just being a mother was a big enough challenge. To me, it was the most important job in the world, and I desperately wanted to do it right. Before I learned my baby had problems, I'd worried whether I would give my child the right mix of love, understanding and discipline.

Now, that worry became panic. *I'm not sure I can handle this!* I agonized. But then the doctor asked, "Jennifer, do you want us to do everything to save your baby?"

For a moment I just stared at him. *"Do everything . . . ?"* His words echoed in my mind. *What is he saying?* I thought. And as it suddenly clicked in, a fierce love unlike any I'd ever felt rose up in me.

Of course I want them to do everything they can for my baby! I thought, as a huge wave of protectiveness washed over me. This was my child—how could I want anything else?

"I'm going to have this baby," I told the doctor tearfully. "And I'm going to love him—no matter what."

That night, doctors induced my labor. When they put little Andrew in my arms, I showered him with kisses. He looked like a little angel, and my heart twisted as doctors took him to surgery. *Be safe, little one,* I thought. *Mommy loves you.*

Andrew's surgery was a success, and when we took him home I was filled with joy. But I cringed at the looks of pity my friends and coworkers gave me when they saw little Andrew.

It's not so horrible! I thought. But I felt sorry for Andrew too. "There's so much in life he'll never do," I sobbed. "It just isn't fair."

Desperate for help, I got in touch with a Down's syndrome support group the hospital suggested. Listening to other parents talk about their hopes, I knew I was not alone. And I learned Andrew would probably be able to work, make friends and live on his own. Most of all, he'd be happy. What more could a mother ask?

When Andrew took his first steps and babbled his first "Dada," I didn't worry about how far behind he was. Instead, I rejoiced—and did everything I could to help him achieve more.

I enrolled him in early intervention classes for speech and physical therapy, and at home we did special exercises to increase his motor skills. When he fed himself or threw a ball, we both clapped and laughed.

Andrew is five now, and he constantly amazes me. He's going to a school and making friends, and I don't worry that other kids will tease him—they adore him.

Sometimes my heart still breaks when I think of the things he'll never do. But then I remember all the wonderful things he has done, and all the things he will do in his own good time. And I know that with courage and love, you can do just about anything.

Jennifer Hill
As told to Chet Dembeck

A Mother's Fight for a Special Child

No language can express the power and beauty and heroism of a mother's love.

Edwin H. Chapin

Frank and Lee married in 1948 after serving in the Catholic church, he as a seminary student and she as a nun. When they started a family, Lee decided that she wanted six children. The first arrived in 1951, with five more following in the next 11 years. But by the time the fifth child, Tom, arrived, Lee was at the point where she wasn't sure she'd be able to care for another.

At six months, Tom still wasn't able to take spoon feedings or hold his head up. Lee felt that he was developing slowly in general. So she took him to the pediatrician, who told her that she was making a big deal over nothing.

"Lots of babies have trouble adjusting to spoon feedings," he told her. "This is normal."

"I think I know what's normal and not normal," she told him evenly. "I've had four others. There's something wrong."

So she took her baby to another doctor, who told her to wait a year to see if he would "grow out of it." So Lee waited—and watched.

Over the next year, Tom did manage to hold his head up, but in many other ways he got worse. He often refused to eat. Or he would eat only squash, until his skin turned an orange tinge. But the most worrisome development involved his violent outbursts. He would attack his older siblings while they watched television, or hit Lee from the back seat of the car while she tried to drive. Lee knew that temper tantrums are normal for a toddler, but the intensity of Tom's tantrums worried her.

When he was a year and a half, Lee made the rounds to the doctors and the specialists again. This time, no one told her Tom was normal. One doctor diagnosed PKU, a metabolic disease that can result in retardation. Another said it wasn't PKU, but brain damage at birth that had deprived the brain of oxygen. After a year, meeting this doctor and that doctor, Lee was told that Tom could never lead a normal life and should be institutionalized.

Lee was horrified. How could she send her child, only three years old, away to an institution, where the possibility of growing up healthy could be jeopardized forever? When Lee and Frank visited the institution the doctors suggested, all the children she saw there were seriously mentally disabled, many unable to communicate. Tom had problems, Lee decided, but this was not the place to send him.

Then a visiting nurse told Lee about a hospital in Ann Arbor that might be able to help Tom. The doctors and psychiatrists there concluded that he was mentally disabled and would never be able to finish high school. A social worker at the hospital suggested that Frank and Lee would find it a problem to raise a son with such limited capabilities, since they both had been to college.

"He'll never be anything more than a ditch digger," she said.

"So?" she retorted. "Let me tell you something. I don't care what he does for a living. I love all of my children. I don't love them based on their intelligence. It doesn't make me love Tom any less if he's not a genius."

But Tom exceeded the doctors' expectations. Reluctantly, the doctors agreed to let Tom attend a regular school. Although he experienced periods of difficulty, he not only graduated from high school, but also completed two-and-a-half years of college. Somewhere along the way, his mental disability was found to be emotionally based and was treated properly.

I'm glad Lee didn't give up on that child, because that child with the rough start in life was me. Today I'm on medication to control my emotional ups and downs. And when I look back on my early years, I thank God I had a mother who was so stubborn that she wouldn't listen to the doctors' pessimistic predictions for my bleak future. My mother loved me enough to listen to what her heart told her instead—that the best weapon in a fight for a child is a lot of faith and a lot of love.

Tom Mulligan

Welcome to Holland

I am often asked to describe the experience of raising a child with a disability—to try to help people who have not shared that unique experience to understand it, to imagine how it would feel. It's like this . . .

When you're going to have a baby, it's like planning a fabulous vacation trip—to Italy. You buy a bunch of guidebooks and make wonderful plans. The Coliseum. The Michelangelo *David.* The gondolas in Venice. You may learn some handy phrases in Italian. It's all very exciting.

After months of eager anticipation, the day finally arrives. You pack your bags and off you go. Several hours later, the plane lands. The stewardess comes in and says, "Welcome to Holland."

"Holland?!" you say. "What do you mean, Holland?? I signed up for Italy! I'm supposed to be in Italy. All my life I've dreamed of going to Italy."

But there's been a change in the flight plan. They've landed in Holland and there you must stay.

The important thing is that they haven't taken you to a horrible, disgusting, filthy place, full of pestilence, famine and disease. It's just a different place.

So you must go out and buy new guidebooks. And you

must learn a whole new language. And you will meet a whole new group of people you would never have met.

It's just a *different* place. It's slower paced than Italy, less flashy than Italy. But after you've been there for a while and you catch your breath, you look around . . . and you begin to notice that Holland has windmills . . . and Holland has tulips. Holland even has Rembrandts.

But everyone you know is busy coming and going from Italy . . . and they're all bragging about what a wonderful time they had there. And for the rest of your life, you will say, "Yes, that's where I was supposed to go. That's what I had planned."

And the pain of that will never, ever, ever, ever go away . . . because the loss of that dream is a very, very significant loss.

But . . . if you spend your life mourning the fact that you didn't get to Italy, you may never be free to enjoy the very special, the very lovely things . . . about Holland.

Emily Perl Kingsley

4

ON MOTHERHOOD

A mother's love is like a circle, it has no beginning and no ending. It keeps going around and around ever expanding, touching everyone who comes in contact with it. Engulfing them like the morning's mist, warming them like the noontime sun, and covering them like a blanket of evening stars. A mother's love is like a circle, it has no beginning and no ending.

Art Urban

Reprinted by permission of Benita Epstein.

Mom's the Word

Mother is the name of God in the lips and hearts of little children.

William Makepeace Thackery

"Mom," a girlish voice calls out in a busy Wal-Mart. I turn to the child's voice. So do several other women. It doesn't matter that I have gone to the store alone, that my daughters, much older than the owner of the helpless little voice, are safely ensconced in school. When I hear the cry "Mom," I stand on alert, poised for action, ready for rescue.

Sure, she said "Dada" first, but we women know it's just because her mouth couldn't quite reach the round wonder of the word "Mom." In those three letters, so much is said. Like Esperanto, "Mom" holds international meaning: It's a complete Morse code of messages and wants.

"Mom, Mom." The voice is a vapor trail through my jet-lagged sleep. She has dropped her bottle, her blanket is out of reach. I stumble into her room and pick up the comforting container of milk. I smooth the threadbare silky "blankey" over her, lean into the crib, kiss her and whisper my love. Eyes closed, I wander back to bed. I don't need any lights: Too well, I know the way.

"Mom!" The voice stabs at me, even after I have driven away from the city's premier day care center, a place where all the teachers have college degrees and are certified in kindness, the rooms are brightly colored, the children diverse and the classroom sizes small, and the educational content stimulating, but not overwhelming. But the center of my loins cries when I walk out of this Cadillac of care, wailing as though I am dumping her alone in a stench-ridden hovel.

My car bucks the traffic, wanting to turn back to rescue this child from her prison. Once in my office, I call the day care center, expecting to hear her screams permeating the background.

"Oh, Jessica stopped crying the moment you left," the teacher assures me.

The dictionary defines "Mom" as "a female parent." But my children have used that word to mean so much more.

Sarah is four and she cries, "Maaawwm!" I know she has misbuttoned her shirt, jammed her zipper.

Jessica, age seven, shrieks "Mo-hom," in a rushed accusatory tone. She can't find a matching sock and she mistakenly thinks this is my responsibility.

Jessica's tone changes when she gets older. She learns to lilt the word, to speak it sweetly: Will I please iron her yellow dress? Already late for school, Sarah, at age 13, spits out the word in a Bernhardt voice. "Mom!" means "I'm desperate for new clothes, I can't believe I exist in these rags."

Now Jessica drives herself to school. Still, she "Mom's" when her clothes are all dirty. "Mom" translates into "May I please please please borrow your new silk blouse?"

"Mom?"

She is older now and rarely knocks on my door in the morning. Yet I recognize the vulnerability of her voice.

"Do you want help typing your paper?" I ask her, getting out of bed quickly, as I have always done, to see what she needs.

She nods, clutching a stack of history books. Then she bursts out crying.

"I don't like John anymore." Her words are smeared by the sobbing. "He's mad at me and I don't know why and he won't talk to me, and . . ."

I put my arm around her and lead her to the kitchen. I make tea, hand her a box of tissues and wait for her to talk. Part of me wants to shield my child from the cruel beasts of relationships. Part of me knows she gains her strength from understanding the boys who come into her life.

"Mom, what should I do?"

The word burrows into my heart like an arrow. I wish the answer were simpler: I wish I could find a sock, iron a skirt, lend a blouse and once again be her hero.

I am exhausted by too much work and too little time. I feel the psychic drain of being responsible for myself and my daughters. I am tired of being a grown-up. I talk to my friends and they empathize. I talk to my brother and he problem-solves.

Then I dial the familiar number I called from college, from my trailer in Alabama, from the duplex in Germany, from a series of homes and apartments throughout the Midwest.

"Hello," says the voice, uncertain, crackled, the voice that has lived through so much.

"Mom?" I say.

"Honey, are you all right?" my mother says.

Somehow, that is everything I want to hear.

Deborah Shouse

Motherhood—A Trivial Pursuit?

You've no doubt heard of Trivial Pursuit, the popular board game based on answering trivia questions. I've often thought that mothering is similar to such a game. It seems we spend much of our time in a maze of trivia, fumbling through the daily minutiae of family living, never quite sure whether we're ahead of the game or not.

With that in mind, I have devised my own trivia game for mothers. The rules are simple—you'll start with 10 marbles, and collect or deduct marbles as you play the game.

Are you ready? Okay, let's go . . .

Square 1. You are awaiting the arrival of your firstborn child. If you look at your rapidly expanding waistline and say, "As soon as the baby is born I'll be a size 6 again," deduct 2 marbles—for wishful thinking.

Square 2. It is two years later and your second child is soon to be born. To avoid sibling rivalry you have prepared carefully for the event, spending "quality time" with your firstborn, giving him his own baby doll to feed, bathe and cuddle. When the new baby comes home, older brother is fine. But deduct 1 marble—it's the dog who's jealous.

Square 3. Your number one son has just announced at the supper table that he is to be an oak tree in the school play and needs a costume by tomorrow morning. If you stay up until 3 A.M. making an imaginative and innovative costume, deduct 3 marbles for setting an impossible example for the rest of us. On the other hand, if you stick him into a brown paper bag with a hole for head and arms and tape green leaves all over front and back, collect 5 marbles. You've just taken the rest of us off the hook.

Square 4. The kids now number three and are all in school. You have discovered that "mother" is synonymous with "taxi service." On a typical day you drop the youngest off at her music lesson, then go with the boys to their Little League practice. Then back to pick up daughter and drop accumulated Little Leaguers off at their assorted homes. It's dinner on the fly because somebody has to be at choir practice at 7 P.M. It's now bedtime and you discover you have an extra kid. But you don't panic . . . it's happened before and soon the phone will ring as another mother discovers she's missing one. Collect 5 marbles for endurance.

Square 5. The little darlings that you tucked lovingly into bed for so many years suddenly treat you as though you lost your brains in kindergarten. They are embarrassed to be seen with you. Guess what: You are the parent of teenagers, those strange creatures who think they are eight feet tall and bulletproof. If you survive this age with your senses intact, collect 8 marbles for heroism under fire. Until then, always remember that you hold the ultimate weapon—you have the car keys!

Square 6. You can tell your oldest child is home from college when you see the pile of dirty laundry in the front hall. If you take the clothes downstairs to sort, wash and press as in days of old . . . deduct 3 marbles and shame on you! If, instead, you take him by the hand and show him the room where the automatic washer and dryer have been housed since he was small, collect 5 marbles. Some of the most important things in life are not taught in college, you know.

Square 7. The children, by some miracle, have grown into responsible adults. By chance you overhear your now grown-up son telling the same bedtime stories to his firstborn that you so long ago told to him, and the tears fall silently down your cheeks. Don't despair—these are the pearls of parenting, and that is what the game is all about.

* * * * *

Congratulations. You have crossed the finish line and it's time to add up the score. The game you have just played is called "Motherhood"—and if you haven't lost all your marbles—you win!

Jacklyn Lee Lindstrom

"Of COURSE I'd like to be the ideal mother. But I'm too busy raising children."

Reprinted by permission of Bil Keane.

Art 101

When I was 34 years old and the mother of three children, I took Art 101 at Motlow State Community College in Tennessee. One day our instructor announced that the project we had done on the first day of class was to be included in the notebook that would be a major part of our grade. "May I do another project?" I asked somewhat anxiously. "I just don't have the first one anymore."

The instructor asked what had happened to it. Somewhat embarrassed, I replied, "It's on my mother's fridge."

Author Unknown
Submitted by Jana Barrett

A Mother's Letter to a Son Starting Kindergarten

Dear George,

When your big brother and your little dog and I walked you up to school today, you had no idea how I was feeling.

You were so excited, you had packed and unpacked the washable markers and safety scissors in your backpack a dozen times.

I am really going to miss those lazy mornings when we waved your brother and sister off to school. I'd settle in with my coffee and newspaper, handing you the comics to color while you watched *Sesame Street.*

Because you are my youngest, I had learned a few things by the time you came along. I found out that the seemingly endless days of babyhood are gone like lightning. I blinked, and your older siblings were setting off for school as eagerly as you did this morning.

I was one of the lucky ones; I could choose whether to work or not. By the time it was your turn, the glittering prizes of career advancement and a double income had lost their luster. A splash in the puddles with you in your bright red boots or "just one more" rereading of your favorite book, *Frog and Toad Are Friends,* meant more.

You didn't go to preschool and I'm not exactly Maria Montessori. I hope that doesn't hold you back. You learned numbers by helping me count the soda cans we returned to the store. (You could usually charm me into letting you pick out a treat with the money we got back.)

I'm not up on the Palmer method, but you do a fine job of writing your name on the sidewalk in chalk, in capitals to make it look more important. And somehow you caught on to the nuances of language. Just the other day, you asked me why I always call you "Honey" when we're reading stories and "Bud" when you're helping with chores. My explanation of the difference between a cuddly mood and a matey one seemed to satisfy you.

I have to admit that in my mind's eye, an image of myself while you're in school has developed. I see myself updating all the photo albums and starting that novel I always wanted to write. As the summer wound down and more frequent quarrels erupted between you and your siblings, I was looking forward to today.

And then this morning, I walked you up the steep hill to your classroom with a picture of the president on one wall and of Bambi on the opposite. You found the coat hook with your name above it right away, and you gave me one of your characteristically fierce, too-tight hugs. This time you were ready to let go before I was.

Maybe someday you will deliver a kindergartner with your own wide-set eyes and sudden grin to the first day of school. When you turn at the door to wave good-bye, he or she will be too deep in conversation with a new friend to notice. Even as you smile, you'll feel something warm on your cheek . . .

And then, you'll know.

Love,
Mom

Rebecca Christian

"All that crying and clinging. I thought the mothers would never leave!"

Tale of a Sports Mom

It's a chilly Saturday in May. I could be home sweeping cobwebs from the corners of the living room or curled up on the couch with a good mystery. Instead I'm sitting on a cold metal bench in the stands of a baseball park in Kirkland, Washington. An icy wind creeps through my heavy winter jacket. I blow on my hands, wishing I'd brought my woolen mittens.

"Mrs. Bodmer?" It's the coach my son Matthew admires so much that he gave up soda pop to impress him with his fitness. "I'm starting your son today in right field. He's worked hard this year and I think he deserves the opportunity."

"Thanks," I say, feeling proud of my son who has given this man and this team everything he has. I know how badly he wants this. I'm glad his hard work is being rewarded.

Suddenly I'm nervous for him as the team members, in their white pinstriped uniforms, trot onto the field. I search for my son's number. It isn't there. Instead, Eddie, the most inexperienced player on the team, takes right field. I look again, unbelieving. How can that be?

I want to run over and ask the coach what's going on,

but I know Matthew wouldn't like that. I've learned the proper etiquette for moms; talking to the coach is not acceptable unless he initiates it.

My son, gripping the chain-link fence in front of the dugout, is yelling encouragement to his teammates. I try to read his expression, but I know he, like most males, has learned to hide his feelings. My heart breaks because he has worked so hard and received so much disappointment. I don't understand what drives boys to put themselves through this.

"Atta boy, Eddie," yells the right-fielder's father, proud that his son is starting. I've seen this same man walk out of games in disgust when his son dropped a ball or made a bad throw. But for now, he is proud of his son, who is starting, while my son is on the bench.

By the fourth inning my fingers are stiff from the cold, and my feet are numb, but I don't care. Matthew has been called into the game. He stands, chooses a batting helmet, picks up a bat and struts out to the plate. I grip the metal seat. He takes a couple of practice swings. The pitcher looks like an adult. I wonder if anyone has checked his birth certificate.

Strike one. "Nice swing!" I yell. The next pitch is a ball. "Good eye! Good eye!" Strike two. I pray. I cross my fingers. The pitcher winds up. I hold my breath. Strike three. My son's head hangs, and he slowly walks back to the dugout. I wish with all my heart I could help. But I know there's nothing I can do.

For eight years I've been sitting here. I've drunk gallons of terrible coffee, eaten tons of green hot dogs and salty popcorn. I've endured cold and heat, wind and rain.

Some people may wonder why a sane person would go through this. It's not because I want to fulfill my dream of excelling at sports through my kids. I also don't do this for the emotional highs. Oh, yes, I've had some. I've seen my two sons score winning goals in soccer, hit home runs in baseball, and spark come-from-behind wins in basketball. I've seen them make some incredible leaping catches in football. But mostly I've seen heartache.

I've waited with them for that phone call telling them they'd made the team. The call that never came. I've watched coaches yell at them. I've watched them sit on the bench game after game. I've sat in emergency rooms as broken bones were set and swollen ankles x-rayed. I've sat here year after year, observing it all and wondering why.

The game ends. I stretch my legs and try to stomp life back into my frozen feet. The coach meets with the team. They yell some rallying cry and then descend on their parents. I notice Eddie's dad has a big grin and is slapping his son on the back. Matthew wants to get a hamburger. While I wait for him, the coach approaches me. I can't bring myself to look at him.

"Mrs. Bodmer, I want you to know that's a fine young man you have there."

I wait for him to explain why he broke my son's heart.

"When I told your son he could start, he thanked me and turned me down. He told me to let Eddie start, that it meant more to him."

I turn to watch my son stuffing his burger into his mouth. I realize then why I sit in the stands. Where else can I watch my son grow into a man?

Judy Bodmer

"We need a strikeout. I have to go to the bathroom."

Reprinted by permission of Dave Carpenter.

No More Oatmeal Kisses

A young mother writes: "I know you've written before about the empty-nest syndrome, that lonely period after the children are grown and gone. Right now I'm up to my eyeballs in laundry and muddy boots. The baby is teething; the boys are fighting. My husband just called and said to eat without him, and I fell off my diet. Lay it on me again, will you?"

Okay. One of these days, you'll shout, "Why don't you kids grow up and act your age!" And they will. Or, "You guys get outside and find yourselves something to do . . . and don't slam the door!" And they won't.

You'll straighten up the boys' bedroom neat and tidy: bumper stickers discarded, bedspread tucked and smooth, toys displayed on their shelves. Hangers in the closet. Animals caged. And you'll say out loud, "Now I want it to stay this way." And it will.

You'll prepare a perfect dinner with a salad that hasn't been picked to death and a cake with no finger traces in the icing, and you'll say, "Now, there's a meal for company." And you'll eat it alone.

You'll say, "I want complete privacy on the phone. No dancing around. No demolition crews. Silence! Do you hear?" And you'll have it.

No more plastic tablecloths stained with spaghetti. No more bedspreads to protect the sofa from damp bottoms. No more gates to stumble over at the top of the basement steps. No more clothespins under the sofa. No more playpens to arrange a room around.

No more anxious nights under a vaporizer tent. No more sand in the sheets or Popeye movies in the bathroom. No more iron-on patches, rubber bands for ponytails, tight boots or wet knotted shoestrings.

Imagine. A lipstick with a point on it. No baby-sitter for New Year's Eve. Washing only once a week. Seeing a steak that isn't ground. Having your teeth cleaned without a baby on your lap.

No PTA meetings. No car pools. No blaring radios. No one washing her hair at 11 o'clock at night. Having your own roll of Scotch tape.

Think about it. No more Christmas presents out of toothpicks and library paste. No more sloppy oatmeal kisses. No more tooth fairy. No giggles in the dark. No knees to heal, no responsibility.

Only a voice crying, "Why don't you grow up?" and the silence echoing, "I did."

Erma Bombeck

YOU KNOW YOU'RE A MOTHER WHEN...
IT TAKES YOU AN HOUR AND A HALF TO READ A 12-PAGE BOOK
ONCE UPON A TIME (YES, THAT'S A CHOO-CHOO) IN A TINY TOWN (A RED CHOO-CHOO, VERY GOOD!) THERE LIVED A (YOU'RE RIGHT, IT'S REALLY A TRAIN, BUT HE CAN CALL IT A CHOO-CHOO, OKAY?) A FUNNY LITTLE MAN WITH (I DON'T KNOW WHY HE DOESN'T HAVE A BEARD) A BIG RED NOSE AND (NO, THEY DON'T SHOW HIM SHAVING, DO THEY?) A LITTLE RED ENGINE. (THE STORY DOESN'T SAY IF HE HAS A TV OR NOT...)
chambers

The Signs of Advanced Momhood

Maybe it starts when you realize rock concerts give you a headache. Or that you're offering to cut up other people's food. Or you catch yourself ending a discussion with, "Because I'm the mother, that's why."

You've reached a new level of motherhood. All the warning signs are there. You know you've crossed the threshold into advanced mommydom when:

You count the sprinkles on each kid's cupcake to make sure they're equal.

You want to take out a contract on the kid who broke your son's favorite toy car and made him cry.

You have time to shave only one leg at a time.

You hide in the bathroom to be alone.

Your child throws up and you catch it.

Someone else's kid throws up at a party and you keep eating.

You consider finger paint to be a controlled substance.

You've mastered the art of placing large quantities of pancakes and eggs on a plate without anything touching.

Your child insists that you read *Once Upon a Potty* out loud in the lobby of Grand Central Terminal, and you do it.

You cling to the high moral ground on toy weapons; your child bites his toast into the shape of a gun.

You hope ketchup is a vegetable because it's the only one your child eats.

You convince your child that FAO Schwarz is a toy museum, not a store.

You can't bear the thought of your son's first girlfriend.

You hate the thought of his wife even more.

You find yourself cutting your husband's sandwiches into unusual shapes.

You fast-forward through the scene when the hunter shoots Bambi's mother.

You become a member of three aquariums because your kid loves sharks.

You obsess when your child clings to you upon parting during his first month at school, then obsess when he skips in without looking back the second time.

You can't bear to give away baby clothes—it's so final.

You hear your mother's voice coming out of your mouth when you say, "*Not* in your good clothes."

You stop criticizing the way your mother raised you.

You lose sleep.

You use your own saliva to clean your child's face.

You read that the average five-year-old asks 437 questions a day and feel proud that your kid is "above average."

You hire a sitter because you haven't been out with your husband in ages, then spend half the night checking on the kids.

You say at least once a day, "I'm not cut out for this job," but you know you wouldn't trade it for anything.

Liane Kupferberg Carter

Forever, For Always, and No Matter What!

There is no friendship, no love, like that of the mother for the child.

Henry Ward Beecher

Our daughter Ariana moved from baby to toddler with her share of the usual bumps and scraped knees. On these occasions, I'd hold out my arms and say, "Come see me." She'd crawl into my lap, we'd cuddle, and I'd say, "Are you my girl?" Between tears she'd nod her head yes. Then I'd say, "My sweetie, beetie Ariana girl?" She'd nod her head, this time with a smile. And I'd end with, "And I love you forever, for always, and no matter what!" With a giggle and a hug, she was off and ready for her next challenge.

Ariana is now four-and-a-half. We've continued "come see me" time for scraped knees and bruised feelings, for "good mornings" and "good nights."

A few weeks ago, I had "one of those days." I was tired, cranky and overextended taking care of a four-year-old, twin teenage boys and a home business. Each phone call or knock at the door brought another full day's worth of work that needed to be done immediately! I reached my breaking point in the afternoon and went into my room for a good cry.

Ariana soon came to my side and said, "Come see me." She curled up beside me, put her sweet little hands on my damp cheeks, and said, "Are you my mommy?" Between my tears I nodded my head yes. "My sweetie, beetie mommy?" I nodded my head and smiled. "And I love you forever, for always and no matter what!" A giggle, a big hug, and I was off and ready for my next challenge.

Jeanette Lisefski

To My Children

DEAR FIRSTBORN:

I've always loved you best because you were our first miracle. You were the genesis of a marriage and the fulfillment of young love.

You sustained us through the hamburger years, the first apartment (furnished in Early Poverty), our first mode of transportation (1955 Feet), and the seven-inch TV we paid on for 36 months.

You were new, had unused grandparents, and enough clothes for a set of triplets. You were the original model for a mom and dad who were trying to work the bugs out. You got the strained lamb, the open safety pins and three-hour naps.

You were the beginning.

DEAR MIDDLE CHILD:

I've always loved you best because you drew a tough spot in the family and it made you stronger for it.

You cried less, had more patience, wore faded hand-me-downs, and never in your life did anything first. But it only made you more special. You were the one we relaxed with, who helped us realize a dog could kiss you and you wouldn't get sick. You could cross a street by yourself long before you were old enough to get married. And you helped us understand the world wouldn't collapse if you went to bed with dirty feet.

You were the child of our busy, ambitious years. Without you, we never could have survived the job changes and the tedium and routine that is marriage.

TO THE BABY:

I've always loved you best because while endings are generally sad, you are such a joy. You readily accepted the milk-stained bibs, the lower bunk, the cracked baseball bat, the baby book that had nothing written in it except a recipe for graham-cracker pie crust that someone had jammed between the pages.

You are the one we held on to so tightly. You are the link with our past, a reason for tomorrow. You darken our hair, quicken our steps, square our shoulders, restore our vision, and give us a sense of humor that security, maturity and durability can't provide.

When your hairline takes on the shape of Lake Erie and your own children tower over you, you will still be our baby.

—A Mother

Author Unknown
Submitted by Barbara Wiltberger

Breaking In Baby

I have a son who began as a baby and has successfully reached the age of three without becoming an ax murderer (as far as we know). In addition, I have spent a number of hours thinking about babies, and I have observed them in other people's cars at traffic lights. Thus I am eminently qualified to tell you how to bring up your baby. Here is my advice:

Taking Your New Baby Home

There is nothing quite like the moment a young couple leaves the hospital, walking with that characteristic new-parent gait that indicates an obsessive fear of dropping the baby on its head. Finally! It's just the three of you, on your own!

This independence will last until you get maybe eight feet from the hospital door, where you'll be assaulted by grandmothers offering advice. The United States Constitution empowers grandmothers to stop any young person on the street with a baby and offer advice. They will always offer this advice in a tone of voice that makes it clear they do not expect your baby to survive the afternoon in the care of such incompetents as yourselves.

The best way to handle advice from random grandmothers is to tell them that you appreciate their concern, but that you feel it is your responsibility to make decisions about your child's welfare. If that doesn't work, try driving them off with sticks. Otherwise, they'll follow you home and hang around under your windows.

The Basic Baby Mood Cycle

All babies settle into this once they get over being born.

Mood One: Just about to cry.

Mood Two: Crying

Mood Three: Just finished crying.

Your job is to keep your baby in Mood Three as much as possible. Here is the traditional way to do this. When the baby starts to cry, you and your spouse should pass it back and forth repeatedly and recite these words in unison: "Do you suppose he's hungry? He can't be hungry. He just ate. Maybe he needs to be burped. No, that's not it. Maybe his diaper needs to be changed. No, it's dry. Do you think maybe he's hungry?" And so on, until the baby can't stand it anymore and decides to go to sleep.

When Should You Feed Your Baby?

During the day, you should feed your baby just before the phone rings. At night, you should feed your baby immediately after you have fallen asleep. After each feeding, you should pat your baby gently on the back until it throws up on your shoulder.

What Is Colic?

Colic is when your baby cries all the time, and people keep telling you how their kid had colic for 71 straight months. If your baby gets colic, you should take it to the pediatrician so he can say, "There's nothing to worry about," which is of course absolutely true from his perspective, since he lives in a colic-free home many miles from your baby.

Baby's Development During the First Six Months

The first six months are a time of incredibly rapid development for your baby. It will learn to smile, lift its head, sit, play the cello and repair automatic transmissions.

Ha, ha. Just kidding; poking fun at new parents who watch like hawks for their babies to pass the Major Milestones of Infant Development, when the truth is that during the first six months, babies mainly just lie around and poop. They haven't even developed brains at this point. If you opened up a baby's head—and I am not suggesting for one moment that you should—you'd find nothing but an enormous drool gland.

Disciplining a New Baby

During the 1950s and '60s, parents were told to be permissive with their children, and the result was juvenile delinquency, Watergate, Pac-Man, California, etc. So we experts now feel you should start disciplining your baby right after birth. At random intervals throughout the day, you should stride up to your baby and say, in a strict voice, "There will be no slumber party for you tonight, young lady."

You may think this is a waste of time, but scientists have determined that babies as young as three days old can tell, just from the tone of an adult's voice, when they are being told they can't go to a slumber party.

Baby-Sitters

The best baby-sitters, of course, are the baby's grandparents. You feel completely comfortable entrusting your baby to them for long periods, which is why most grandparents flee to Florida.

If no grandparents are available, you will have to rent a teenager. You don't want a modern teenager, the kind that hangs around the video-game arcade. No, you want an old-fashioned, responsible teenager, the kind who belongs to the 4-H Club and wants to be a nun. Even then you don't want to take any chances. The first time she takes care of your baby, you should never actually leave the house. Drive your car until it's out of sight; then sneak back and crouch in the basement, listening for signs of trouble. In later visits, as you gain confidence in the sitter, you should feel free to eat sandwiches in the basement, and maybe even listen to the radio quietly. After all, this is your night out!

Baby's First Solid Food

We're using the term "food" loosely here. What we're talking about are those little jars on store shelves with the smiling baby on the label and names like "Prunes with Mixed Leeks." Babies hate this stuff. Who wouldn't?

The way babies eat food is by absorbing it directly into their bloodstreams through their faces. So the most efficient way to feed a baby is to smear the food on its chin.

Unfortunately, many inexperienced parents insist on putting food into the baby's mouth. They put in spoonful after spoonful of, say, beets, sincerely believing they are doing something constructive, when in fact the beets are merely going around the Baby Food-Return Loop, which all humans are equipped with until the age of 18 months. After the parents finish "feeding" the baby, they remove the bib and clean up the area, at which point the baby starts to spew beets from its mouth under high pressure, like a little beet volcano, until its face is covered with beets, which it can then absorb.

Walking

Most babies learn to walk at about 12 months, although nobody has ever figured out why they bother, because for the next 12 months all they do is stagger off in random directions until they trip over dust molecules and fall on their bottoms. You cannot catch them before they fall. They fall so quickly that the naked adult eye cannot even see them. This is why diapers are made so thick.

During this phase, your job, as parent, is to trail along behind your child everywhere, holding your arms out in the Standard Toddler-Following Posture made popular by Boris Karloff in the excellent parent-education film *The Mummy,* only with a degree of hunch approaching that of Neanderthal Man so you'll be able to pick your child up quickly after it falls, because the longer it stays on the ground the more likely it is to find something horrible to put in its mouth.

Bedtime Songs

I advise against "Rock-a-bye Baby" because it's really sick, what with the baby getting blown out of the tree and crashing down with the cradle. Some of those cradles weigh over 50 pounds. A much better song is "Go to Sleep":

Go to sleep
Go to sleep
Go straight to sleep
And stay asleep until at least 6:30 A.M.

Dave Barry

"They look so sweet and peaceful when they're asleep. You wonder how they could ever yell at us during the day."

When a Child Goes Off to College

How do you know the fruit is ripe? When it leaves the bunch.

André Gide

I thought I was taking her to kindergarten; then what am I doing on this college campus? Isn't this the blanket I made for her nap time? Why am I putting it on this strange bed? What are we doing here? She's so excited, and I—I'm pretending the stone sitting on my heart isn't there. Where did the 18 years go?

There's nothing left to do. The bed's made, suitcases unpacked, she's even putting up posters and pictures. Does this mean I'm supposed to leave? I kiss her goodbye, smile and tell her to have a good time—but not so good she forgets to study. Then I walk out the door into golden autumn, unlock the car, slip behind the steering wheel and cry.

The drive home is long and lonely. I walk into the house; it's so still, as though everyone is gone forever. Her room is so bare and quiet and oh, Lord, it's so empty! I can't believe it; you can even see the carpet! Her bed is made all neat and tidy, not even a lump from a lost sock. The curtains are straight at the windows and the closet is almost vacant. But . . . what's that? The junk is still under the bed!

So that's where my missing cups and the crystal glass disappeared to—all sitting on the dresser, surrounded by pictures of cast-off boyfriends. And there's her favorite blouse in the corner. She forgot it. Will she forget my teachings as easily as the blouse?

I hear the school bus rumbling its way up our road, and my heart leaps because for one sharp instant I think she's home. And then with a ragged sigh I remember: The school bus doesn't stop here anymore. The driver rounds the corner, shifts gears and drives on, and I stare at the empty driveway. No more schoolgirl, the house full of friends, the trail of clutter, the messed-up bathroom. Just clean, tidy, dull, quiet.

This morning I was a mother, 18 years on the job. Then, just like that, I've been phased out. What do I do now? Whom do I nurture? So I want her to be independent, and I know I'm supposed to work my way out of a job, but why didn't they tell me how one corner of your heart falls off when the time comes?

Wasn't it just yesterday she cuddled in my lap, her baby curls shining in the sunlight? Then she turned a corner and her biggest catastrophes were skinned knees and loose teeth. Now she's running down a whole new path, and the catastrophes loom larger—like broken hearts and dreams. And I no longer can heal her hurts with a kiss; Band-Aids and chocolate chip cookies just won't do it anymore. I yearn to save her from tears and hurt—but I can't. She has to learn it all by herself, cry her own tears and deal with her own heartaches.

I thought I was ready for this, had it all planned. I started a new career, dug out projects and filled up my calendar. I wasn't about to sit around and indulge in the empty-nest syndrome. Not me; I was smarter than that. Why, I'm the "new" woman: bright, efficient, self-assured. Then why am I clutching my daughter's old Raggedy Ann doll and crying?

Then I remember. Another autumn, another place. I was the young girl going away to college, standing on the threshold of dreams, the air crisp and sparkling with the excitement of new tomorrows. It was my father who stood waving good-bye, his whole body slumped with sorrow. Oh, my father, now at last, I understand!

A phase of living gone, a child you nurtured no longer needing you, an empty spot in your heart and days.

I expect I'll recover and pursue new dreams, relish unlimited time, love not picking up clutter and grow to adore tidy bathrooms. But right now, for a little while on this golden autumn afternoon, I think I'll just sit here in a young girl's bedroom, clutch an old and much loved doll, cry my tears and remember.

Phyllis Volkens

Mother's Helper

The year I came to Dallas, I learned that true mothering isn't reserved for mothers. I had just moved into my new job as the female prime-time news anchor for the NBC affiliate in the Dallas-Fort Worth television market. As a former Miss America, I knew the risk of being stereotyped as a beauty queen, so I was determined to work doubly hard to prove myself. I didn't mind that because I loved the work—but I also loved my family. The pressures of the job, a new home, four kids and a Texas heat wave were proving too much to handle.

My hardest challenge was finding day care for Tyler, my three-year-old. In Oklahoma City, he'd had three years of baby-sitting with the most wonderful family right in my neighborhood, who had treated him like an adopted member of the clan. If I was to have peace of mind in Dallas, I needed to find an arrangement as ideal. But checking out one institutional day care option after the next was getting to be a nightmare, and with my new job needing my attention, I needed some ideas fast.

Just when I thought things were hopeless, my friend Carmen came to the rescue. She had an aunt in San Antonio who might be willing to come to Dallas on a trial basis. A personal referral was just what I needed, and I was ready. So I sent for Mary right away, and my hopes soared as I waited for her arrival.

The woman who appeared on my doorstep did not match my preconceived image of the ideal nanny. She was tiny and quite old. Her clothes were ragged, mismatched, and held together with safety pins. Painfully shy, speaking broken English, she barely spoke a word, even when I asked her a question. And when she smiled, her teeth revealed a life of hardship and poverty. How could I hire her? How would I be able to give her instructions or trust her to make decisions? Did I want to take care of yet another person?

Tyler settled those questions from the first moment, dismissing my unspoken reservations. He took her hand, led her into the house, and spent the next few hours jabbering happily as Mary listened and smiled. They sat in the same small chair and watched television, then colored together on the floor. She kept saying that Tyler was "so smart," but I could see that they were learning equally from each other.

The clothes we bought Mary stayed tucked away in her closet for special occasions. But Tyler didn't notice—or even care—that Mary always looked different from most people. He was just proud of her friendship. Every afternoon, without fail, she walked to his school, sat on a little bench in the hall, and watched the children. When the final school bell rang, Tyler would find her for the journey home. The first time it rained hard, I scurried around to arrange a ride home for Tyler, but he wouldn't hear of it. He wanted to walk home with Mary so he could play in the puddles with her. After that, regardless of rain, wind or snow, Mary and Tyler walked home together, wrapped in a loving friendship that most people can only imagine.

My favorite example of their devoted partnership is the trip to the ophthalmologist. Mary was timid and shy in public places, and the prospect of visiting a big eye institute made her nervous. But I insisted that her eyes needed checking, and off we went. She looked especially dwarfed and vulnerable in the big examination chair, and Tyler must have sensed her uneasiness, too. I saw him move an inch or two closer to her when the lights went off. As the doctor flashed letters on the wall, Mary hesitantly whispered the top line and struggled as the letters got smaller. Then I caught a glimpse of movement out of the corner of my eye. Tyler had managed to sneak up right beside her chair and was leaning over the arm with a big grin on his face—telling her the answers!

Thank God mothering isn't reserved only for mothers. Thank God for women and men in the world who have the capacity to give and nurture and love others. How wonderful when children have access to *several* adults who love them—child care workers, Girl Scout leaders, Little League coaches, teachers, nurses, neighbors, aunts and uncles. Thank God for people like Mary, one of his special angels.

Jane Jayroe

The Stepmother

Since our amicable divorce a few years before, Eric and I had maintained a comfortable relationship, remaining good friends. We had agreed on consistent parenting rules and visiting schedules, and our son, Charley, enjoyed a nice balance between our two homes. He seemed well-adjusted and happy.

So when I first met Eric's fiancée, the woman who was to become my son's stepmother, I was bound to be a little nervous. There was no doubt that Bonny would have an influence on my child's life. What I didn't appreciate at the time was the effect she would have on mine.

At that first meeting, I was struck by how opposite we were. Her clothes had a "dress for success" look, while I wore "rumpled nonchalance." She was attractive, composed and confident, while I was disheveled and nervous, prattling on about nothing. I was uncomfortable and suspicious, scrutinizing her every mannerism and inflection, sizing her up as my son's future parent. My prevailing thought was: "What will she do to my precious baby?"

Before this moment, I'd had various fantasies about who my "ex" might someday marry. One was of a wicked witch, a raving shrew from whom my son would run screaming. He would, of course, be running to me, his real mom, who would supply endless patience and wisdom, as only a true mother can.

Another fantasy was scarier. In this one she was the rock, his bridge over troubled water, where he could find solace from his nagging mom, who never understood him. Or even worse, she was the fun one, as in, "I can't come home tonight, Mom. Bonny got us the luxury suite for the Bulls championship."

Unfortunately, the latter of my fantasies wasn't a fantasy. This was a real person who was about to become my son's other mother, and all I could do was watch and wait.

Over time, I grew less wary and more natural around Bonny. She grew less coolly professional and more familiar around me. We found an easy way of working through the routines of pick-up and drop-off times, school conferences and soccer games.

Then one night my new husband and I invited Eric and Bonny to our house for coffee after a school conference. Charley, who loved to have us all together, was delighted. Over the course of the evening, tensions and pretensions melted away. Bonny and I let our walls down a bit and spoke more frankly. Instead of a complicated configuration of "ex's" and "steps," we were now just friends.

A few months later, the four of us got together to talk about Charley's grades. Instead of bringing her usual outlines, lists, data and literature—as if she were making a case before a committee—Bonny opened up and confessed her vulnerability. She talked about her insecurities and despair in dealing with Charley's adolescence. Was she demanding too much or asking too little? Was she pushing him or coddling him?

My heart went out to her. These were the same thoughts and fears that kept me up at night. She was thinking, feeling and behaving just like a mother—which is what she had become.

So Charley's second mom is neither an evil witch who would hurt my son, nor a fairy godmother who would steal him away. She's a woman who loves my little boy. She will worry over him, fight for him and protect him from harm.

I've gone from dreading Bonny's appearance to being grateful for her presence in Charley's life and mine. I welcome her unique perspective, her ideas—and even her lists. I was wrong to want to hold my child to my chest, like a toy. I didn't want to share. Maybe I was the first to love him, but that doesn't mean I should be the last. Now there's one more person in this world watching over him. And for that, I happily share the title *Mom.*

Jennifer Graham

I'd Rather

I'd rather be a mother
Than anyone on earth
Bringing up a child or two
Of unpretentious birth.
I'd rather nurse a rosy babe
With warm lips on my breast
Than wear a queen's medallion
Above a heart less blest.
I'd rather tuck a little child
All safe and sound in bed—
Than twine a chain of diamonds
About my foolish head.
I'd rather wash a smudgy face
With round, bright baby eyes—
Than paint the pageantry of fame,
Or walk among the wise.

Meredith Gray

5

BECOMING A MOTHER

Every child born into the world is a new thought of God, an ever-fresh and radiant possibility.

Kate Douglas Wiggin

"Mom's not going to go to the hospital. She's going to have the baby delivered."

Reprinted by permission of Dave Carpenter.

Joy to the World

The pains began as a dull ache deep in the pit of my stomach. I didn't take them seriously. After all, it was Christmas Eve, my baby wasn't due until February, and there was a lot to do. Probably something I ate, I told myself.

That year, 1973, my husband, Bill, and I were celebrating our first Christmas in a small Maine town, a few miles from the base where Bill, a career Air Force man, was stationed. Our parents were far away, but I had planned cherished holiday customs from both families—his mother's chestnut stuffing, my mother's Yorkshire pudding, his family's ritual of decorating the tree the night before Christmas, my family's tradition of attending midnight Mass.

One thing I hadn't planned on was the weather. All afternoon, snow had been falling steadily—giant featherlike flakes that blanketed the earth in cold silence. It had taken Bill over an hour to drive the 10 miles home from the base, which was shrouded in fog. As a result, we decided to stay home by the fire rather than go out to midnight Mass.

The house smelled of stuffing and pine. Carols played on the stereo, and logs crackled merrily in the fireplace.

Everything was picture-perfect. There were only two problems. My upset stomach was getting worse, and so was the snowstorm.

At about seven o'clock, Bill and I had a light supper—mainly indigestion medicine for me. Then we started decorating the tree with bright red and gold balls I had purchased the day before. Just as I was stretching to fix the star to the top branch, a searing pain ripped down my back and I let out a scream.

Bill rushed to my side and helped me to the bathroom. My water had broken, and I was in active labor. "But it's too early!" I mumbled in disbelief, while my husband frantically tried to time the contractions. Each one seemed to merge with the next, following no particular pattern.

"We'd better get to the hospital while we still can," said Bill, remembering the weather.

"Maybe it's a false alarm?" I gasped, as the tidal wave of pain subsided.

"We're going anyway," he said.

Bill helped me into my coat and carried me to where our car was parked. By that time, the snow had changed to frozen rain. I brought along some old towels to sit on; he tucked a warm afghan around me and slipped in behind the wheel. The engine started nicely, but we had several tense minutes as the tires spun and skidded, trying to get a grip on the ice.

Eventually they caught and we were on our way. To calm us both, Bill turned on the radio. The uplifting, familiar strains of "Joy to the World" filled the car. It was as if an invisible choir was singing to us in the dark, but it did little to quiet my pain and rising fear.

The nearest town lay in a valley six miles away. From there, the base hospital was another four miles—and weather conditions were treacherous. The car struggled through driving sleet and pockets of dense fog as we inched our way downhill. It was impossible to see a foot in front of us on the two-lane road.

"Am I over the line?" asked Bill, switching off the radio. He leaned forward and peered into the dark. "God, I can't see a thing!"

He did not mean it as a prayer, but now I realize it was just that. We could see no traffic behind or ahead of us, but suddenly, from out of nowhere, an old station wagon with a distinctive silhouette passed us on the left. Instead of going on, however, the driver slowed down, his rear lights showing us the way down the hill. Wherever he was going, we would go; we had no choice.

The station wagon slowly led us off the road and into the parking lot of a church on the outskirts of a nearby town. Through the fog I could make out parked cars and the blurred gold rectangle that was the church door. We followed the wagon across the lot to the front of the rectory, where we came to a stop. The wagon continued on and out the other side of the lot.

Bill rushed out of our car and into the rectory to get help. The priests were already in the church to conduct midnight Mass, but the housekeeper was still there and knew just what to do. After calling for an ambulance, she helped Bill maneuver me into the back seat and then stationed herself at my side. Five minutes later our tiny daughter was born to the strains of "Joy to the World" coming from the church. By the time the ambulance arrived, she was 10 minutes old, small and perfect. Her bald head peeked from the priest's sweater we had wrapped around her as a swaddling cloth.

The housekeeper, a maternal take-charge type, insisted on coming with me in the ambulance to the nearest hospital, while Bill followed in our car. "The fathers can get their own breakfast for once," the housekeeper said, winking.

She smiled down at the little bundle in my arms. "You can call her Carol," she suggested "or maybe Noelle or Gloria."

"I think we'll call her Joy," I said, thinking of the song that had accompanied me throughout this eventful night. "And maybe Dorothy for a middle name—after my mother."

The housekeeper approved. "Dorothy means 'gift of God,'" she said.

It wasn't until several hours later, on Christmas morning, that I remembered to ask about the driver who had led us down the hill. We had had no time to thank him before he disappeared after doing his good deed.

"I wonder who he was," I said to the housekeeper, describing the distinctive old station wagon in the hope that she would recognize it as belonging to a parishioner. But she had no clue, nor did any of the other townspeople we talked to later. Yet the driver had known exactly where to lead us.

Over the years, friends have suggested that perhaps we were visited by an angel that night. Perhaps we were. Some things can never be explained. But whether our mysterious driver was human or divine, one thing I do believe—God was with us that night our daughter, Joy, was born to the world.

W. Shirley Nunes

An Indescribable Gift

In the sheltered simplicity of the first days after a baby is born, one sees again the magical closed circle, the miraculous sense of two people existing only for each other.

Anne Morrow Lindbergh

She slips into this world, and into my arms, placed there by heaven. She is straight from God. An indescribable gift. As I look upon her, peace and purity fill the air around her. Through joyful tears I whisper in her ear, "We are glad you are here. We waited so long to see you." She opens her eyes, and I am transformed—a timeless moment filled with the infinity of what life is. In her eyes I see total recognition, unconditional love and complete trust. I am a mother. In that instant I feel, and in my heart I know, everything I need to know to guide her.

Lying on the bed, she sleeps between her daddy and me. We count the toes and fingers and marvel at the perfection in such a tiny form. We look for ways she looks like us, and ways she is uniquely herself. We have nothing to say, but our hearts and minds are full of thoughts—of our hopes and dreams for her, of who she might be, of what gifts she brings with her and how she might touch the world. Just looking at her and feeling the love and sweetness she brings, it seems the stress and weight of the world are lifted from us, and what is important and true in the world becomes apparent—as being in the presence of a great, wise sage. It is hard to close our eyes to sleep.

As the days and years pass, we are awed at the transformation of who she is becoming. The first smile, the first word, the first step—all according to plan, yet in her own time and special way. She teaches us how to play again; to slow down and see the world again. To rediscover the things we used to see, and know. It is clear there is much she remembers, feels and sees that we no longer can, and maybe never could.

Time will fly; suddenly she will be grown, a young adult, ready to soar into the world and give what she came here for. Letting go will be wrenching, and yet we know that she is not ours to keep. She came to us to teach us our lessons, to give us joy, to make us whole and to connect us to God.

Jeanette Lisefski

Motherwit

I was near the end of my first pregnancy and confined to round-the-clock bed rest. After a near miscarriage, we weren't taking chances. Lying in bed, I didn't have much to do except talk to my baby and enjoy her movements. She'd greet me every morning at nine like clockwork, move around, dance all over the place, find a comfortable resting spot, and move some more.

Two weeks before Angelica's due date, I woke up and felt nothing. One of my pregnancy books said that this could happen, so I tried to relax. But when Phil Donahue came and went, with Oprah coming on at 10 A.M. and still no movement, I was really anxious. So I called my doctor. "Don't worry," he told me. "These things happen all the time. If eight hours pass with no movement, then we'll be concerned." Exactly what the book said.

And that's when my "motherwit" kicked in. I didn't care what the experts said—I knew something was wrong. I called the doctor back to say I was on my way over so they could let me hear a heartbeat. I didn't care if everyone thought I was overreacting. I was going on instinct.

My husband met me there from work as the nurse hooked me up to the monitor. My baby's little heart was beating, steadily but weakly. But at 11:30, an ultrasound showed that her heart was the only thing moving!

I was rushed to the hospital in a state of shock, under doctor's orders for an emergency C-section. Was my baby going to die? The nurse at the hospital whisked us past the front desk. "We're ready for you!" The scene was like a code blue on *ER.* By the time my husband parked the car, I was on a gurney with an I.V. in my arm, prepped for surgery.

I squeezed my husband's hands for dear life—Angelica's life—throughout the surgery. She came out blue. The doctor spanked her once, twice, again. *Please, God, please don't take her.* And then she let out a wail that was the most beautiful sound I've ever heard. Through our tears, we kissed our daughter and welcomed her into the world. She had become tangled up in her umbilical cord, and if I hadn't called when I did, we would have lost her.

What made me call? It was motherwit, that sixth sense mothers have about their children. I marvel and give thanks that my mothering instinct kicked in before I was officially a mother, telling me to take action to save my child.

And my Angelica? She's now a healthy and precocious 10-year-old. Guess what her favorite bedtime story is. "Tell me again about the time I was born, Mommy."

Amy Hilliard-Jones

She Looks Like Us

Three months before my first child was born, I began gathering baby things. I already had some clothes of mine that my mother had saved, some of my dad's that my grandmother had saved, and some that my mother and grandmother had crocheted years before in much too early anticipation of this event.

There were a few dresses, a long white cotton one of my dad's being the most beautiful and fragile, two buntings, booties and some tiny caps that we tried on over my husband's fist.

I'm not very good at crafts, but it was important to me to handmake the pillows and quilts and skirts for a bassinet for this baby to sleep in. I had pictures of me in my long white baby's gown, and it seemed the right way to start a new life. So I made one, with white eyelet, satin ribbons and bows—the only thing I ever made—and it turned out great.

Then I went shopping. Diapers, bottles, rattles, bibs, blankets, a stroller, a car seat, approved teething devices. It takes a lot of stuff to keep a modern baby in the manner to which we've become accustomed.

The soft, fresh things were arrayed in the pale yellow

room that would soon be a nursery and already smelled of baby powder. I played with them while we waited.

We weren't kept waiting too long. She arrived on her due date in the tradition of the great Caesar. She was red in the face from trying for 21 hours to get into the world the hard way, but her head was beautifully shaped, perfectly bald and, of course, perfectly beautiful. Eight pounds, one-half ounce, 19-and-one-half inches, 12:53 post meridiem, January 5, 1980.

Why are these details of infants told so carefully? Because every single thing about them is fascinating and important, that's why.

When she was placed in my arms, I looked down at her face, she opened her eyes into mine and she smiled. I know, they say infants don't smile. To that I say, "Ha!" To her I said, "Hi."

Back in the gathering months, my husband and I had compiled long lists of names, and by comparing and discussing and eliminating, decided on Katherine for a girl and Benjamin for a boy. Either one was going to have my dad's name for the middle: Lindsey. And, of course, Farris.

Katherine Lindsey Farris.

When I called my parents to announce her birth and told them the name, my dad asked me to repeat it. It was one of my early pleasures as a new mother to hear my literate, well-spoken father at a loss for words.

When it was time to bring her home, we dressed her in Dad's delicate baby dress and small, pretty cap and a pair of the crocheted booties, which turned out to be huge.

The first friends we talked to asked what she looked like and I blurted out, "She looks like us!" Before that moment, I hadn't even thought about it. But 10 months later, someone else thought she did too: the judge who approved our adoption.

Judy Farris

READER/CUSTOMER CARE SURVEY

If you are enjoying this book, please help us serve you better and meet your changing needs by taking a few minutes to complete this survey. Please fold it & drop it in the mail.

Please Print

Name:______________________________

Address:______________________________

____

Telephone Number: ________________________

(1) Gender: 1) ____ Female 2) ____ Male

(2) Age: 1)____ 18-25 3)____ 36-45 5)____ 56-65
2)____ 26-35 4)____ 46-55 6)____ 65+

(3) Marital status: 1)____ Married 2)____ Single 3)____ Divorced/Wid.

(4) Was this book: 1)____ Purchased for self?
2)____ Received as gift?

(5) How did you find out about this book?

1)____ Mail Order Catalog
2)____ Best Seller List
3)____ Book Store
4)____ Website
5)____ Price Club
6)____ Other Retail Store
7)____ TV/Radio Talk Show
8)____ Feature Article or Book Review
9)____ Word of Mouth

(6) Which subjects do you enjoy reading about most?

Please rank in order of importance:

6)____ Self-improvement/Motivation
7)____ Religious/Inspiration
8)____ New Age/Alternative Healing
9)____ Health and Wellness
10)____ Women's Issues/Relationships
11)____ Recovery
12)____ Family Issues and Aging

(13) When do you buy books?

1)____ Holidays (Christmas, etc.)
2)____ Special Occasions (Birthdays, etc.)
3)____ Anytime

(14) What do you look for when choosing a personal growth book?

Please rank in order of importance:

14)____ Subject
15)____ Title
16)____ Author
17)____ Price
18)____ In Store Location

(19) Where do you buy your books?

Please rank in order of importance:

19)____ Bookstore
20)____ Price Club
21)____ Department Store
22)____ Supermarket Drug Store
23)____ Health Store
24)____ Gift Store
25)____ Book Club
26)____ Mail Order
27)____ Airport

(28) Which magazines do you read?

1)____ Crafts & Hobbies
2)____ Family/Parenting
3)____ Women's Issues
4)____ Religious
5)____ New Age/Spirituality
6)____ Business/Professional
7)____ Other (Sports, Current Affairs, etc.)

Additional comments you would like to make to help us serve you better. ____________________

____

____

____

> As a special **"Thank You"** we'll send you exciting news about interesting books and a valuable Gift Certificate. *It's Our Pleasure to Serve You!*

FOLD HERE

NO POSTAGE
NECESSARY
IF MAILED
IN THE
UNITED STATES

BUSINESS REPLY MAIL

FIRST-CLASS MAIL PERMIT NO 45 DEERFIELD BEACH, FL

POSTAGE WILL BE PAID BY ADDRESSEE

HEALTH COMMUNICATIONS, INC.
CHICKEN SOUP FOR THE MOTHER'S SOUL
3201 SW 15TH STREET
DEERFIELD BEACH, FL 33442-9875

Mom

I did not become a mother in the conventional way. I could have chosen to get pregnant, but my husband and I decided to start our family instead through adoption—the adoption of special-needs children waiting for home and family.

We knew we were going to face the raised eyebrows and rude questions, but we still felt this was the right route for us. Someday, I may give birth to a child, and I know that experience will be incredible and moving in its own special way. Just as the night I first became a mother.

We were adopting brothers—Jesse, age five, and Mario, age four. One look at the pictures of the boys as they had been discovered, dangerously underweight and sickly, had banished any doubts we might have had. We had accepted them wholeheartedly before we even met. But would they accept us?

Rather than sharing a first bath, or feeding my child for the very first time, I found myself sitting cross-legged on the floor of a stranger's home, trying unsuccessfully to snap two pieces of plastic together in order to form a Lego submarine with one of my new sons.

I couldn't keep my eyes off my boys' faces. Mario's hands flew over the speedboat he was constructing, though occasionally he would stop to look at me and make sure I was still there. He was gorgeous—long eyelashes dusting his cheeks, big hazel eyes fixed intently on the project at hand. I couldn't believe he was four; he was so small, looking more like a two-year-old, and I cringed as I thought about the "before" pictures I had seen earlier. Now, he looked almost stout—chubby legs running back and forth, carrying toys he wanted to show us. He was so happy, so trusting.

Jesse, on the other hand, seemed much older than his five years. Though he was due to turn six in just a few months, he carried himself more like an eight- or nine-year-old—very serious and extremely concerned about his brother's welfare and behavior. We watched as he corrected Mario several times throughout the evening and protectively hovered over him, ensuring that these strangers—his new parents—wouldn't harm the little brother he had worked all of his short life to protect and raise.

Would he ever let us take over the parenting chores so that he, himself, could be a child—not again, but for the very first time? I hoped there was still a small window where the ability to trust a grown-up could enter Jesse's young life. Had I taken on more than I knew how to handle?

"Mom, will you hand me that piece?" I heard a small voice next to me ask.

Then the voice came again, this time a little louder.

"Mom, will you hand me that piece, please?"

I turned to look at Jesse to let him know his foster mother had left the room for a minute, but I stopped in mid-sentence because I could see he was looking at me.

Mom . . . ?

"Do . . . do . . . you mean me, Jesse?" I asked quietly.

He nodded his head solemnly and pointed over my shoulder.

"I need that piece on the table," he said, his dark eyes focusing on mine.

I reached behind me, took the small, blue piece from the coffee table and handed it to him. He smiled.

"Thank you," he said politely, snapping it into place.

"Um, can I hug you? Would that be okay?" I was scared to ask this. It was like asking a 30-year-old. But I so wanted him to be five. It was time to be five.

He hesitated, then looked at me. I could see he was thinking hard. Could he trust me?

Then he nodded. "Yeah," he said, putting down his submarine.

I reached out, and he came to me and sat on my lap. I enveloped him with my embrace and held him as closely as I could. I could feel him put his arms around my neck and hug me back.

In that moment I knew that he was giving me the gift of being a mother. And maybe, just maybe, I could give him the gift of being a child.

Barbara L. Warner

I Don't Want a New Baby

"I don't want a new baby."

This was my oldest son Brian's response when I told him his father and I were expecting a third child. We'd survived the first round of sibling rivalry when his brother, Damian, was born. But now three-year-old Brian had made his stand about this new baby, and neither logic, reason nor persuasion could budge him.

Puzzled, I asked him, "Why don't you want a new baby?"

With wide and teary eyes, he looked straight at me and said, "Because I want to keep Damian."

Rosemary Laurey

Out of Our Hands

When the doorbell sounded that afternoon, I answered numbly. It was the worst possible time for a repairman to come to the house. I was nearly five months pregnant, and I had never been more emotionally on edge, waiting for the phone to ring. In fact, it was the worst possible time for our alarm system to malfunction, period. Not only were our emotions on overload, we didn't need another repair bill.

Our finances were shaky. I had morning sickness from the get-go with my pregnancy, and it became so bad I had to stop working, a loss of income we hadn't counted on quite yet. Although that was difficult, we were too excited to complain. We'd tried for a year and a half to have a baby and had even gone through the first phase of fertility testing, with no conclusive results. The next month, though, we got the call we'd dreamed about. I was pregnant!

The first trimester had been normal, except for the debilitating morning sickness, which I knew was temporary. I looked forward to each doctor visit, relishing the fact that we were learning more and more about our child. So when the doctor asked me if I wanted to have an optional blood test that would screen for spina bifida, among other things, in the growing fetus, I didn't hesitate to say yes.

When the results came back, our doctor had called immediately. In a professional yet concerned voice, he said that the test numbers were so low they were off the charts. Instead of suggesting spina bifida, the blood count suggested Down's syndrome.

The doctor immediately scheduled an amniocentesis. Even though my husband, Joe, and I were apprehensive, that day was also a thrill. The technician also used an ultrasound, so for the first time we got to see the baby move. It suddenly seemed all so real to me. We were really going to be parents, and the little person was a boy! Something cataclysmic couldn't really be wrong with him—could it?

Reality set in when we were told it would take two weeks for the results to come back. We were counseled that all the waiting for results was pushing us toward the end limit for a safe pregnancy termination. However, whatever the diagnosis, we didn't feel that was an option for us.

The wait was on. Never have I known two weeks to seem so endless. I tried to involve myself, to think about other things, but those words "off the charts" kept replaying in my mind. It didn't help when our home's built-in alarm system would blare for no reason when we least expected it. Joe, of course, went to work every day. I felt alone and helpless.

Finally the day arrived when we were supposed to get the answer. I'll never forget how nervous I was, at home all morning by myself, waiting for the phone to ring. It was silent. By noon I couldn't stand it any more. I called in, but the nurse said there were still no results.

Morning turned to afternoon. When the doorbell rang, I just about flew out of my skin. On automatic pilot, I let the repairman in, showed him the alarm system, and quickly left. Overwhelmed, my only thoughts about his arrival were a combination of, "This is gonna really cost us!" and, "Could there be any worse timing?" The faith that I'd been taught in "God's perfect timing" was beginning to show serious signs of wear and tear.

About two hours later, the nurse called. As I recall what she said, it almost started off like a bad joke: There was good news and bad news.

The good news was that our son did not have Down's syndrome. The bad news was that he did have two chromosomes that were joined. She explained that if either Joe or I had the same condition, our son should be okay. However, if neither of us had it, that meant there was something missing in the makeup of our baby's genes.

"Something missing?" I tried not to screech. "Like what? What does that mean?"

"I'm sorry, Mrs. Horning, there is no way we can tell what's wrong with him until he's born. Now, the best thing is for you and your husband to come in right away for a blood test."

"Right away? We can find out today?"

"We can do the test today. We'll have the results in five days."

Five days?

That's when I lost control. I became hysterical. I don't remember ever screaming or crying like that in all of my 34 years of life. It felt as if someone had punched me in the stomach, and I had regained my breath long enough to have it done again.

I remember calling Joe at work, still hysterical.

"Colleen, honey, listen to me. I want you to go next door to the neighbor's house, okay? Colleen? I'll leave as soon as I can, but I don't want you to stay there alone."

But his words and frantic urgings for me to get help couldn't cut through the panic that had overtaken me. I let the phone drop into the cradle.

As I sat gasping by the phone, I realized that the repairman was still working in the front room. I couldn't believe he had heard all of this. Deeply chagrined, I felt I had to apologize. I walked around the corner, still weeping.

He was standing in the doorway, as if he were waiting for me. Before I could say anything, he guided me to a chair. "Sit down," he instructed. "Just sit down and catch your breath."

The specific instructions and the gentle tone caught me off guard. As I sat and breathed, I felt myself calming down.

This stranger sat down right across from me. In a quiet voice, he told me how he and his wife had lost their first child. The baby had been born dead because they didn't realize his wife had developed diabetes during her pregnancy.

He went on to explain how hard it was for them to accept this, but they finally had to give it up and admit it was something that was beyond their control.

He looked at me and said, "I understand how badly your heart is hurting right now. But there's nothing you can do but have faith, and realize what's happening with your baby is out of your control. The more you try to take it back, to try to keep control of the baby, of the tests, the worse your inability to change anything is going to tear at you."

He took my hand and told me their second child was born a few months ago. This time there were no problems. He and his wife were blessed with a healthy little girl.

He told me he still thinks about his first child, who was a little boy, but for whatever reason, that wasn't meant to be. He asked me to please try to keep faith about my baby, and that he felt our situation would turn out all right.

Then, as quietly as he told me his story, he got up and walked to the front door. He turned around and told me that he was finished, the alarm was fixed.

He had helped me in a way that no one else could have—what could I possibly say? All that came out was a meek thank-you.

Then I remembered I hadn't paid him.

He smiled and said I didn't owe him anything. All he asked was for me to keep faith.

The timing, as it turned out, was perfect.

Colleen Derrick Horning

Editor's Note: Colleen and Ted's son was born four months later. He weighed 9 pounds, 2½ ounces, and is the picture of health.

A Treasure Without Price

I had waited nearly five years for this moment. Five years enduring the empty arms of childlessness, the baby showers for someone else, and the well-meaning question from friends, "Are you pregnant yet?"

I longed for a baby of my own, and at last it was happening. Our baby was due to arrive anytime. My husband and I waited with bated breath, our hearts pounding with anticipation. Soon, he would be here—soon! We had been told it was a boy. A son of our very own. What joy!

Years ago, before we knew of the long, painful journey ahead in our quest for a child, I had chosen a boy's name. For some reason, we had never been able to settle on a girl's name, but the boy's name had come quickly, with no hesitation and no second thoughts. Our son would be Nathan Andrew, meaning "Gift from God" in the Hebrew language. I was unaware of the name's meaning when I first began sounding it out on my tongue. I just liked the way it flowed—the fine, masculine ring it produced in my ear. I chose my son's name long before he was ever conceived, when he was still a desire deep in my heart. Once I discovered the significance of the name, I was doubly pleased. How fitting a name for such a precious gift from God.

Now we waited for Nathan Andrew to arrive. The painful months and years we had endured would soon become a dim memory.

A car drove up and parked in front of the house. We pressed close to the window, eagerly watching as a woman stepped out of the car with a blanket-wrapped baby carrier. As she walked up the sidewalk, I held my breath, my eyes never leaving the shrouded bundle she carried. I would soon hold my baby in my arms. Yes, God had chosen to answer our prayer through adoption.

The scene was suddenly thrown into slow motion, and questions flashed through my mind with the speed of light. What of the girl who had borne him? What of the young man who had fathered him? What were they doing on this day?

A single act of passion had touched off a chain of events that culminated in the life of this innocent child. What wrenching discussions must have filled the homes of these teenagers a few months after that act.

She could have had an abortion. No doubt it would have been easier than bearing the shame of being an unwed 16-year-old mother. It would have been easier than watching the fresh, young skin across her belly stretch into an enormous mound, the tissue underneath breaking, leaving permanent scars. It would have been easier than experiencing the pain of childbirth when she was hardly more than a child herself. It would have been easier than carrying a baby in her body for nine months, feeling the kicks, the hiccups, the heartbeat, and then kissing it good-bye as soon as it was born.

I thought of this young girl, 10 years younger than I. She was somewhere in this city, recuperating from the birth of her baby that was no longer her baby. Hormones must be raging in her body, making tears a frequent companion—and her arms were empty.

After nine months of waiting, she had given life to a little boy. After five years of waiting, we were taking that little boy and giving him the life he deserved. We would be the mother and father who would love him, providing for his physical, emotional and spiritual needs in ways that a young girl was not yet capable of.

With tears in my eyes, I silently thanked a stranger whose baby would become my own. At peril to herself, she had carried and nourished him in her body, she had endured the pain of delivery, and would carry the scars of childbirth until her dying day. And then, she had given him to me.

I was his mother now, and for the rest of his life. I slipped the blanket from its tent-like perch on the handle of the baby carrier and stared into the face of my son. Big, gray eyes fringed with thick, black lashes solemnly stared back at me. I touched the tiny, perfectly formed fingers and toes. He was beautiful!

With heartfelt words of gratitude, I whispered, "Thank you!" not only to God for answering our prayers and sending us a son, but to a girl I would never meet. A girl whose gift was a treasure without price. Thank you.

Sandra Julian

The Chosen One

Not flesh of my flesh
Nor bone of my bone,
But still miraculously my own.
Never forget for a single minute,
You didn't grow under my heart,
But in it.

Anonymous

It was my all-time favorite story. "We'd looked after kids for years, but after a while they had to go back to their parents. Now we wanted our own baby, one we could keep forever."

I was usually sitting on my mother's lap when she started the story, but as I got older, I liked to sit opposite her so I could watch her face. I'd seen some of these other kids in the photograph album: black, brown and white, looking wistful, staring straight ahead, leaning against the dog. In the most recent pages, laughing straight into the camera, was a plump, happy baby, and that was me.

She'd continue, "It was November 1947, and bitterly cold—in fact, it was the coldest winter for over 100 years.

The train was already standing at the station when we got there, puffing out big clouds of steam. We hadn't been anywhere for years, because of the war, so after we got in, we could hardly sit still, we were so excited. We didn't even mind the cold too much; it all looked so beautiful. It seemed as if the whole country had been frozen. It was white everywhere."

My mother always stopped here and smiled, and I imagined a snowy fairyland, trees shrouded in ice, stalactites dripping from roofs, snowflakes in bright constellations on the train windows.

"At last we arrived and took a bus to a big house. The matron was expecting us, and gave us a cup of tea to warm up. Then she took us around. There were dozens and dozens of babies! Roomfuls of them! Boys and girls, some with fair hair, some with dark. There were blue-eyed babies and ones with brown eyes, like yours. We looked around for a long time—there were so many, and lots of them were very pretty. Your dad and I just didn't know how we were going to choose."

If I was sitting on her lap, she would squeeze me then as she looked down, kissing the top of my head. If I was opposite, she would have a faraway look, lit up by the memory. I couldn't wait for the next bit, and wriggled like a worm.

"Suddenly," she continued, "we came into a new room, and there, in the second crib, we saw you. You were sniffling up at us, as if you'd been waiting for us your whole life, and we knew immediately you were the one we wanted, that we'd been waiting for you, too. We thought you were the prettiest one in that whole house, with your lovely brown skin and thick black hair. They told us your name was Susan and you were four months old.

" 'Is this the one?' asked the matron, and we said, 'Yes, this is definitely the one.' We wrapped you up and went back to the station. On the train, people kept coming up to us. 'Oh, what a lovely baby. Is she yours?' they'd ask, and we'd say, 'Yes, we just went to choose her.'

"'Well,' they'd say, 'you chose the best one by the look of her,' and we'd say, 'Oh, yes, we did.'"

I would snuggle down, scrunching my toes, feeling very special. Sometimes I even felt sorry for the children of ordinary births. For years, whenever we got on the train, I thought the couples we saw whispering together in the compartment were going off somewhere to get a baby of their own.

We chose you must be the sweetest words in any language.

Sue West

6

SPECIAL MOMENTS

Make a memory with your children,
Spend some time to show you care;
Toys and trinkets can't replace those
Precious moments that you share.

Elaine Hardt

The Day We Flew the Kites

"String!" shouted my brother, bursting into the kitchen. "We need lots more string."

It was Saturday. As always, it was a busy one, for "Six days shalt thou labor and do all thy work" was taken seriously back then. Outside, Father and Mr. Patrick next door were doing chores.

Inside the two houses, Mother and Mrs. Patrick were engaged in spring cleaning. Such a windy March day was ideal for "turning out" clothes closets. Already, woolens flapped on backyard clotheslines.

Somehow the boys had slipped away to the back lot with their kites. Now, even at the risk of having Brother impounded to beat carpets, they had sent him for more string. Apparently, there was no limit to the heights to which kites would soar today.

My mother looked at the sitting room, its furniture disordered for a Spartan sweeping. Again her eyes wavered toward the window. "Come on, girls! Let's take string to the boys and watch them fly the kites a minute."

On the way we met Mrs. Patrick, laughing guiltily, escorted by her girls.

There never was such a day for flying kites! God doesn't make two such days in a century. We played all our fresh twine into the boys' kites, and still they soared. We could hardly distinguish the tiny, orange-colored specks. Now and then we slowly reeled one in, finally bringing it dipping and tugging to earth, for the sheer joy of sending it up again. What a thrill to run with them, to the right, to the left, and see our poor, earth-bound movements reflected minutes later in the majestic sky-dance of the kites! We wrote wishes on slips of paper and slipped them over the string. Slowly, irresistibly, they climbed up until they reached the kites. Surely all wishes would be granted.

Even our fathers dropped hoe and hammer and joined us. Our mothers took their turn, laughing like schoolgirls. Their hair blew out their pompadours and curled loose about their cheeks; their gingham aprons whipped about their legs. Mingled with our fun was something akin to awe. The grownups were really playing with us! Once I looked at Mother and thought she looked actually pretty. And her over 40!

We never knew where the hours went that day on the hilltop. There were no hours, just golden breezes. I think we were all beside ourselves. Parents forgot their duty and their dignity. Children forgot their combativeness and small spites. *Perhaps it's like this in the kingdom of heaven,* I thought confusedly.

It was growing dark before, drunk with sun and air, we all stumbled sleepily back to the houses. I suppose we had some sort of supper. I suppose there must have been a surface tidying-up, for the house on Sunday looked decorous enough.

The strange thing was, we didn't mention that day afterward. I felt a little embarrassed. Surely none of the others had thrilled to it as deeply as I. I locked the memory up in that deepest part of me where we keep "the things that cannot be and yet they are."

The years went on, then one day I was scurrying about my own kitchen in a city apartment, trying to get some work out of the way while my three-year-old insistently cried her desire to "go park and see ducks."

"I can't go!" I said. "I have this and this to do, and when I'm through I'll be too tired to walk that far."

My mother, who was visiting us, looked up from the peas she was shelling. "It's a wonderful day," she offered, "really warm, yet there's a fine, fresh breeze. It reminds me of that day we flew kites."

I stopped in my dash between stove and sink. The locked door flew open and with it, a gush of memories. I pulled off my apron. "Come on," I told my little girl. "You're right, it's too good a day to miss."

Another decade passed. We were in the aftermath of a great war. All evening we had been asking our returned soldier, the youngest Patrick boy, about his experiences as a prisoner of war. He had talked freely, but now for a long time he had been silent. What was he thinking of—what dark and dreadful things?

"Say!" A smile twitched his lips. "Do you remember—no, of course you wouldn't. It probably didn't make the impression on you it did on me."

I hardly dared speak. "Remember what?"

"I used to think of that day a lot in POW camp, when things weren't too good. Do you remember the day we flew the kites?"

Winter came, and the sad duty of a call of condolence on Mrs. Patrick, recently widowed. I dreaded the call. I couldn't imagine Mrs. Patrick facing life alone.

We talked a little of my family and her grandchildren and the changes in the town. Then she was silent, looking down at her lap. I cleared my throat. Now I must say something about her loss . . . and she would cry.

When she looked up, Mrs. Patrick was smiling. "I was just sitting here thinking," she said. "Henry had such fun that day. Frances, do you remember the day we flew the kites?"

Frances Fowler
Submitted by Ruth Rogness

Dance with Me

When we're young and we dream of love and fulfillment, we think perhaps of moon-drenched Parisian nights or walks along the beach at sunset.

No one tells us that the greatest moments of a lifetime are fleeting, unplanned and nearly always catch us off guard.

Not long ago, as I was reading a bedtime story to my seven-year-old daughter, Annie, I became aware of her focused gaze. She was staring at me with a faraway, trancelike expression. Apparently, completing *The Tale of Samuel Whiskers* was not as important as we first thought.

I asked what she was thinking about.

"Mommy," she whispered, "I just can't stop looking at your pretty face."

I almost dissolved on the spot.

Little did she know how many trying moments the glow of her sincerely loving statement would carry me through over the following years.

Not long after, I took my four-year-old son to an elegant department store, where the melodic notes of a classic love song drew us toward a tuxedoed musician playing a grand piano. Sam and I sat down on a marble bench nearby, and he seemed as transfixed by the lilting theme as I was.

I didn't realize that Sam had stood up next to me until he turned, took my face in his little hands and said, "Dance with me."

If only those women strolling under the Paris moon knew the joy of such an invitation made by a round-cheeked boy with baby teeth. Although shoppers openly chuckled, grinned and pointed at us as we glided and whirled around the open atrium, I would not have traded a dance with such a charming young gentleman if I'd been offered the universe.

Jean Harper

The Prognosis

A young mother who had been diagnosed with a treatable form of cancer returned home from the hospital, self-conscious about her physical appearance and loss of hair following radiation. Upon sitting down on a kitchen chair, her son appeared quietly in the doorway, studying her curiously.

As his mother began a rehearsed speech to help him understand what he was seeing, the boy came forward to snuggle in her lap. Intently, he laid his head to her chest and just held on. His mother was saying, "And sometime, hopefully soon, I will look the way I used to, and then I'll be better."

The young child sat up thoughtfully. With six-year-old frankness, he simply responded, "Different hair, same old heart."

His mother no longer had to wait for "sometime, hopefully soon" to be better. She was.

Rochelle M. Pennington

The Family Dinner

I looked at my twin teenagers and I wanted to cry. He wore baggy pants, orange hair and earrings. She wore a nose ring, a fake tattoo and three-inch nails. It was Passover and we were on our way to the relatives . . . for dinner . . . to celebrate.

What would the family say? I could just imagine the whispers of their aunts and uncles, the looks, the clucking of tongues and shaking of heads. I could have started an argument right there, at the door, before we left. I could have threatened and ridiculed and grounded. But then what? I knew I didn't want a fight and harsh words said on this day.

It would have been easy if they were only nine. "March back into your rooms and put something respectable on!" I would have said. But they were 16, and what they had on—to them—was respectable.

And so we went. I was ready for the looks, but none came. I was ready for the whispers. None came. My kids sat (looking a bit awkward) around the table of 20. They sat alongside the scrubbed and perfect shiny faces of their little cousins. They participated in the service and they sang the holiday songs. My son helped the younger ones read. My daughter helped clear the dishes in between courses. They laughed and joked and helped pour coffee for the elders.

I realized as I watched their beautiful faces that it didn't matter what anyone else thought. Because I thought they were terrific. They were carrying on our tradition with enthusiasm and love. And it was coming naturally—from their hearts.

Sitting across from them at the table, I studied them. I knew that the hair, the baggy clothes and fake tattoos were just a statement of who they were for the moment. This would change with time. But their participation in the songs and ceremonies of our holidays and the closeness of our family would be within them always. As they grew older, I knew this would never change.

Soon, the Passover celebration would be over. The loud music, friends and chaos would again be a part of our lives. I didn't want this special night to end. These were precious moments that sneak up on us as mothers. I don't think it matters how young or old our children are. Sometimes, it's just a quick, funny smile, or a small gesture they make that sparks that overwhelming feeling of total love.

I watched my son and daughter and felt their peace and happiness. At that moment, I wanted to jump up and hug them. I wanted to tell them what great kids I thought they were. But I didn't. At that moment, I wanted to walk over and pinch their cheeks as I did when they were nine, and tell them I thought they were beautiful. But I didn't. Instead, I sat in my place and sang and ate, and talked with the others.

Later, on the way home I would tell them. In private, I would say how much their presence at the table meant to me. I would tell them how great they were and how proud I was to be their mom. Later, when we were alone, I would tell them how much I loved them. And I did.

Shari Cohen

"If my parents like it, can I exchange it?"

Bouncing Back

I have been through some very bad times in my life, and because I'm Joan Rivers, I've had to go through them publicly. At times being a mother has been overwhelming for me. When my business partner, my best friend and more importantly, my beloved husband, Edgar, committed suicide, it made things tough for me and my daughter, Melissa. Even for a mother and daughter who *don't* lose a man to suicide, things can still be tough. A daughter's teenage years can be a mother's attempt to make contact with a UFO: Unintelligible Female Opponent. Restoring my relationship with Melissa after Edgar's death was a long and often agonizing process for me.

Yet by the time she returned to college for her senior year, we were enjoying each other's company, and when graduation neared, she told me that her classmates wanted me to speak at their ceremony. At first the invitation delighted me. But then I thought: I don't want to turn this into "Commencement Starring Joan Rivers."

"I'm very flattered," I told Melissa, "but I think I shouldn't. This is your moment, and I don't want to steal it from you."

"Mom," she said warmly, "even if you just sat in the balcony, the spotlight would still be on you. It would mean a lot to me if you spoke."

And so I addressed her college graduating class of the University of Pennsylvania. I told a few jokes and gave the graduates the usual commencement advice. But there was nothing usual about the way I felt on that graduation day. My daughter had been through more pain in two years than any woman deserves in a lifetime, and she had come through. Not only had she graduated with her class on time, but she had graduated with honors. Even more important, she had retained her kind and sensitive heart.

When I finished my speech, I looked into the audience and saw Melissa and the friends who had helped her through the last two years. Few events on earth are more moving than a college graduation. Melissa and her friends looked so brave and confident as they prepared to head into the big scary world. And I knew that waiting for them were sharks that belonged in *Jaws.* These kids would need so much courage and luck. They would have to know to never give up. I hoped that some of them were aware that I had never given up.

"I love you, Melissa," I suddenly said, as if the two of us were alone, and she answered by blowing me a kiss from her seat. I was so overwhelmed by joy and pride and relief that we had found our way back to each other that I could barely hold myself together long enough to leave the podium.

And then the entire class rose and gave me a standing ovation. My stand-up career should have ended right there, for knocking 'em dead at Buckingham Palace would have been just a lounge act compared to this. Of course, this was the first applause I'd ever gotten that wasn't really for me. It was for my daughter. I wanted to applaud right along with them. Melissa and I had survived those teenage encounters, and also an encounter with unthinkable tragedy. Now we were bound to each other—not just by love, but by friendship, too.

Joan Rivers

My Daughter, My Teacher

Children reinvent your world for you.

Susan Sarandon

Children teach us something every day. As a parent, I have learned to expect this. Yet sometimes the extent of what my daughter teaches surprises me.

When Marissa was six months old, it seemed she was always looking up. As I gazed upward with her, I learned the magic of leaves dancing on trees and the awesome size of the tail of a jet. At eight months she was forever looking down. I learned that each stone is different, sidewalk cracks make intricate designs and blades of grass come in a variety of greens.

Then she turned 11 months and began saying "Wow!" She spoke this marvelous word for anything new and wonderful to her, such as the assortment of toys she spotted in the pediatrician's office or the gathering of clouds before a storm. She whispered, "Oh, wow!" for things that really impressed her, like a brisk breeze on her face or a flock of geese honking overhead. Then there was the ultimate in "Wow," a mouthing of the word with no sound, reserved for truly awesome events. These included the sunset on a lake after a magnificent day in Minnesota and fireworks in the summer sky.

She has taught me many ways to say "I love you." She said it well one morning when she was 14 months old. We were cuddling. She buried her head in my shoulder and, with a sigh of contentment, said "Happy." Another day (during her terrific twos) she pointed to a beautiful model on the cover of a magazine and said, "Is that you, Mom?" Most recently my now three-year-old walked into the kitchen while I was cleaning up after supper and said, "Can I help?" Shortly after this she put her hand on my arm and said, "Mom, if you were a kid, we'd be friends."

At moments like this, all I can say is, "Oh, wow!"

Janet S. Meyer

The Broken Doll

Here's a story a friend of mine once told me, in her own words:

One day my young daughter was late coming home from school. I was both annoyed and worried. When she came through the door, I demanded in my upset tone that she explain why she was late.

She said, "Mommy, I was walking home with Julie, and halfway home, Julie dropped her doll and it broke into lots of little pieces."

"Oh, honey," I replied, "you were late because you helped Julie pick up the pieces of her doll to put them back together."

In her young and innocent voice, my daughter said, "No, Mommy. I didn't know how to fix the doll. I just stayed to help Julie cry."

Dan Clark

A Child's Vision

My child took a crayon
In her little hand
And started to draw
As if by command.

I looked on with pleasure
But couldn't foresee
What the few simple lines
Were going to be.

What are you drawing?
I asked, by and by.
I'm making a picture
Of God in the sky.

But nobody knows
What God looks like, I sighed.
They will when I'm finished
She calmly replied.

Sherwin Kaufman

May Day

Mr. Kobb wrapped the half-dozen carnations in plastic wrap, with some green leafy things and those little teeny weeny white baby's breath flowers. He was even kind enough to put a bow around this gift I was bringing my mother for May Day.

"How are you getting these home, Ernie?" he asked me.

"I'm carrying them."

"You're riding your bike in this?"

We both looked out the flower shop window to observe the trees bending to the sidewalk. That was a nasty wind. I nodded my answer.

"How about I wrap that bouquet in a stronger bag?" He took the flowers and rolled them up in a couple of layers of strong brown paper. Handing the bundle to me, he said, "Good luck, kid."

"Thanks," I said. I stuck the bouquet inside the front of my coat and zipped it up as far as it would go. The petals tickled my neck and chin, but I didn't think they would last too long if I tried to hold them in a hand that needed to be stuck on a handlebar. I didn't know much about flowers, but I knew my mother deserved more than a ripped-up bundle of stems.

Now, there's wind, and then there's pick-you-up-and-blow-you-two-blocks-away wind. The wind that day was the second kind. Riding against it was not easy. I felt my feet pedaling, my hands gripping, my lungs gasping, and wind against my face, but every time I looked up, I was still in front of the same store on the same block. At least it seemed that way.

My nose ran. I had no tissues to wipe it. It didn't take too long for my lips to chap. My ears hurt way deep inside, like someone was poking my eardrums with toothpicks. My eyes were so dry I couldn't blink. Every muscle in my body hurt.

The highway got more and more crowded with cars as the sun started setting. The wind knocked me out of the bike lane and into the street enough for me to worry about getting hit. One truck driver swerved and honked his horn to avoid me. A man in a Cadillac yelled out his window for me to get my you-know-what home.

It was after dark when I finally neared my block. My parents should have been worried sick by that point. I kept looking for Dad's mini-van or Mom's station wagon. They must have been out looking for me, I figured. At any moment they would drive past, stop, and load me, the bike and my flowers inside for a nice warm drive the rest of the way home. The longer I went without seeing their familiar headlights, the angrier I got.

I was only doing this stupid bike ride for Mom. The least she could do was save my life.

Four blocks from home, worn out, I stopped and took the flowers out of my jacket. I was going to throw them into the wind. Mom didn't deserve them anymore.

What stopped me was the sight of the white carnations. They weren't quite as perky as they had been, and the baby's breath was all munched, but as a whole, the bouquet still looked nice. It had been so much work getting them this far, it would be stupid to waste it all now.

I stuck the paper-wrapped stems of the bouquet into my mouth and rode super slowly so the wind wouldn't hurt them. Soon enough I came to the hill leading down to my house. I kept my feet still on the pedals, and my hands gripped the brakes on the handlebars. It didn't matter. With the wind at my back, my neighbors' houses became a blur as I whizzed by. I tried to stop and swerve into my driveway.

The bike skidded and went down. I landed at least three feet away after sliding across the driveway, stopping only when my head hit the soft grass of the front lawn. The flowers scattered across the yard, petals ripping off and flying about like confetti.

Ignoring my scratches, I ran around my front yard to gather up what I could of Mom's bouquet. By the time I had clumped together the six stems again, little was left of the pretty parts. Sloppily, I re-tied the bow around them.

Mom rushed out the front door, frantic to know what the crash had been. I hid the flowers behind my back.

"Are you okay?" Mom asked, looking my face over for serious wounds.

"I'm fine," I said, through the knot forming in my throat.

"Are you sure?" she double-checked. "Why are you hiding your hands?"

"My hands are fine. See?" I revealed the mess that used to be a bouquet of flowers. "I'll get you something else," I muttered as I started to cry.

Mom grasped the flowers, with my hands still holding them, and sniffed them so long I thought they might go up her nose. At last she lowered them, and I saw that she was crying, too.

"I love them. Thank you."

Right then I remembered why I had bought them for her. It was more than a day on a calendar; it was because she was always so good at showing me how much she loved me, no matter what. The flowers were dead, but in Mom's hands they looked alive and beautiful.

Ernie Gilbert
As told to Donna Getzinger

How Santa Knew

Nineteen years ago, I was going through a terrible divorce. Near Christmas, I took my young daughter, Kim, to see Santa at a local department store. I thought I knew what she wanted, so I didn't listen closely. But on Christmas morning, she seemed very disappointed. She wouldn't tell me why.

During the next year, I met and married a wonderful man named Sam. On our first Christmas, there was a huge box under the tree for me. It was a 12-place setting of beautiful dishes—something that I'd needed and wanted but that was too much of a luxury before.

I asked Sam how in the world he'd known how much I wanted new dishes. He explained that he'd never forgotten the little girl who had sat on his lap the previous Christmas—and who told him that all she wanted for Christmas was new dishes for her mom.

Fay Porter

The Day I Was Too Busy

"Mommy, look!" cried my daughter, Darla, pointing to a chicken hawk soaring through the air.

"Uh huh." I murmured, driving, lost in thought about the tight schedule of my day.

Disappointment filled her face.

"What's the matter, sweetheart?" I asked, entirely dense.

"Nothing," my seven-year-old said. The moment was gone. Near home, we slowed to search for the albino deer that comes out from behind the thick mass of trees in the early evening. She was nowhere to be seen.

"Tonight, she has too many things to do," I said.

Dinner, baths and phone calls filled the hours until bedtime.

"Come on, Darla, time for bed!" She raced past me up the stairs. Tired, I kissed her on the cheek, said prayers and tucked her in.

"Mom, I forgot to give you something!" she said. My patience was gone.

"Give it to me in the morning," I said, but she shook her head.

"You won't have time in the morning!" she retorted.

"I'll take time," I answered defensively. Sometimes no matter how hard I tried, time flowed through my fingers like sand in an hourglass, never enough. Not enough for her, for my husband, and definitely not enough for me.

She wasn't ready to give up yet. She wrinkled her freckled little nose in anger and swiped away her chestnut brown hair.

"No, you won't! It will be just like today when I told you to look at the hawk. You didn't even listen to what I said."

I was too weary to argue; she hit too close to the truth.

"Good night!" I shut her door with a resounding thud.

Later, though, her gray-blue gaze filled my vision as I thought how little time we really had until she was grown and gone.

My husband asked, "Why so glum?"

I told him.

"Maybe she's not asleep yet. Why don't you check," he said with all the authority of a parent in the right. I followed his advice, wishing it was my own idea.

I cracked open her door, and the light from the window spilled over her sleeping form. In her hand I could see the remains of a crumpled paper. Slowly I opened her palm to see what the item of our disagreement had been.

Tears filled my eyes. She had torn into small pieces a big red heart with a poem she had written titled, "Why I Love My Mother!"

I carefully removed the tattered pieces. Once the puzzle was all put back into place, I read what she had written:

Why I Love My Mother!

Although you're busy, and you work so hard
You always take time to play
I love you Mommy because
I am the biggest part of your busy day!

The words were an arrow straight to the heart. At seven years old, she had the wisdom of Solomon.

Ten minutes later I carried a tray to her room, with two cups of hot chocolate with marshmallows and two peanut butter and jelly sandwiches. When I softly touched her smooth cheek, I could feel my heart burst with love.

Her thick dark lashes lay like fans against her lids as they fluttered, awakened from a dreamless sleep, and she looked at the tray.

"What is that for?" she asked, confused by this late-night intrusion.

"This is for you, because you are the most important part of my busy day!" She smiled and sleepily drank half her cup of chocolate. Then she drifted back to sleep, not really understanding how strongly I meant what I said.

Cindy Ladage

"Between the time spent going to school and doing my homework it's hard to spend quality time with my doll."

The Play's the Thing

Forgive me, Lord,
for all the tasks
that went undone today.
But this morning when my child
toddled in and said, "Mommy play?"
I simply had to say yes.
And between the puzzles and trucks
and blocks and dolls and old hats and
books and giggles,
we shared a thousand special thoughts,
a hundred hopes and dreams and hugs.
And tonight, when prayer time came
and he folded his hands and softly whispered,
"Thank you, God, for Mommy and Daddy and
toys and French fries, but 'specially
for Mommy playing,"
I knew it was a day well wasted.
And I knew You'd understand.

Jayne Jaudon Ferrer

Swift Second

As far as Will was concerned, the regular Levi's 501 jeans were not cool enough to wear to school. He wanted to wear the dirty stonewashed pair in the laundry. He argued with me when I insisted he wear the clean 501s, and he ran out the door to catch the school bus in a huff. We did not have our usual good-bye hug. I felt a little upset we had angrily parted ways, yet I felt proud of my 10-year-old son for being strong-willed.

I was running late; it was already 7:20 A.M., and I needed to be at the office early for a meeting. I showered and was drying off when I heard the doorbell ring. I threw on the sweat clothes I'd just taken off, and with dripping wet hair hesitantly opened the front door. I *felt* something was wrong.

A frightened, wide-eyed little girl breathlessly announced that Will had just been hit by a truck. My heart sank. I stood there petrified until something deep inside made me run toward the bus stop. I was only halfway there when I spotted him lying lifeless in the street. Sheer fear of what I might encounter momentarily slowed my pace. Then I heard him crying for me and his voice made me run faster than I ever have in my life. He was lying face down, trumpet case nearby, with a blanket thrown over him—a thoughtful neighbor's way of helping.

There was a chill in the air on that school day in September, and the sun was glaring upon the scene. It was the blinding sun that contributed to the accident, and a 16-year-old boy in a small truck. It took only one split second, a level motion, and Will was hit by the truck at a speed of around 20 miles an hour. Apparently, upon impact he was thrown at least 10 feet up in the air and landed some distance away, falling on his knees and trumpet case. Thank goodness for all those Saturday afternoons at soccer games, where he learned how to fall to minimize injury, and for the trumpet case, which prevented him from hitting his head.

Will was coherent, talking to me and making little jokes—his way of reassuring me of the outcome. I felt terrified inside, but I knew I needed to stay positive and strong. I realized I could have lost him in the blink of an eye; instead, for some unknown reason, he was lying here, sweetly, telling me anecdotes.

I heard sirens, and the fire department emergency crew arrived first, with an ambulance not far behind. Their initial exam showed no evidence of injuries to his head, back or arms. The fireman was gently cutting the legs of his 501 jeans to make certain no bones were broken when Will said, lightheartedly, "Mommy, it looks like I won't ever have to wear these anymore." I laughed and knew instinctively as we were getting into the ambulance that he was going to be just fine.

Will was very lucky—I was very lucky. According to the police officer, it was a miracle he was not severely injured or dead. Staying home that day, we talked and cried about many things; being more careful, never leaving a person you love when you are mad, and how important it is to live in the "now" and appreciate your life.

While he was resting, I washed the stonewashed jeans and clung to the 501s, sobbing. I had an overwhelming awareness of how your life can change, without notice, in a swift second. This happened seven years ago, and when I need a reality check, or a gentle reminder that our time together is a precious gift, I pull out those neatly cut 501s.

Daryl Ott Underhill

When Mother Came to Tea

I had no idea she would be there. My apologies for her absence had been well-rehearsed.

When my high school home economics teacher announced that we would be having a formal mother-daughter tea, I felt certain I would not be serving my mother at this special event.

So I will never forget walking into the gaily decorated gym—and there she was! As I looked at her, sitting calmly and smiling, I imagined all the arrangements this remarkable woman must have had to make to be able to be with me for that one hour.

Who was looking after Granny? She was bedridden following a stroke, and Mom had to do everything for her.

My three little sisters would be home from school before Mom got there. Who would greet them and look at their papers?

How did she get here? We didn't own a car, and she couldn't afford a taxi. It was a long walk to get the bus, plus at least five more blocks to the school.

And the pretty dress she was wearing, red with tiny white flowers, was just right for the tea. It brought out the silver beginning to show in her dark hair. There was no money for extra clothes, and I knew she had gone into debt again at our coal company store to have it.

I was so proud! I served her tea with a happy, thankful heart, and introduced her boldly to the group when our turn came. I sat with my mother that day, just like the rest of the class, and that was very important to me. The look of love in her eyes told me she understood.

I have never forgotten. One of the promises I made to myself and to my children, as young mothers make promises, was that I would always be there for them. That promise is difficult to keep in today's busy world. But I have an example before me that puts any lame excuses to rest. I just recall again when Mother came to tea.

Margie M. Coburn

Finding Her There

Every year my birthday followed the same ritual. My mother would come to see me, on that late fall day, and I would open the door. She would be standing on the step with wind swirling leaves around her feet.

There would be a chill in the air, and in her hands she would hold my birthday gift. It would always be something small and precious, something I had needed for a long time and just never knew it.

I would open this gift from my mother with great care, then I would tuck it carefully away with all my heart's possessions. How fragile these gifts were, from my mother's hands.

If my mother could come to me today on my birthday, I would bring her into the warmth of my kitchen. Then we would have a cup of tea, and watch the turning leaves press themselves against the windows.

There would be no rush to open my gift, because today I would know that I had already opened it when I opened the front door to find her there, with the wind swirling leaves around her feet . . .

Christina Keenan

7

MIRACLES

Miracles are instantaneous; they cannot be summoned, but they come of themselves, usually at unlikely moments and to those who least expect them . . .

Katherine A. Porter

Angel in Uniform

Where there is great love there are always miracles.

Willa Cather

This is a family story my father told me about his mother, my grandmother.

In 1949, my father had just returned home from the war. On every American highway you could see soldiers in uniform hitchhiking home to their families, as was the custom at that time in America.

Sadly, the thrill of his reunion with his family was soon overshadowed. My grandmother became very ill and had to be hospitalized. It was her kidneys, and the doctors told my father that she needed a blood transfusion immediately or she would not live through the night. The problem was that Grandmother's blood type was AB-, a very rare type even today, but even harder to get then because there were no blood banks or air flights to ship blood. All the family members were typed, but not one member was a match. So the doctors gave the family no hope; my grandmother was dying.

My father left the hospital in tears to gather up all the family members, so that everyone would get a chance to tell Grandmother good-bye. As my father was driving down the highway, he passed a soldier in uniform hitchhiking home to his family. Deep in grief, my father had no inclination at that moment to do a good deed. Yet it was almost as if something outside himself pulled him to a stop, and he waited as the stranger climbed into the car.

My father was too upset to even ask the soldier his name, but the soldier noticed my father's tears right away and inquired about them. Through his tears, my father told this total stranger that his mother was lying in a hospital dying because the doctors had been unable to locate her blood type, AB-, and if they did not locate her blood type before nightfall, she would surely die.

It got very quiet in the car. Then this unidentified soldier extended his hand out to my father, palm up. Resting in the palm of his hand were the dog tags from around his neck. The blood type on the tags was AB-. The soldier told my father to turn the car around and get him to the hospital.

My grandmother lived until 1996, 47 years later, and to this day no one in our family knows the soldier's name. But my father has often wondered, was he a soldier or an angel in uniform?

Jeannie Ecke Sowell

The Healing

The shock of events of the past 30 hours overwhelmed Jim all at once. His body felt numb, and while the world was moving along, he felt removed from it.

Jim and his wife, Connie, had just lost their beautiful four-month-old son. Preliminary diagnosis: SIDS, sudden infant death syndrome.

Thirty hours ago Jim had driven to the baby-sitter's home to pick up Joshua. It was a routine trip, like the one he made five days every week . . . until he arrived, and little Joshua could not be awakened from his nap. The next few hours were a blur. Wailing sirens, swift-moving paramedics, critical-care doctors and reassuring nurses, holding hands and praying. A decision to life-flight Joshua to Children's Hospital 60 miles away . . . but all in vain. Twelve hours later, the doctors had exhausted all attempts at revival. There was no brain activity. The decision was to turn off life-support. Little Joshua was gone. Yes, they wanted all of Joshua's usable organs to be readied for donation. That was not a difficult decision for Jim and Connie, a loving and giving couple.

The next morning dawned. More decisions and arrangements. Telephone calls and funeral plans. At one point Jim realized he needed a haircut, but being new to the community, he didn't have his own regular barber yet. Jim's brother volunteered to call his hairdresser and get Jim an appointment. The schedule was full, but after a few words of explanation, the salon owner said, "Just send him right over and we'll take care of him."

Jim was exhausted as he settled into the chair. He had had little sleep. He began to reflect on the past hours, trying desperately to make some sense of it all. Why had Joshua, their firstborn, the child they had waited so long for, been taken so soon . . . he had barely begun his life . . . The question kept coming, and the pain in Jim's heart just enveloped him. He thought about the words spoken by the hospital chaplain. "We don't fully understand what part we have in God's plan. Perhaps Joshua had already completed his mission on earth." Those words didn't ease the bitterness that was creeping in.

The hairdresser expressed her sympathy, and Jim found himself telling her all about the events of the last 30 hours. Somehow it helped to tell the story. Maybe if he told it enough times, he would gain some understanding.

As Jim mentioned the organ donations, he looked at his watch and remembered what was happening 60 miles away . . . where he had said good-bye to his beloved Joshua a few short hours earlier. "They are transplanting one of his heart valves right now."

The hairdresser stopped and stood motionless. Finally she spoke, but her voice quivered and it was only a whisper. "You're not going to believe this . . . but about an hour ago the customer sitting in this chair wanted me to hurry so she could get to Children's Hospital. She left here so full of joy . . . her prayers had been answered. Today her baby granddaughter is receiving a desperately needed transplant . . . a heart valve."

Jim's healing began.

Sandy Jones

Adopting a Dream

Michael or Michelle.

Before Richard and I married, we agreed that this would be the name of our first child. We had it all planned.

Two years later, Richard walked across the stage to receive his college diploma. It was time to make our dream come true for a family.

For the next two years, we prayed that I would get pregnant. Yet month after month was filled with disappointment, until one day in the spring of 1985, I was so sure I was pregnant that I made an appointment to see the doctor.

With a smile, he said, "You're pregnant."

I wanted to dance around the room. My due date was set for the first week of November, "around the third," my doctor said.

The next six weeks were filled with preparations. We did everything but take out an ad in the newspaper. Richard began preparing the room that would be the nursery.

We tried to imagine what our son or daughter would be like. My thoughts were consumed with the child growing inside me.

"I'm concerned that we haven't heard a heartbeat," my doctor told me on my third visit.

A half-hour later, I cried in his office when he explained that a blood test showed no sign of my ever having been pregnant.

"A false pregnancy," he said. "Your mind wanted it so badly, your body believed it."

Little Michael or Michelle didn't exist. There was no baby to mourn, yet we grieved.

So began nearly a decade of infertility tests and watching enviously as our friends and siblings had babies. My heart ached as I forced smiles when they talked of their children.

More pregnancy tests. More pacing and praying. Negative. They were always the same. The dream died again and again.

We plunged into our work—Richard into his teaching and I into my writing. Yet our desire for a child was strong, and in 1992 we attended an adoption orientation class.

I looked around the crowded room of nervous couples. Could our dream really come true?

I was afraid to hope.

"This is our chance," Richard whispered.

We began our required parenting classes. Every Monday evening for 10 weeks we listened, role-played, and discussed the joys and trials of parenting these children who needed new homes.

With all the work came the joy of preparation. How long before our child arrived? Would he or she come with a broken heart and spirit? How long would it take to bond with our child, and he with us? Would our child be anything like the one I'd imagined so long ago?

Together Richard and I prepared our extra bedroom. Would it be a nursery or child's room? There were so many plans to make, yet so little information to help us. Lovingly I placed bottles of lotion and powders beside bibs and books, inside dresser drawers.

Often, I sat on the floor in the yellow and white room and dreamed of the child who would sleep and play there. I bought a few toys and stuffed animals. They waited quietly for small hands to hold them.

Then, on November 3, 1993, the phone rang and our lives changed.

"Kathy, is there something you've been wanting for Christmas?" our caseworker asked.

I could almost hear her smiling. I clutched the phone and whispered, "Yes."

"Well, we've got some good news."

Then she told me about an eight-month-old girl. A baby girl! Would I awake and find it just another dream?

"Here name is Theresa Michelle. But her foster parents call her Michelle," I was told.

I was stunned. Michelle. Eight years ago, we'd dreamed of our Michelle. Then it hit me. It was November 3. If I had had that child in November of 1985, "around the third," my doctor had said, he or she would be eight years old. How wonderful God was to us, how our prayers had been answered!

I tried to imagine what it would be like holding this child.

Within two weeks, we began our three days of visitation. I looked into my daughter's face. She smiled and held her arms out. I held her and breathed in the scent of baby powder and milk, as sweet smelling as a garden of roses.

Our Michelle had arrived.

On November 23, she came to live in our home and hearts. Every day our love for her grows. Nearly four years old now, she loves to hear the story of her adoption, of how we waited and longed for her.

Hopes and dreams don't have to die. We watched ours come back to life and call us Mama and Daddy.

Kathryn Lay

Honey, You'd Better Sit Down

If you ask me, life can be quite unpredictable. For example, on an ordinary day, one phone call can change everything.

My husband, Gary, views life a little differently than I do. A big, kind and quiet man, I'm sure he didn't know what he was getting himself into when he proposed to me. For one thing, I was the mother of four children, now mostly grown; Gary was a lifelong bachelor. I'm a talker; he often feels more comfortable writing things down. (For example, his marriage proposal came in the form of a multiple-choice questionnaire with ring attached.) I like to "go with the flow." He takes comfort in daily routine.

Our differences seemed to complement each other, and we settled happily into marriage. As great as he is with my grown kids, I occasionally wondered if he didn't mind not raising a child himself. But he knew I was past child-bearing age when he proposed to me, and he asked me anyway.

From the beginning of our marriage, every evening Gary would come home from work and ask me, "How was your day, dear?" He often seemed amused by my sometimes unexpected answer to that question. One day, two years after we were married, I replied, "Honey, you'd better sit down for this one."

My oldest daughter, Mia, had recently been transferred by her company from near our home in Florida to Texas. Once there, she had hired four new trainees and accompanied them back to company headquarters in Tampa for 10 days of training. When she called me from the motel where they were staying, which was 40 minutes from our house, all trace of managerial calm was missing from her voice.

"Mom, you won't believe what just happened! It's like something you'd hear about on *Oprah!*"

"What is it, Mia?" She'd certainly piqued my curiosity.

"One of the young women I hired was up all night with a severe stomach ache. We finally called an ambulance. Well, the hospital just telephoned—and she had a baby! No one knew she was pregnant, including her!"

"Yes, right," I said, amused but skeptical.

"I'm telling you, I interviewed her and she didn't look the least bit pregnant. And I'm sure if she knew, she wouldn't have switched jobs, or come away for a 10-day training seminar when she was due. This is incredible! I'm going to the hospital."

A veteran of four very noticeable pregnancies, I shook my head and laughed, and went about my day.

Around 4:00, Mia called again. "Mom, you're not going to believe this. Since no one back in Texas knew Judy was pregnant, she's going home tomorrow just like nothing happened!"

"Like nothing happened?" I asked, confused. "But what about the baby?"

"She's going to leave it here. She's sure social services will find someone who wants it."

I was stunned. "But . . . you can't just leave a child with no instructions. It could bounce from foster home to foster home for years! I'd take that child myself before I'd let that happen!"

"Mom," Mia sputtered, "you'd do *what?*"

"I'd—uh—well . . . well, you talk with the mother and see if she'd like to have a name and a phone number to leave the child with instead of losing her in the system for 18 years." Even as I said it, I knew there was impulsive, and then there was *impulsive.* I added, "I guess I'd better talk to Gary when he gets home."

That was the day when Gary came home at his usual time and asked his usual question and I replied, "Honey, you'd better sit down for this one."

I told the story, and in disbelief Gary replied, "Yes, right, it's gonna get left behind. Uh, huh, right, we're going to adopt."

Oddly, the more absurd it sounded, the more I was sure it was right. "Honey," I said, "this is a once-in-a-lifetime opportunity. If Mia hadn't been transferred, if she hadn't hired that particular woman or brought her here for these 10 days. . . . Here's a child on a golden platter. If you ever want a child of your own, this is the only way it's gonna happen!"

Overwhelmed, he answered, "Well, you can't make a life-changing decision like this in minutes!"

Knowing that he woke up in the mornings well before I did, and that writing about big decisions was more his style, I said, "Sleep on it, and leave me a note in the morning."

The next morning Gary was gone early, as usual—but there was no note. I was disappointed because I was so sure this was right, was meant to be!

Promptly at 9 A.M. the phone rang. "Hi, Sherry! This is Sue. I'm a social worker from the hospital. I just talked to the mother and she said you can have the baby. Want to come and get her?"

What should I do? Here I was, ready to turn our world upside down, and Gary, it seemed, preferred to deal with the well-ordered life we already had.

But as I searched for words, I heard footsteps on the stairs. To my surprise, it was Gary, not at work at all.

He sat down on the bed and whispered, "Who are you talking to?"

I grabbed a piece of paper and wrote, "How would you like to pick up your baby daughter?"

He took the pen and scribbled on the paper, "What if she gets sick? Do we need an attorney? What's it going to cost? What if the mother changes her mind?"

I read it and tore the paper in half, returning the original question: "How would you like to pick up your baby daughter?"

"Do you have an attorney?" Sue was asking.

"No," I said. "About how much would all this cost?"

"Let me find you an attorney and check into it," she said, and hung up.

Five minutes later came the return call. "I found an attorney and he said since no one was involved until now, it will cost about $2,000. Have you got that much handy?" *Gee,* I thought, *$2,000 dollars. And just when I finally paid off my credit cards.* Then—"That's it! We can adopt her with a cash advance!"

Gary, who still seemed stunned, finally headed for work. I rushed to Wal-Mart for diapers and formula, then tried to go about my day as calmly as possible. The lawyers and agencies were beginning the legal proceedings, but it still seemed unreal. And if it seemed unreal to me, I still wasn't sure whether Gary was ready to go along with this whole thing.

That night, Gary came with me to a book signing. Not exactly a party animal, he wore his usual calm (or was it bored?) look throughout. When it was over, I thought: *Now or never.*

"Honey," I said, when it was over, "let's go see her."

"We can't," he answered pragmatically. "Visiting hours are over in 10 minutes, and it's a 20-minute drive to the hospital."

"Oh, come on," I said, as I tugged him outside and into the car.

When we got to the hospital, a whispering hum followed us through the corridors. At the nurses' station where we were directed, the nurses on duty explained, "This has been an unusual event for all of us. If the paramedics had suspected that girl was pregnant, they would have taken her to a birthing hospital down the street. We don't even have a maternity ward here!" There were grins and giggles all around.

They gave us directions, and Gary and I walked down a long hall. My big, quiet husband hesitantly pulled down the handle of the door.

Beyond us was a huge, empty room. Empty, that is, except for one little crib standing in the middle of the floor.

Together we approached, and saw a tiny newborn. Gary leaned down to touch her. As he did, she reached out and wrapped her tiny fingers around his. I watched and heard Gary whisper in his deep voice, "Hi, honey! This is your daddy."

As unexpected as it was, it was as if daddy and daughter had been waiting just for each other.

Some things, I guess, are meant to be.

It might be awhile, however, before Gary is completely relaxed when he asks, "How was your day, dear?"

Sheryl Nicholson

A Promise on Mother's Day

Sue and Kenny Burton had tried for more than two years to have a baby, and things weren't going well. Month after month, despite many medical tests, they continued to be disappointed. People in their tiny, close-knit town of Frankfort, Kansas, knew about the Burtons' dream and were praying for them.

At that time, Sue sang contemporary Christian songs in a sextet formed by women from Frankfort's United Methodist Church. The group, ironically named Special Delivery, performed regularly at mother-daughter banquets, Elk and Moose club meetings, and other functions. "Usually during a program we each share a little personal history with the audience," Sue explains. "Since we range from teenage to grandmother status, people can relate to all of us."

The other singers, knowing Sue's longing for a baby, encouraged her to share that with audiences too, and she did. The response was tremendously supportive. After the Christmas concerts, many people came up to assure Sue that they would add their prayers to those of her neighbors. In March, a woman from South Dakota even predicted that a year from then, Sue would have a baby daughter. Although Sue and Kenny seemed no closer to decorating a nursery, it helped to know so many people cared.

On Mother's Day weekend, Sue drove her mother to Kansas City to spend some time with Sue's sister, Shelley, who attended college there. The three visited shopping malls all day Saturday, and Sue conscientiously pressed the automatic door lock every time they parked and got out of her car. "We joked about being overly cautious in the big city, but there was no point in being careless," Sue says.

Sunday morning, the trio awakened to a steady rain. They lounged around in Shelley's apartment and had an early lunch. The downpour continued, so eventually the three decided to go out, anyway. Dodging raindrops, they splashed across the parking lot to Sue's car. "Hurry up! I'm getting soaked!" Shelley laughed as Sue unlocked the driver's door, then pressed the switch to open the other doors.

Shelley and Sue scrambled into the front seat, while their mother got in back. "Look at this!" she exclaimed as her daughters turned around. On the backseat was a pink baby bootie.

"Where did that come from?" Sue asked. "It wasn't there yesterday, was it, Mom?"

"No," her mother said. "I was in and out of here all day, and I never saw it."

"Could it have been stuck down in the seat, maybe left by one of your friends in Frankfort?" Shelley wondered.

Sue shook her head. "I doubt it. My friends' children are all older. I don't think a baby has ever been in this car."

The women pondered over that awhile.

"Someone must have found it lying near the car just now and tossed it in, thinking it was ours," Shelley tried again.

"But," Sue pointed out, "the car was never open—you know I've locked the doors whenever we got out. And why would anyone think a bootie belonged to us? No one here knows us."

"Look how muddy and wet it is outside," Sue's mother added. "But this bootie is clean and dry."

The women fell silent again, turning over possible explanations in their minds. But no solution emerged. The bootie's position looked deliberate, as if someone had wanted to be sure it was seen.

"What if . . . ?" Sue couldn't finish her sentence. But the others knew what she was thinking. Was the bootie a message from heaven, a sign that all those prayers ascending from the Kansas plains were about to be answered?

Sue hardly dared to hope. She took the bootie home, put it in her Bible, and waited. Waited until she realized she was indeed pregnant, had been pregnant on that Mother's Day morning, and would, just as the lady from South Dakota predicted, be a mother—of a daughter—very soon. "When people asked how I could be so sure of a girl, I would simply show them the bootie," Sue says. "Would God send pink for any other reason?"

Today, five years later, the bootie hangs over Paige Elizabeth Burton's bed as a constant reminder that God answers prayers. In fact, he answers in abundance, for Paige now has a little sister. "I have no doubt that an angel left the bootie there as a sign for me," Sue says.

For Sue, every day is Mother's Day.

Joan Wester Anderson

Mother and Child Reunion

Until this past April, Kellie Forbes and Shauna Bradley had never met or spoken to each other. Their husbands worked at different companies, their children went to different schools. Now, as Kellie and Shauna prepare to celebrate their first Christmas together, their only regret is that they didn't meet sooner. For more than 14 years, these two Utah women unknowingly shared a connection as close as blood; yet only through the most unlikely of circumstances did they find out exactly what it was. Call it chance, call it fate—or call it, if you prefer, a miracle.

In 1992, life looked bleak for Kellie, with three deaths in her family. Then just after moving to a new home, she and her husband were laid off from work. The accumulated problems left her feeling overwhelmed and depressed.

Her company offered layoff counseling with psychotherapist Shauna Bradley. Shauna couldn't help noticing that her client bore an amazing resemblance to her son, Jake, whom she had adopted as an infant. She felt Kellie's dimples, freckles, dark hair and hazel eyes looked exactly like Jake's. But she passed it off as an odd similarity.

During their second session, Shauna asked Kellie about future plans. Kellie said, "I want to write a book about my adoption experience." As a teenager, she told Shauna, she gave up a baby boy to a couple she never met. Kellie went on to a happy marriage and three other children, but she never stopped thinking about that first son, who would soon celebrate his 14th birthday. She hoped that writing about her experience might help other young women.

Kellie's attitude impressed Shauna. She knew she'd be happy to meet her own son's birth mother if she were like Kellie. She told Kellie that as an adoptive mother, this subject was close to her heart.

Grateful to have found a compassionate listener, Kellie tearfully spoke of her one regret: She had not been allowed to hold her son before surrendering him. When asked why, she replied, "Kanab is a small town, and that's just how they did things," referring to the town hundreds of miles away where she'd grown up.

Startled, Shauna dropped her notebook. Her son had been born in Kanab 14 summers ago. "Did you say Kanab?" she cried. Cautiously, Kellie replied yes.

Suddenly, Shauna felt like she couldn't breathe, as if someone had hit her in the stomach. Then she started hyperventilating. She shook, trembling hands covering her mouth as she repeated, "Oh, my gosh! Oh, my gosh!"

Kellie's words emerged slowly. "Do you have him?"

Shauna nodded, "I think I do."

Taking turns, they shared their stories with each other. As a teenager, Kellie felt ridiculed by classmates in her small-town school. She told Shauna, "I allowed myself to have a physical relationship because I wanted so badly to be accepted."

The result was an unexpected pregnancy when Kellie was 18. She broke up with her boyfriend soon after the pregnancy was confirmed and decided to place the baby up for adoption. When her child's future parents were selected, all Kellie was told were their ages, descriptions, and religious and educational backgrounds.

Jim and Shauna Bradley were married for four years when they applied for adoption after "a lot of infertility work." A year later, they were selected to be parents of a baby from Kanab. Three days after his birth, Jake was presented to the Bradleys. The Bradleys told Jake about his adoption as soon as he could understand, emphasizing that his birth mother gave him up because she loved him. On his birthday, Shauna would say, "You know who's thinking about you today."

Standing in the counselor's office, Kellie didn't know whether to rejoice or be wary. After all she'd endured in the past year, she felt she couldn't risk another bitter disappointment if this woman wasn't her son's mother.

Kellie began, "So his birthday is . . ."

"June 29, 1980."

"And the attorney was . . ."

"Mike McGuire," said Shauna. "And wasn't your maiden name Robinson?"

Her heart pounding, Kellie nodded yes. The impossible had happened.

"The odds that we would meet like this do not exist," says Shauna. The two women talked long after the appointment ended. Shauna told Kellie that she wanted to wait until Jake was 18 to tell him about her, feeling he would be better able to handle the news as an adult. Kellie, happy in the knowledge that her son had a loving home, agreed.

That evening, Jim Bradley could tell that his wife was excited, as if she'd had the best workday ever. After their children were asleep, he found out why Shauna was so overjoyed and shared her excitement.

In the days that followed, Kellie and husband, Thayne, on a counselor's advice, decided to tell their children about the amazing meeting. Their children already knew they had a half-brother who had been given up for adoption to another family. They excitedly asked when they would be meeting Jake.

In the meantime, the Bradleys experienced their own dilemma. Weighing options, they concluded Jake was old enough to tell now. They felt if they waited and he found out they already knew—or if someone else told him—he'd possibly lose trust in them. But if they told him, he could grow into the knowledge of who his birth mother was, and they could be there for him.

When Kellie heard that the Bradleys now wanted to tell Jake as soon as possible, it was her turn to be anxious. "Please don't tell him because you think I want you to," she urged. Now she felt apprehensive. What if she didn't meet Jake's expectations?

One morning, Shauna and Jim came into Jake's room and woke him up. Shauna said, "Jake, the weirdest thing happened. I was counseling with a woman and we realized that she's your birth mother."

Jake burst into a grin. He asked, "What does she look like? When do I get to meet her?" His mother gave him a picture of Kellie. Thrilled, the teen ran off to show the photo to his grandmother.

When Shauna called to say, "We've told him. Can we meet for dinner?" Kellie promptly said yes, thinking: "I'd stop my life for this."

Kellie was first to arrive at the restaurant, and tried to keep her emotions under control. Jim, driving straight from work, was next. Then Shauna drove into the parking lot with Jake. She hadn't even parked the car before Jake jumped out and handed her a beautiful violet.

Kellie's voice quavered, "I've got to give you a hug—I've waited so long for this." As they embraced, Jake's eyes filled with tears and he turned back toward his mother. Shauna comforted him. "It's okay to be emotional, honey. This is a big deal!"

In the restaurant, an excited Jake told Kellie about his hobbies and activities. He was happy that his biological mother shared his love for music, and that his talent for fixing things came from Kellie's father, a mechanic.

Both birth mother and son wept as Kellie said the words she'd always longed to tell him. "There were so many things I knew I couldn't do for you. I wanted you to have a home with a mom and dad. Although I knew I was doing the right thing by giving you up, it was really, really hard."

After their first successful meeting, Shauna and Kellie brought their children together. "Our kids acted as if they'd known each other for a long time," says Kellie.

Today, Kellie and Shauna talk regularly, still amazed at the astonishing coincidence that brought them together. "I'm so happy for Jake," says Shauna. "A piece of his life puzzle has been solved." Adds Kellie, "I'm thrilled Jake has the family he does—they've far exceeded my expectations."

Carolyn Campbell

After 40 Years

When I came home from my nursing job on June 13, 1992, I did my daily chauffeuring of our four kids, then rummaged through the mail. I was pleased to see that a copy of my birth certificate had arrived from Nebraska. That put me one step closer to my passport, which I needed for a much anticipated 25th high school reunion cruise with my husband, Mike.

Humming, I tore open the envelope—and the bottom dropped out of my world.

Across the top of the paper the words boldly proclaimed, "Adoptive Birth Certificate."

There must be some mistake. You don't just open the mail when you're 42 and have a paper claim you were adopted!

My parents, Beatrice and Albert Whitney, were both deceased, so when I came to my senses, I called someone of their generation who would know—my uncle. He was evasive and uncomfortable. He hemmed and hawed, but I wouldn't let it go. He finally said yes, I was adopted when I was two years old, but my parents had made everyone promise not to tell me. Reeling, I called my older sister, Joan. She, too, hesitantly confirmed the truth.

I was devastated. It felt as if my whole life had been a lie. I thought I knew who I was, but it turned out I had no idea. As illogical as it sounds, I felt betrayed by the Whitneys and abandoned by my own birth mother.

Mike and the kids understood some of what I was going through. Finally Mike said, "Honey, why don't you try to find your birth parents?"

"Not every story ends happily," I retorted. "My mother didn't want me once. Why should she want me now?"

"Look. No matter what happens, you can't feel worse than you do right now. If you found them, if nothing else, you could probably get some medical information that would be helpful to both you and our children."

After some consideration, I realized he was right. But where should I start?

Though I'd grown up in Riverside, California, I knew I'd been born in Omaha, Nebraska. Then Joan, who was 10 years my senior, remembered a crucial piece of information: my biological parents' first names. I contacted social service agencies and started the long search process. A friend suggested I place an ad in the classified section of the Omaha paper. I almost sloughed off the suggestion. Who reads newspaper classifieds unless they're looking for a job or a used car?

On the other hand, it couldn't hurt. There was a remote chance that someone who knew either my biological or adoptive parents would see it. I decided to give it a try. The ad read: *My name is Linda, born to a Jeannie and Warren in Omaha on 8/7/50 and given up for adoption. My adoptive parents are deceased. I do not wish to cause any problems but am seeking available info or possible reunion.* It gave the phone number of a social services agent in Omaha who'd been helping me. I didn't put much stock in this particular avenue of search. I paid the paper for the first few weeks, and went on about my business.

The first ad ran on Sunday, November 1. On Monday, the telephone rang. It was the social services agent. "Linda," he said, "I think you're going to have a very merry Christmas."

A woman named Jeanenne Curtis had seen the ad, read it over and over again, and finally called the agency. She had information about me no one else could have known. "Shall I give her your number?" he asked.

When the phone rang that afternoon, I was nearly too nervous to answer. Mike held my hand. The woman on the other end said, "Is this Linda?"

"Yes," I answered. "Is this my mom?"

And two strangers burst into tears.

When I regained my voice, I said, "I can't believe you happened to look in the classified on the one day I placed the ad!"

Softly, she replied, "Honey, I've been looking for your ad in that newspaper every day for many years."

I thought at this point that nothing else could surprise me, but the story that she told left me gasping for breath.

She had been married when she was 17, and had me that same year. By the time she was 18, she and my father had realized it was all too much for them, and had divorced. She was thankful to find a full-time job in Omaha and felt blessed to find a lovely older couple, the Whitneys, to care for me. The only problem was that the Whitneys lived all the way across town, an hour-and-a-half each way on the streetcar. Though she hated to do so, she agreed to leave me with the Whitneys during the week and pick me up on the weekends.

For a year, the arrangement worked well. I was obviously well cared-for and enjoyed the Whitneys' 12-year-old daughter, Joan. But one day, my mother received a frantic phone call from Beatrice. She said that social services had found out about our arrangement, and unless the Whitneys and my mother quickly signed some routine papers, I would be taken from all of them. Mom hurried to the lawyer. He told her the same story. She didn't really understand the legal terms in the paper, but she kept telling the lawyer she'd do anything not to lose me. She never wanted to give me up.

It seemed the crisis was averted. The very next weekend was my second birthday, and Mom excitedly came to get me, bearing presents. But when she arrived, the Whitneys' apartment was empty. They were completely gone.

She did everything she could to find me. The Whitneys' lawyer refused to talk to her. Mr. Whitney's boss knew nothing except that he'd quit abruptly. Suddenly worried that the papers she'd signed were adoption papers, she called social services, but they said all adoption information was confidential.

Without money to hire a lawyer or private investigator, she kept doing what she could by herself. For years, then decades, she scoured phone books from all over the U.S. And every day, she read the classifieds, searching. For 40 years, she'd never given up hope.

My first emotion was rage at the Whitneys, who, with twisted logic, had loved me so much that they'd stolen me from my mother. But then I thought of my birth mother, and the heartache she'd suffered for decades. My suffering of a few months felt like nothing in comparison. But my third thought was a joyous one: Mom did love me. She did want me!

I can't explain the immediate bond we had. We burned up the phone lines. Mom was married, had a son who had died, and a daughter named Debbie. She and her husband had also adopted a son from Vietnam. Mom had graduated from college when she was 53. I poured out all the details of my life as well.

We actually met, as fate and the electronic age would have it, when someone from the *Faith Daniels* show saw the story of our reunion in the Omaha paper and flew us to be on the show. I'm sure it made great TV: We fell into each other's arms, weeping copiously.

That Thanksgiving, my new family came to celebrate with us in Utah. On Christmas day, I flew to be with Mom in Omaha for two weeks.

I have too much faith to believe that finding Mom was coincidence. Even the timing seemed preordained. You see, we had time to get to know each other, and to become soul companions, for the next year and a half. After that, she suddenly became very ill with a kidney disease and died.

But that year and a half was a precious gift. As painful as discovering the truth was, I'm so grateful that it happened.

I no longer think of the classifieds as a place where you find jobs and used cars.

I know that sometimes, just sometimes, you find your heart there, as well.

Linda O'Camb

Four Angels

I glanced out the rear windows of the ambulance, which was making its strange reverse trip, hospital to home. I stroked the back of my mother's limp hand in a slow, steady rhythm, trying to comfort myself as well as her.

She was breathing so shallowly, I concentrated upon her now-tiny body (tiny except for the huge, swollen abdomen) before I detected a slight, uneven movement of her swaddled form. I stopped breathing myself as I death-watched her, utterly transfixed with terror.

I breathed out a desperate prayer: *Please God, wait until we get her home. Let it happen in her own bed, in peace.*

"Is there anything in particular you want to talk about?" my mother asked, but with a stranger's voice. Her throat was so raw from the tubes and machines that even the simplest words were thickly coated with involuntary and sometimes almost unintelligible inflections.

I could not answer her question at first. I looked down at my hands clasped in my lap.

"Just everything, Mom. I just want to talk about everything."

Every little big thing and every little thing that will happen to me for the rest of my life, I thought to myself. *I want your advice on raising my daughter, your first granddaughter, who, now too young to know you, will have to borrow my memories. But most of all let's talk about how, exactly how, step by step, I am going to live the rest of my life without you—my one and only safe harbor of unconditional love.*

This is what I wanted to say, but I remained silent instead. Spoken words could not do this moment justice, I painfully realized.

"I know," she said, in the saddest tone yet of that stranger's voice, as if she had just read my thoughts from the worried lines of my face.

I stared at her, momentarily shocked by the sudden change in her eyes. My mother's extraordinary ocean-blue eyes were now filled with the pale-yellow tears of a dying woman. When had this happened? Last night? Last minute, when my head was turned down? This was the ultimate deprivation, to be robbed of seeing her unique qualities, to see her only, and finally, in terms of dwindling bodily functions.

"The bottom line is that she has a tumor that is growing rapidly and will result in her death in the next 24 hours."

This is what her oncologist said to us late last night in the hospital corridor, his eyes dropping to the floor.

"It could be a particularly agonizing kind of death," he added, now speaking directly to our feet.

My sisters stood there with me, flanking our father. I clutched a notepad to my chest, where I had carefully written down all of our questions. Somehow we figured that if we just asked this man the right question, he would finally give us the answer we hoped for. But now none of the questions about the quality of our mother's life mattered anymore, after being given the answer of death. Still, my father choked one out.

"Will she make it until we get her home?"

The doctor gave my father a look I had seen on his face once before. It was 10 months earlier, when the diagnosis had been made, and after listening to his clinical speech, my mother asked him a single question. The room was so quiet, I remember thinking I actually heard the sound of our hearts breaking as she spoke.

"Do I have one good year left?" she had asked.

And the doctor had answered my mother with this same wary expression.

Unfortunately he had been right. It had not even been a year, and certainly not enough of what had occurred since then had been good.

My father flinched at the silent message on the doctor's face. And then he spoke in a voice I remembered from over 20 years before, an incredibly resonant, strong voice, the way as a child I had imagined God sounded.

"I have arranged for a private ambulance to take my wife home as soon as she wakes up tomorrow morning. I expect you to be there, and take every damn tube, and I mean every one, out of her so that she can go home the way she should—the way a person who is as loved and cherished as she is should."

"Yes, of course," the doctor said simply.

The doctor was visibly relieved. There was nothing else for him to do, and best of all, nothing else he was expected to do. The passing of the torch, so to speak, for the home stretch.

"Have we gone over the bridge yet, darling?" my mother asked, waking surprisingly alert.

I looked out for a familiar landmark and saw that we were slowing down to glide through the sleepy Maryland eastern-shore town that my parents had retired to a few years earlier. I recognized a few of our neighbors outside their houses, standing in a solemn salute to the ambulance passing through, acknowledging its precious cargo.

They had been there for her, the way only a rural community still knows how to be. Leaving freshly baked, still-warm casseroles on the doorstep at five o'clock, weeding her flower garden when she was away for chemotherapy, clearing brush from the shoreline so that she could see the water from her bed. People made of solid gold.

"Mom, we're almost there. We're going through town." The ambulance crept up our driveway, and I could see my father and sisters standing outside the front door, waiting. The sight of their wretched vigil struck me, and I burst into tears. So, this is how I must look, how we all look, the exposed faces of premature grief.

How terrible for her to remember us this way. How equally terrible for us to remember her this way. I threw myself angrily against the doors, just as they opened, and gasped the rain-filled air as I scrambled out.

I have only the filmiest memories of those first hours of my mother's return. But at some remarkable point during the early evening, right before our eyes, she turned her own corner, one that no physician had foreseen or even held out the remotest possibility of existing. And the next morning she woke up, her abdomen completely flat, got out of bed, and made a pot of coffee for her incredulous family.

"There were four angels with me last night," she announced quietly, her soft voice restored.

My sisters and I smiled at the same time, each of us thinking that she was referring to her four daughters because, angels or not, we had taken turns listening, every moment of the night, our ears pressed against a baby monitor, to the sounds of her continued breathing.

"No," she said, reading our thoughts. "Four angels came in the night, and each held one corner of the sheet a few inches above my stomach."

She looked across the table solemnly at each of us in

succession. My father looked down at his hands, but the rest of us held her gaze, steady, utterly believing.

"And they are still waiting for me, but they said that I must have faith because there is still some time left. And I know what all the doctors have said, but you all must listen to me because the angels told me. And so, let's make some plans, now."

And then she proceeded to give us her wish list. To pick up the new boat and go on a family ride across the creek. To have my daughter flown out to see her one more time. To arrange a small dinner party to thank her closest friends. Small wishes. Yet, the day before, they had been beyond our most far-reaching prayers.

My sisters made a grocery list in preparation for the dinner, and I followed my mother back into the bedroom.

"Mom," I started to say, not even knowing what my question was.

She adjusted her brightly colored silk scarf around her bare scalp, and looked up at me defiantly.

"Darling, it was not a dream. It was not even a vision. It happened, and they were here, as surely as you are standing here right now. And," she added, pointing to Danny, our aged golden retriever in his favorite position on the end of her bed, "he had to shove one of the angels aside last night before he could find a place to lie down. I watched him nudge an angel gently with his nose so that he could sleep here."

We both stared at the dog, who rolled his chestnut eyes toward me, tilting his head up proudly, as if he knew full well the importance of being sole witness to my mother's story.

"So you see, you have time to fly back to California and bring my granddaughter here so that I can see her again."

I buried my face in the dog's neck, hiding my bewilderment, and listened blissfully to her plans for her short but still existent future. I had always believed that if God had to choose one animal to enter heaven, it would be a golden retriever. My mother's revelation only strengthened my convictions.

"The angels told me that God has chosen my time," she said, "but he is allowing me to choose the hour."

And so indeed he did. In the next few weeks she hosted her dinner party, although informally attired in her bed clothes, and she had Communion in her living room, the minister stepping good-naturedly over the sleeping dog on the floor so as not to spill the blessed wine. And she went out on the water for a short ride on a calm day in my father's new boat. And she saw my daughter once more and listened to her giggle abandonedly the way only a two-year-old, untouched by the closeness of death, can. And more small things, but enormous to us by the mere fact of their occurrence. Each one a gift, from God, through her, to us. The gift of answered prayers.

And then, six weeks later, my mother chose her hour. She was home, sleeping in her bed, holding my father's hand. I did not ask, but I am sure our God was somewhere nearby. And I am surer still, that even closer to her side were those special friends that only my mother and our dog had been granted the privilege to meet, returning once more to reclaim their precious charge.

Jacquelin A. Gorman

8

LETTING GO

That which the fountain sends forth returns again to the fountain.

Henry Wadsworth Longfellow

Home Run for Mom

When my five-year professional baseball career with the St. Louis Cardinals came to an end in 1990, I prayed for the chance to play closer to New York. My mother, Grace, had been diagnosed with breast cancer. She was living on Long Island, and I wanted to spend more time with her. My wish came true when I signed with the Philadelphia Phillies for the 1991 season. Philadelphia was just three short hours from her home.

As the 1991 baseball season progressed, Mom's condition took a turn for the worse. The cancer was spreading, and she couldn't hold on for much longer. My fiancée and I even got married four months earlier than planned so Mom could attend.

My performance was also taking a turn for the worse. After the All-Star break, my playing time was reduced, and the few games I played were anything but impressive. Over the next six weeks, I went hitless in 18 consecutive at bats. This was a long slump, and I felt everything from self-pity to loneliness.

My downturn came to an end in the September 1 game against the Atlanta Braves. Playing in Philadelphia on a gorgeous Sunday afternoon, I entered the game as a leadoff pinch-hitter in the bottom of the tenth. With the score tied 4–4, I batted against one of the hardest-throwing pitchers in the league, Mark Wohlers. I just wanted to do anything to get on base so that we could win the game.

I took the first two pitches as the count reached one ball and one strike. Then I fouled off the next two pitches on fastballs that were clocked in excess of 95 mph! After those two healthy cuts, I finally felt a competitive spirit rise up inside me again.

With the count two balls and two strikes, I stepped out of the box and mentally prepared myself for the hardest pitch my adversary could possibly throw, determined not to be late again. The fastball was delivered over the inside corner, and the ball jumped off my bat with a thunderous crack usually reserved for superstar home-run hitters.

Right-fielder David Justice went back to the wall and watched the ball sail over the fence for a game-winning home run. Mobbed by my teammates at home plate, I could feel my heart pumping so fast I thought it was going to come crashing through my jersey. What a feeling!

Two weeks later, I visited Mom, eager to show her a videotape of the home run. But when I walked into her room, I was shocked to see the physical condition of my dear mother. I knew that this would probably be the last visit I would ever have with her.

We were both watching the tape for the first time, so I didn't anticipate the commentator's story that would unfold. After I hit the home run, the announcer, Harry Kalas, explained that it had been six long weeks since my last hit. Mom and I held hands and listened to Kalas continue. "John Morris has really struggled the second half of this season, and this couldn't have happened to a nicer guy." I could feel the tears building up inside the two of us, as he showed a slow motion replay of my dramatic home run. As the pitcher wound up, Kalas uttered the sweetest words my mom had ever heard. "John's mom has been quite ill for some time," and as the ball connected with the bat, he finished, "and this one was probably for his mom."

Mom and I broke down. She hugged me as tightly as she could and whispered into my ear, "I love you son, and I'm very proud of you. I'm going to miss you very much."

The season was ending the last weekend of September when I received a call that Mom was not expected to make it through the weekend. That Sunday afternoon, the last out of the season was recorded, and on Monday morning she passed away with me at her bedside. It was as if she knew the season was complete, and that it was all right to let go.

John Morris

Remembering Will Have to Do

And when one of us is gone
and one of us is left to carry on,
then remembering will have to do,
our memories alone will get us through.
Think about the days of me and you.
You and me against the world.

The lyrics to this song kept turning over in my mind like a record that wouldn't stop. I got off the chair and walked to the window. It was near dawn and lights were being turned on. A new day was beginning. All around me life was going on. But in this room, life was coming to an end.

With the exception of the faint beeping sound of a nutrition pump, it was quiet. I walked over to the bed and straightened the blanket that covered the tiny, fragile body. I smoothed the silver-gray hair that was once so neatly combed. I could see life slipping away, but there was nothing I could do to hold it.

I heard someone enter the room. The shift was changing and the day nurses were arriving. Daylight broke and sunlight trickled through the window. We had made it through the night. But what would this day bring?

I stared at the person who'd had more influence on me than anyone else in my life. There was so much I wanted to say to her, things that I never said but took for granted that she knew. Somehow she always knew. But right now I needed to be sure.

I felt confused. When had I gone from being taken care of to the one who is now the caretaker? It had happened so smoothly that I was totally unaware. This was the woman who had raised three children alone because she was widowed at a very young age. This was the woman who'd taught me that I was capable of doing whatever I set my mind to. She had shared my laughter and had cried my tears. She was as solid as a rock. She had always been there for me. Now it was my turn to be there for her.

Tears formed in my eyes as I looked at the freshly dressed bandages on her arms. Her eyes opened and she smiled at me. Oh, her eyes. I've seen that look in my children's eyes a hundred times, the look that says, "I'm scared, please don't let anyone hurt me." A lump formed in my throat. I was on the verge of breaking down, but I knew I had to be strong.

She closed her eyes and slept. I walked over to the chair and sat down. I needed to regain my composure. I was so focused on myself that I failed to see her breathing had changed. It had become slower and more shallow. I ran to find a nurse, only to have her confirm what I already knew.

I stood at the bedside and held the hand that once held mine. Her breathing grew faint. I held on tightly. I was not ready to let her go.

Very slowly my mother opened her eyes. She looked up at me with a smile, whispered, "I love you," and with this took her last breath.

I stood there for some time, unable to move. I felt so alone. With tears rolling down my face, I needed her to hold me, to make things better the way she always had.

"She's just sleeping," I told myself, but I knew better. The beautiful face that had always tried to hide the pain was now very peaceful.

It was over. There was nothing more I could do. When I left the room and walked down the hall, life was going on as usual. Once again the same lyrics played in my mind.

> *. . . then remembering will have to do,*
> *our memories alone will get us through.*
> *Think about the days of me and you.*
> *You and me against the world.*

"I love you, Mom."

Somehow I'm sure she knew.

Victoria A. Lapikas

Celebrating My Mother

When I stopped seeing my mother with the eyes of a child, I saw the woman who helped me give birth to myself.

Nancy Friday

Almost five years ago at her 80th-birthday celebration, my mother, feeling fine and looking wonderful, closed her eyes and died in my living room.

Her death made no sense to me, and for a year I stumbled through the motions of living, probing the dimensions of the hole that her passing left in my world.

To me she had been larger than life, larger certainly than other people's moms. She would lean out of the car window to lecture knots of smoking teens on the evils of tobacco. If she caught us watching *American Bandstand,* she snorted and asked about the dancers on screen, "Why aren't those children out playing?!"

She was fiery and funny. She was brave and honest. But most of all, she was compassionate. For 30 years she and my Aunt Grace owned and ran a summer camp for girls and enjoyed nothing more than watching young people blossom in confidence and happiness. She married late and then suffered seeing the marriage dissolve quickly. But she raised her two girls with joy and without a backward glance. We felt safe with her; we felt loved. "Be careful what you pray for," she once said to us. "I prayed for children all my adult life." She paused, for meaning. "I never prayed for a man." And her eyes twinkled.

The month before Mom turned 80, my sister, Nan, and I had talked with our husbands about the great birthday event. "Instead of celebrating in October," one of us had suggested, "how about we do it in December, when the whole family can gather in New England? How does the 20th sound?"

About eight weeks ahead of time, I sent out the invitations. Inside was a photo of our mother as a baby, along with the caption, "How did this baby, who was so good and sweet and neat and quiet through *most* of her early years, turn out?" On the back was a recent photo of her smiling broadly. "For a more personal viewing," the invitation continued, "come to her 80th birthday celebration."

On her real birthday, October 26, my sister sent her a grandmother's ring with the birthstone of each of her four grandchildren; it thrilled her. I gave her a watch with a large dial, specially suited to her dimming sight, and a jacket with a mandarin collar, made in China, which she immediately put aside. "I'll wear this at my party in December," she vowed.

October and November passed; the 20th approached. Nan and her family flew up from their home in Florida. The party was to be at my house, and the morning of the big day, my family and I were all up early. We talked and laughed excitedly as we polished silver, set out glasses and mixed the punch. Snow had fallen during the night, for an added touch of magic.

Just before two, my sister called Mom to say that I was on my way over to pick her up. "I feel like a bride," she said to Nan on the phone. She looked like one too, a bride dressed in a Chinese jacket with a mandarin collar. Her face glowed.

At my house, as we walked together into the living room, everyone turned toward her and began applauding. "Oh, say," she cried, bowing her head in a mixture of modesty and strong emotion.

The time came to cut the cake and offer formal congratulations to this family matriarch. We gathered in the dining room. During the toast, I read two documents that she and I had recently unearthed from the depths of her desk. They were written by her father—grandfather to almost everyone in the room—who had been dead for 30 years.

One was a series of small envelopes enclosed in a leather pouch, labeled in his small, precise hand, "Caroline's Account with Time." Each envelope had once held five dollars, marking a significant stage in her life (the first "for learning to crawl and walk, and eat with a spoon," the second "for starting school," and on up).

The other was a letter he had written to her at college on the eve of her 20th birthday. "How glorious it must be to be 20," he wrote. "At that age, I was filled with hope and courage, both of which, thanks to God, have never left me. . . . I had good health and was not afraid to match myself with anyone. But I never dreamed then that in this or any other year I would have a fine daughter like you . . ."

As I read, tears streamed down our mother's face. I finished the toast, and we raised our glasses. Mom turned to her sister and said, "Oh, Grace. Did you feel that? It was as if he was *in the room with us.*"

Well, perhaps he was. Because 20 minutes later, she left us to join him. She was sitting in her favorite wing chair in my living room, chatting and holding a plate of pastries on her lap. Then she closed her eyes and was gone. It was that easy, that graceful.

In the year that followed, I grew fearful and jumpy; I imagined all of the people I loved dying before my very eyes. I forgot appointments, dented the car, grieved deep and long. On a rainy April day, in a burst of poor judgment, I took my three children to see her grave for the first time.

It had not been sodded. It had sunk some six or eight inches in the thawing spring. We sat in the rain on the base of the large headstone marking the family plot, and we wept. Then we drove to a mall to try to cheer ourselves up. There was a wishing well there, and we threw in some pennies. "I wished that Grandma would be happy where she is," said my third-grade daughter. "I *know* Grandma is happy, so I wished *we* could be," said her sixth-grade sister. "I just threw my penny into the dark," said their three-year-old brother, miserable.

But time has passed and healed us all. Slowly I recalled things she said to me in the months before she died. This came back among them: One night, just weeks before her party, we were chatting on the phone in an aimless, comfortable fashion, the way we always had done. Then her tone changed. "You are so kind, Terry, so compassionate, and you bring such light into people's lives. You girls both have that gift: a talent for liveliness . . ." I stopped her there.

"Mom! That's not me you're describing; it's you." But she would have none of that.

Maybe she was trying, that last fall, to hand down to us her set of attributes, to state for one last time the values that she'd lived by. Or was it more mystical than that—"Here, I give these gifts to you"? I don't know. I guess I never will. But although the hole that her passing left in my life is still there, I feel that I can look into it now without the terrible vertigo I felt at first. Slowly I have come to see the closing of her "Account with Time" not as the cruel parody of a birthday celebration, but as something else entirely—a celebration of her entire life, with the people she loved most all around her—a launching, almost.

Every day of my life since then, I have worn her large-faced watch. Always, I tell her stories. "You know, you sound a lot like your mother," people tell me more and more lately.

"Where do the dead go—our own closest dead?" we ask ourselves. We don't know, of course. But I sense that the woman who mothered me is someplace not far off. Inside, or all around. In a sudden familiar twinkle in the eyes of one of my children. Even in my very mirror.

Terry Marotta

A Motherless Child

It was when I had my first child that I understood how much my mother loved me.

from *For Mother—A Bouquet of Sentiments*

My mother's death was quick and brutal—she had a stomach virus Friday night and was lifeless by Monday morning. There was no time to say good-bye. There was no preparation for losing her. But then, how do you explain death to a two-year-old child? I asked my father how I reacted.

"You were so small, you were easily distracted," he said. His quick answer told me that he didn't discuss my mother's death with me then, and he talks about it now only when pressed.

Almost all the characters in my childhood books had no mothers: Cinderella, Dumbo, Bambi and Snow White. Little Annie was an orphan. Dorothy grew up with her Auntie Em. Motherlessness is a technique that storytellers often use to give their characters hero status and make them more lovable. And I did love my storybook characters as a child—not because I saw them as abandoned and vulnerable, but because we had something in common.

Women who have mothers expect me to be able to articulate the sorrow they're sure I felt. They want to hear about the coping skills I developed to compensate for growing up without a mother, someone to guide me through the rites of passage that girls shouldn't have to navigate alone. The truth is that I *didn't* navigate them alone; I was not a hero like the motherless children in my fairy tales. Thanks to my grandmother, aunts, sisters and dad, my supper was hardly ever late. My hair was braided. I was read to. I wore a training bra. And someone explained to me what those mysterious machines in the women's restrooms sell. I don't ever remember not feeling loved enough or hugged enough as a child. After all, a child is self-centered, too focused on her immediate needs to be distracted by intangibles.

By the time I was school-age, I had learned how to use the fact that I didn't have a mother in much the same way the storytellers did. It made me special, more important somehow. I realized that once the nuns learned my sad story, they judged me by a different standard than they did the other girls. And I could make a particularly stinging jab at my father when he was late picking me up by whining: "If Mommy were alive, I bet she'd have been on time." During those competitive adolescent years when my friends complained about their mothers, I bested them with, "Well, at least you *have* a mother."

With maturity came the acceptance of motherlessness as a fact of my life—it was neither unusual nor difficult. And so it was a surprise that, when my son was born, I began to miss my mother, and not because I could have used her help in caring for him. With Jacob came the understanding of what a mother gives her child, of what a mother *is.* As I got to know Jacob, I felt an intensity of emotion, a completeness of love that I'd never known one human could feel for another. I learned what I had missed and what I had longed for but could never put into words.

I watched him especially closely when he was five days past his second birthday—the exact age I was when my mother died. I was looking for clues to how her death had affected me. I tried to remember what it was like to be a toddler whose center of life had been stolen. But I couldn't recall the experience. These are what the experts call preverbal memories—the thoughts and feelings that cannot be described by an adult because they occurred before a vocabulary had been learned. I couldn't go back. So I focused instead on my relationship with Jacob—mother to child, not child to mother. I looked at how his tiny, chubby fingers fit into my palm and realized that my mother had held my little hand once too. I gave him our "secret handshake"—three little squeezes while whispering, "I love you." It was something I learned from my mother's mother; perhaps Nana had taught it to Mommy as well, and she had used it on me. I thought about how I comfort Jacob when he cries, how he giggles when I do raspberries on his tummy. All the things I do with Jacob she had certainly done with me.

For the first time, I thought of my mother as a woman who once loved and enjoyed her child with the passion that I feel for mine. And then I wept. It was deep and cleansing. I cried for the woman who was taken from her child. I cried for her little girl. I wanted to hug that child and tell her how sorry I was for her loss, that I would protect her and help her feel safe. I wanted her to know how freely, how deeply she had been loved by her mother. Doing that gave me the freedom to feel all the feelings I had spent my life denying I had. And the hole that I've tried to fill with work, lovers and risky hobbies started to close. It's a wound that will never totally heal. I know that.

Now when I read Jacob his bedtime stories and watch his movies, I still have a special empathy for the characters who must go it alone: E.T., who was separated from his mother ship; Fievel, who traveled West without his parents; the baby dinosaur who lost his mother so early in *The Land Before Time;* the Little Mermaid who had only a dad; and the Beauty who faced her Beast without a mother to advise her. But I also understand now how heartbreaking the idea of a motherless child is. What my life didn't teach me, my child did.

Jane Kirby

Robin

So I am glad not that my loved one has gone,
But that the earth she laughed and lived on
was my earth, too.
That I had known and loved her,
And that my love I'd shown.
Tears over her departure?
Nay, a smile
That I had walked with her a little while.

—Sent to the Bushes by a friend after Robin died

Our son Jeb was just a few weeks old when our daughter Robin woke up one morning and said, "I don't know what to do this morning. I may go out and lie on the grass and watch the cars go by, or I might just stay in bed." I didn't think that sounded like a normal three-year-old and decided she must have what my mother called "spring fever." I took her to our excellent pediatrician, Dr. Dorothy Wyvell. She examined Robin, took some blood, and told me she would call me after the test results were in. She suggested I might want to come back without Robin but with my husband, George Bush. That sounded rather ominous to me, but I wasn't too worried. Certainly Robin had no energy, but nothing seriously wrong.

Dr. Wyvell called, and George met me at her office in the late afternoon. Dorothy was not one to pull any punches. She told us Robin had leukemia. Neither of us had ever heard of it, and George asked her what the next step was: How did we cure her? She talked to us a little about red and white blood cells and told us as gently as possible that there was no cure. Her advice was to tell no one, go home, forget that Robin was sick, make her as comfortable as we could, love her—and let her gently slip away. She said this would happen very quickly, in several weeks. George asked her if she would talk to his uncle, Dr. John Walker, at Memorial Sloan-Kettering Hospital in New York City. She readily agreed. Uncle John also thought Robin had little chance to live, but he thought we should treat her and try to extend her life, just in case of a breakthrough.

The very next day George and I flew to New York and checked Robin into Memorial Sloan-Kettering. Thus began an extraordinary experience, and in a strange kind of way, we learned how lucky we were. We met people there who had only one child. We had three. We met people who did not love each other. We loved each other very much. We had the most supportive family and friends who helped us.

And last, but not least, we believed in God. That has made an enormous difference in our lives, then and now.

Robin was wonderful. She never asked why this was happening to her. She lived each day as it came, sweet and loving, unquestioning and unselfish.

I made up my mind that there would be no tears around Robin, so I asked people who cried to step out of her room. I didn't want to scare our little girl. Poor George had the most dreadful time and could hardly stand to see her get a blood transfusion. He would say that he had to go to the men's room. We used to laugh and wonder if Robin thought he had the weakest bladder in the world. Not true. He just had the most tender heart.

Eventually the medicine that was controlling the leukemia caused other terrible problems, and our baby slipped into a coma. Her death was very peaceful. One minute she was there, the next she was gone. I truly felt her soul go out of that beautiful little body. For one last time I combed her hair, and we held our precious little girl. I never felt the presence of God more strongly than at that moment.

After George's mother died in 1992, I was given an envelope with George's name on it. It contained the following letter, which George had written his mother several years after Robin died and which she had saved all these years.

Dear Mum,

I have jotted down some words about a subject dear to your heart and mine. Last night I was out, and on my way home—late—I said to myself, "You could well have gone to the cemetery in Greenwich tonight" . . . this thought struck me out of the blue, but I felt no real sense of negligence. The part I like is to think of Robin as though she were a part, a living part, of our vital and energetic and wonderful family of men and Barbara.

Bar and I wonder how long this will go on. We hope we will feel this genuine closeness when we are 83 and 82. Wouldn't it be exciting at that age to have a beautiful 3½ year old daughter . . . she doesn't grow up. Now she's Neil's age. Soon she'll be Marvin's—and beyond that she'll be all alone, but with us, a vital living pleasurable part of our day-to-day life. I sometimes wonder whether it is fair to our boys and to our friends to "fly-high" that portrait of Robin which I love so much, but here selfishness takes over because every time I sit at our table with just our candlelight, I somehow can't help but glance at this picture you gave us and enjoy a renewed physical sensation of closeness to a loved one.

This letter . . . is kind of like a confessional . . . between you and me, a mother and her little boy now not so little, but still just as close, only when we are older, we hesitate to talk from our hearts quite as much.

There is about our house a need. The running, pulsating restlessness of the four boys as they struggle to learn and grow, their athletic chests and arms and legs; their happy noises as the world embraces them . . . all this wonder needs a counterpart. We need some starched crisp frocks to go with all our torn-kneed blue jeans and helmets. We need some soft blond hair to offset those crew cuts. We need a doll house to stand firm against our forts and rockets and thousand baseball cards. We need a cut-out star to play alone while the others battle to see who's "family champ." We even need someone . . . who could sing the descant to "Alouette," while outside they scramble to catch the elusive ball aimed ever roofward, but usually thudding against the screens.

We need a legitimate Christmas angel—one who doesn't have cuffs beneath the dress.

We need someone who's afraid of frogs.

We need someone to cry when I get mad—not argue.

We need a little one who can kiss without leaving egg or jam or gum.

We need a girl.

We had one once—she'd fight and cry and play and make her way just like the rest. But there was about her a certain softness.

She was patient—her hugs were just a little less wiggly.

Like them, she'd climb in to sleep with me, but somehow she'd fit.

She didn't boot and flip and wake me up with pug nose

and mischievous eyes a challenging quarter-inch from my sleeping face.

No—she'd stand beside our bed until I felt her there. Silently and comfortably, she'd put those precious, fragrant locks against my chest and fall asleep.

Her peace made me feel strong, and so very important.

"My Daddy" had a caress, a certain ownership, which touched a slightly different spot than the "Hi, Dad" I love so much.

But she is still with us. We need her and yet we have her. We can't touch her, and yet we can feel her.

We hope she'll stay in our house for a long, long time.

Love, Pop

George and I love and value every person more because of Robin. She lives on in our hearts, memories and actions. I don't cry over her anymore. She is a happy, bright part of our lives.

George Bush and I have been the two luckiest people in the world, and when all the dust is settled and all the crowds are gone, the things that matter are faith, family and friends. We have been inordinately blessed, and we know that.

Barbara Bush

Letting Go

I bend, but I do not break.

Jean de La Fontaine

It was January of 1991. Life looked good. The children were doing well.

January 30 was my son Shane's 12th birthday. We had a tradition: on birthday night, the birthday person got to decide on dinner—home-cooked or at a favorite restaurant. Shane picked Red Lobster. He ordered crab legs. The waiters sang "Happy Birthday." It embarrassed him, but he liked it. I could tell. My daughter, Nichole, apologized to Shane because she didn't have a gift. "Want to come skiing with Joey and me this Saturday?" she asked.

Shane's eyes lit up. Offers like that from his 14-year-old sister didn't come very often.

At home that evening Shane sidled up to me while I sat at my dressing table, brushing my hair. He opened my jewelry drawer and took out a small gold cross, one his father had given me at the time of our divorce. "Can I have this?" he asked.

"Sure, honey," I said. "You can have that."

That Friday, before the birthday ski trip, Shane stopped me in the kitchen, pulled down the neck of his sweater and pointed to the cross hanging around his neck. "God is with me now," he said quietly.

I had a hard time falling asleep that night. It wasn't, as the song says, that I thought we'd get to see forever. But I thought we'd have more time than we did. I didn't know the end would come so soon—that I would face a mother's worst nightmare, involving not just one but both of my children.

"Be home by six o'clock!" I yelled as the kids left that Saturday morning for Afton Alps, a ski area south of our home in Stillwater, Minnesota. Nichole promised they would be back on time.

It was a strange day. I felt as if I was waiting for something, but I didn't know what. At 8 P.M. I wondered why the children weren't home yet. I was puttering around the house after 9 P.M. when the telephone rang.

"Mrs. Beattie?" a man asked. "I'm with the Afton Alps Ski Patrol. Your son has been injured. He's unconscious, but I'm sure he'll be fine. Stay where you are. We'll call you back."

The phone rang again in 15 minutes. "Your son's still not conscious," the man said. "We're taking him to the hospital."

Be calm, I thought. *Drive to the hospital and see your son. Be by his side. Everything will be fine.*

A nurse met me in the emergency room. She looked at me differently from anyone who had ever looked at me before. She took my arm and led me to a small room. "Do you have someone you can call?" she said.

Those words broke my heart. I knew what they meant.

Soon I learned what had happened. After skiing the beginner hills all day, Shane decided to finish up by trying an expert slope called Trudy's Schuss. He talked one of Nichole's friends into going with him.

When the two reached the top, Shane shouted, "Let's face it!" He dug his poles into the snow and pushed off. While going over a mogul, he fell, then stood up. Struggling to regain his balance, he was hit from behind by another skier and fell again. This time he didn't move.

In minutes the first-aid sled arrived. When artificial respiration didn't work, someone called an ambulance.

"Help him! That's my brother!" Nichole shouted at the paramedics. As one medic hooked up an I.V., another started to cut off the chain with the cross that hung around Shane's neck. "Leave that on him," Nichole said. They closed the ambulance doors and sped toward the emergency room.

At the hospital I talked to a doctor. He said something about brain injury. Swelling. More tests. All weekend I prayed for a miracle. Sometimes I couldn't bear to be in Shane's room. I felt as if I were going to explode or go insane. The ventilator whooshed as it pushed air into his lungs. I held his hand, gently squeezing his fingers. He didn't squeeze back.

I remember when we were sledding together a few weeks before Shane slammed into a tree and rolled off the sled. He lay there on his back in the snow. "Shane, are you all right?" I yelled, running to him.

He sat up quickly, smiled and said, "Psych?"

"Don't tease me like that," I said. "If anything happened to you, I don't think I could go on. Do you understand that?"

He looked at me, got serious and said yes, he knew that.

Now I kept wishing he'd sit up, smile and say, "Psych." But he didn't.

On the third day the doctors told me we should turn off the life-support equipment. Shane's kidneys had shut down. His body wasn't working. He was brain-dead. Medically there were no more options.

I started screaming, "Damn it! This is my baby you're talking about!" I kicked a door across from me as hard as I could.

After Shane's friends, Nichole's friends, and family members said their good-byes, I entered his room. I cut off a lock of his hair and touched his foot. I always loved his little feet. And I held him while they shut off the ventilator.

"I love you." I said. "I always have. I always will."

When they turned off the machine, a whiff of air escaped from his lungs, and he didn't move again. I knew then he hadn't been breathing, hadn't been alive for days. The machines had made it look that way, but it wasn't so.

Walking out of that room and out of the hospital was the hardest thing I have ever done in my life.

We had balloons at Shane's funeral. When the children were little, they loved balloons. If they lost one into the air, I comforted them by saying, "That's okay. God catches all your balloons, and when you get to heaven, you get a big bouquet of every balloon you've ever lost. So don't cry. They'll all be there waiting for you."

The sky was clear that February day as hundreds of balloons sailed up and up until eventually they passed beyond where we could see.

In the months that followed, I missed Shane terribly. Missed his presence, his voice, the touch of him. Some nights I lay awake until the morning, trying to penetrate the veil that divides this world from the next. But Shane felt far away. Gone forever. All meaning had been drained from my life.

Nichole was also having a bad time. Occasionally we'd cry together, but as time wore on, I realized I was losing Nichole, too. We began arguing. She refused to do homework and skipped school. I didn't like the new crowd of friends she started running with. They were surly, sometimes downright rude. I tried forbidding her to see them, but it didn't work.

We were each adrift in our own cold, dark sea, unable to help each other, unable to do much but swim for our lives. Sometimes we'd bob to the surface, reach out, touch each other's hands and say, "I love you."

On one such occasion, six months after Shane's death, Nichole said to me, "Mom, some people think things like this get better with time. But in some ways it gets worse. I miss Shane more every day he's gone."

Most of the time, however, we each struggled alone.

One night Nichole came home late. When I tried talking to her, she started giggling, then blew me a kiss. She reeked of alcohol.

The next day we had a talk. I set some ground rules, trying to be clear and reasonable. I insisted she see a counselor, but she didn't want to go.

I asked her how often she'd been drinking. She named only two other occasions in the past year: the day after the funeral and once last summer. She assured me she was doing all right.

Then one afternoon the following winter, I was in the kitchen when the door flew open. "I need to talk to you," Nichole said. "I don't know how to say this, but I can't control myself when I drink. Sometimes I go blank, and the next day I can't remember anything. I'm scared. I need help."

"Okay," I said, not knowing what else to offer.

"I'm starting to hate myself," she went on. "I've been looking you right in the face and lying to you about where I'm going and what I'm doing. I've also used cocaine and marijuana."

The next day I admitted her to an inpatient chemical-dependency treatment center for young people. Hugging her good-bye, I held her close. "It'll be all right, baby," I said. "It's a new beginning, the start of the rest of your life."

"I've hurt you," she said. "I feel so bad. I want you to be proud of me someday, Mom."

Christmas, the second since Shane's death, was a quiet day. I brought Nichole's presents to her at the treatment center. "Mom, I'm happy I'm here," she said. "I feel like a new person."

The following week was family conference, something I dreaded. This was the day the dirty laundry got hung out to air in a private session between parent, child and counselor.

I walked into the small office and sat across from Nichole. The counselor, a woman with short hair, sat to the side. "Tell her," she said to Nichole.

Nichole's chin started trembling, and her hands shook. Her voice was soft in the beginning. "I'm sorry, Mom," she said. "I feel so guilty, so bad. I tried to drink it away. I tried to drug it away."

Then she stood up and was yelling. "This whole nightmare is all my fault! You told me to be home by six that night. That's the last thing you said before we walked out that door. And if I had listened, if I had come home when you said, Shane wouldn't be dead now. I'm so, so sorry, Mom."

The next thing I knew, I was holding her. Her body shook so hard I could barely keep my arms around her.

I told her it was an accident; it was nobody's fault. Then before I left, I wrote her a note:

> *Dear Nichole*
>
> *I love you very much. I always have. And if you had called me that night to ask if you could ski later than 6 P.M., I would have said yes. You didn't cause this, baby. And don't ever again think you did.*
>
> *Love, Mom.*

When I got home, the telephone rang. "Thank you, Mom," Nichole said. "Thank you so much. That note means a lot, more than anything."

Right then and there I learned how important it is to get rid of useless guilt. Hers and mine.

There are seasons of the heart. There are seasons in our lives, just as there are seasons to all of nature. These seasons cannot be forced any more than one can force the coming of spring by pulling at tender blades of grass to make them grow. It took me awhile to understand.

I felt a lightness that I hadn't felt in years. Maybe ever. I wondered how long, how long really, I had struggled to get this lesson right.

I didn't have to scramble up and down the mountain from despair to euphoria anymore, trying to convince myself that life was either painful and terrible or joyous and wonderful. The simple truth was that life was both. I hadn't come here to live happily ever after, although I now sensed I could.

Nichole came home in January. We vowed to have the best year a mother and daughter ever had. To celebrate her homecoming, we had a party with her friends. It was a grand day.

The time had come, I realized, to release my balloon, the one I had been carrying since the day of Shane's funeral. To let my heart rise up in joy and hope, the way I thought it never would again.

So I let go. "Thank you for my life," I whispered into the air.

I was surprised to find I meant it.

Melody Beattie

John

I saw him first in April
When they said, "You have a boy,"
I waited long to hear these words
So he became my joy.

And every time his birthday came
I saw him growing tall,
And then he started off to school
In just no time at all.

It seemed I only turned around
And he was in his teens,
He went around in funny hats
And had his favorite jeans.

Then track and football filled his life,
His high school days were fun,
And in his private treasure box
Went medals that he'd won.

And often when he came back home
From being on a date,

He'd whisper at my bedroom door,
"Mom, are you still awake?"

Then we would talk a little while
Before he went to bed,
And I would often breathe a prayer,
"God bless my son," I said.

I saw him last in April
When he said, "Mom, don't you worry,
I'm leaving for Vietnam—
We'll win this in a hurry."

But he will nevermore be back,
My heart still seems to break,
I'll never hear him whisper now,
"Mom, are you still awake?"

Yet I thank God for every joy
For all the love and fun,
And locked in my heart's treasure box
Are memories of my son.

Muriel Cochrane

To Captain Candy and the Women Who Took to the Skies

It was one of the most poignant moments of my life. I was holding my baby in a tiny printing shop called The Sandpiper, on Balboa Island, when I overheard the two women owners murmuring to each other. They were helping a customer make photocopies of an article and were exclaiming over and over, "Look at her picture. She's so beautiful!" I had to wander over to see what they were looking at.

The customer's name was Marilyn, and the article she'd brought in was about one of the first female American pilots to fly missions during World War II. She was as glamorous as a movie star.

"I'm shocked," I told Marilyn. "My father has always worked for the airlines, and even he never told me that women flew in the war. Is she still alive?"

"No. She was killed when her B-25 crashed in 1944. She was only 19." Tears welled up in Marilyn's eyes as she told us this.

I could understand her emotion. While my family has never lost anyone personally in a plane crash, it was my father's job to talk with the families of commercial crash victims. All my life, we stayed glued to the television whenever there was a crash, praying that we didn't know anyone on the flight.

Marilyn went on about the article. "This is the poem they read at the woman's funeral in 1944. It's called 'Celestial Flight,' and it became a bond for all female fliers. They always read this poem at memorials to women pilots."

We were moved—and totally unprepared for what followed.

"They read this poem at my daughter's funeral."

We stared and waited in silence until Marilyn could continue. Her daughter was Captain Candalyn Kubeck—she called her Captain Candy—the pilot who flew the ValuJet that crashed in the Florida Everglades. She had begun flying when she was only 16, and no matter how many times Marilyn had asked her daughter to quit, Candy refused. She loved to fly, to soar in the skies, to feel the freedom of flight. At one point, Marilyn stopped objecting and started supporting her young daughter's passion.

As I stared at her through my tears, my mind flooded with memories of the ValuJet episode, and I imagined what this poor mother had gone through. The news that the pilots and all passengers were dead. The dozens of hearings, the weeks of broadcasts about the crash. At one point her daughter was blamed, but a later investigation declared Captain Candy and the entire crew innocent of wrongdoing. Then my mind jumped back to Marilyn, left behind without her child—a mother who'd had the courage and bravery to let her daughter go into the skies to follow her dream. What could I say to her?

Holding my baby, I could only think to offer the same words that appeared in the news clipping that Marilyn held shakily in her hand:

Celestial Flight

She is not dead—but only flying higher,
Higher than she's flown before,
And earthly limitations
Will hinder her no more.

There is no service ceiling,
Or any fuel range.
And there is no anoxia
Or need for engine change.

Thank God that now her flight can be
To heights her eyes had scanned,
Where she can race with comets,
And buzz the rainbow's span.

For she is universal,
Like courage, love and hope,
And all free, sweet emotions
Of vast and godly scope.

And understand a pilot's fate
Is not the thing she fears,
But rather sadness left behind,
Your heartbreak and your tears.

So all you loved ones, dry your eyes,
Yes, it is wrong that you should grieve,
For she would love your courage more,
And she would want you to believe,

She is not dead.
You should have known
That she is only flying higher,
Higher than she's ever flown.

Good-bye to Captain Candy and to all those other women who took to the skies and are gone. And thanks to all you mothers who let them fly. They didn't reach stardom, but they reached the stars.

Diana L. Chapman

9

A GRANDMOTHER'S LOVE

If your baby is "beautiful and perfect, never cries or fusses, sleeps on schedule and burps on demand, an angel all the time" . . . you're the grandma.

Teresa Bloomingdale

"Know what souvenir I wanna take home with me, Grandma? You!"

What's a Grandmother?

A grandmother is a lady who has no children of her own. She likes other people's little girls and boys. A grandfather is a man grandmother. He goes for walks with the boys, and they talk about fishing and stuff like that.

Grandmothers don't have to do anything except to be there. They're so old that they shouldn't play hard or run. It is enough if they drive us to the market where the pretend horse is, and have lots of dimes ready. Or if they take us for walks, they should slow down past things like pretty leaves and caterpillars. They should never say "hurry up."

Usually, grandmothers are fat, but not too fat to tie your shoes. They wear glasses and funny underwear. They can take their teeth and gums off.

Grandmothers don't have to be smart, only answer questions like, "Why isn't God married?" and "How come dogs chase cats?"

Grandmothers don't talk baby talk like visitors do, because it is hard to understand. When they read to us they don't skip or mind if it is the same story over again.

Everybody should try to have a grandmother, especially if they don't have a television, because they are the only grown-ups who have time.

Source Unknown

I Was Born for This Job

If I'd known grandchildren were going to be so much fun, I'd have had them first.

Anonymous

As a novice grandma, I eagerly looked forward to the first time I'd hear, "Mom, can you keep the baby a couple of days?" My response? "I'm ready! How soon can you get here?"

The calendar was cleared of bridge clubs and tennis matches. The crib was set up in the guest room, and friends were put on alert that I would be holding open house for the debut of our little princess. This cherub, a living, breathing angel, was to be all mine for two-and-a-half days. Talk about your dividends!

And talk about your responsibility! Instinct told me that taking care of my child's child was going to be a whole different diaper pail. (Diaper pail—what we Neanderthals put dirty cloth diapers in before laundering them. Yes, we laundered them.) I invested in a fresh copy of Dr. Spock. I was actually worried that if I didn't do a good job at this baby-sitting routine, they wouldn't let me do it again.

The new parents arrived with a two-week supply of clothes, enough disposable diapers to soak up the Mississippi River, an entire zoo of stuffed animals, stroller, car seat, an itinerary of their hourly whereabouts for the next two days, the phone number of their pediatrician (60 miles away), their personal copy of Dr. Spock (with notes in the margins), and six pages of instructions. They left the collie at home.

The instructions included a 6:30 A.M. to 7:30 P.M. feeding/sleeping schedule. The baby must have read it because she followed it to the letter, even though there was a notation that "these times are estimates." That darling baby had been in this world barely four months, and she had four people ready to do her bidding, willing to keep a record of said bidding and call it a schedule. Our son's parting remarks were classic father-of-first-child edicts.

"Now, Mom, let her cry sometimes." (What kind of sadist did I raise here?!)

"You don't have to pick her up every time she opens her eyes." (I've waited four months to pick this child up whenever I want!)

"It's a matter of discipline, you know, and it must start early." (This from a boy who at 15 needed 45 logical reasons he couldn't hitchhike 300 miles to a high school basketball tournament.)

I was up at 5:30 that first day. She made me sit and watch her breathe until 6:45. Grandpa went to work and didn't get to stay home and watch her breathe. For some reason he didn't think that a major sacrifice.

My beautiful granddaughter and I had a wonderful day. I dressed her in her finest and we danced around the living room and strolled up and down the block. She responded beautifully for all the potential grandmothers who dropped by, then slept most of the afternoon, no doubt worn out from being adorable. She continued to follow the schedule. What a good baby!

What a joyful experience—pleasuring in that first grandchild. As I held her I looked into her father's baby eyes again. They crinkled and sparkled with each toothless giggle. I nuzzled the soft cheeks and inhaled the sweet baby-fresh scent, long forgotten and greatly missed. This grandchild had added a dimension to life impossible to measure or explain. And all her father's sins, from colic to wrecking the family car, were forgiven.

The second night, Baby decided to see how quickly Grandma could get to her crib when she called. Grandma hit the floor running each time. Baby called at 1:00, hungry. I fed her. She called at 2:30, wanting to smile and play. At 4:00 she was chewing her fist. I fed her. At 5:00 what I had fed her at 4:00 reappeared all over her and the crib. We both slept through her 6:30 feeding. I don't think she missed it.

She remained happy and content for the rest of our time together, glorying in her star status, until five minutes before her parents walked in the front door. At that moment she woke up screaming, for no reason I could comprehend other than she had forgotten the schedule. They found me, her parents did, hair stringing, shirttail out, walking the floor and crooning. Her mother grabbed my precious from me. Immediately the crying stopped. I never convinced them that Baby hadn't done that for two days.

But I had passed my maiden grandbaby-sitting test, and they did let me do it again. And again. And again. And so did our other children, so by the time I was rocking my seventh baby grand, my beginner's luck had seasoned to old pro status.

It's been 20 years since I heard the first, "Mom, can you . . .?" and my response is still, "I'm ready. How soon can you get here?"

Billie B. Chesney

"That's not a REAL sitter. It's our grandma. She LIKES to take care of us."

Grandma's Garden

Each year, my Grandmother Ines planted tulips in her flower garden and looked forward to their springtime beauty with childlike anticipation. Under her loving guardianship, they sprang up each April, faithfully, and she was never disappointed. But she said the real flowers that decorated her life were her grandchildren.

I, for one, was not going to play along.

I was sent to stay with my grandmother when I was 16 years old. My parents lived overseas and I was a very troubled young woman, full of false wisdom and anger at them for their inability to cope with or understand me. An unhappy, disrespectful teenager, I was ready to drop out of school.

Grandma was a tiny woman, towered over by her own children and their not-yet-grown offspring, and she possessed a classic, old-fashioned prettiness. Her hair was dark and elegantly styled, and her eyes were of the clearest blue, vibrant, and glittering with energy and intensity. She was ruled by an extraordinary loyalty to family, and she loved as profoundly and sincerely as a child. Still, I thought my grandmother would be easier to ignore than my parents.

I moved into her humble farmhouse silently, skulking about with my head hung low and eyes downcast like an abused pet. I had given up on others, instead cocooning myself within a hard shell of apathy. I refused to allow another soul admittance to my private world because my greatest fear was that someone would discover my secret vulnerabilities. I was convinced life was a bitter struggle better fought on one's own.

I expected nothing from my grandmother but to be left alone, and planned to accept nothing less. She, however, did not give up so easily.

School began and I attended classes occasionally, spending the rest of my days in my pajamas, staring dully at the television set in my bedroom. Not taking the hint, Grandma burst through my door each morning like an unwelcome ray of sunshine.

"Good morning!" she'd sing, cheerfully raising the blinds from my window. I pulled my blanket over my head and ignored her.

When I did stray from my bedroom, I was barraged with a string of well-meant questions from her regarding my health, my thoughts and my views on the world in general. I answered in mumbled monosyllables, but somehow she was not discouraged. In fact, she acted as if my meaningless grunts fascinated her; she listened with as much solemnity and interest as if we were engaged in an intense conversation in which I had just revealed an intimate secret. On those rare occasions when I happened to offer more than a one-word response, she would clap her hands together joyously and smile hugely, as if I had presented her with a great gift.

At first, I wondered if she just didn't get it. However, though she wasn't an educated woman, I sensed she had the simple common-sense smarts that come from natural intelligence. Married at age 13 during the Great Depression, she learned what she needed to know about life by raising five children through difficult economic times, cooking in other people's restaurants and eventually running a restaurant of her own.

So I shouldn't have been surprised when she insisted I learn to make bread. I was such a failure at kneading that Grandma would take over at that stage of the process. However, she wouldn't allow me to leave the kitchen until the bread was set out to rise. It was during those times, when her attention was focused away from me and I stared at the flower garden outside the window of the kitchen, that I first began to talk to her. She listened with such eagerness that I was sometimes embarrassed.

Slowly, as I realized my grandmother's interest in me did not wear off with the novelty of my presence, I opened up to her more and more. I began to secretly yet fervently look forward to our talks.

When the words finally came to me, they would not stop. I began attending school regularly, and rushed home each afternoon to find her sitting in her usual chair, smiling and waiting to hear a detailed account of the minutes of my day.

One day of my junior year, I hurried through the door to Grandma's side and announced, "I was named editor of the high school newspaper!"

She gasped and clapped her hands over her mouth. More moved than I could ever be, she seized both of my hands in hers and squeezed them, fiercely. I looked into her eyes, which were sparkling like mad. She said, "I like you so much, and I am very proud of you!"

Her words hit me with such force that I couldn't respond. Those words did more for me than a thousand "I love you's." I knew her love was unconditional, but her friendship and pride were things to earn. To receive them both from this incredible woman made me begin to wonder whether there was, in fact, something likable and worthy within myself. She awakened in me a desire to discover my own potential, and a reason to allow others to know my vulnerabilities.

On that day, I decided to try to live as she did—with energy and intensity. I was suddenly flushed with an appetite to explore the world, my mind and the hearts of others, to love as freely and unconditionally as she had. And I realized that I loved her—not because she was my grandmother, but because she was a beautiful individual who had taught me what she knew about caring for herself and for others.

My grandmother passed away in the springtime, nearly two years after I came to live with her, and two months before I graduated from high school.

She died encircled by her children and grandchildren, who held hands and remembered a life filled with love and happiness. Before she left this world, each of us leaned over her bed, with moist eyes and faces, and kissed her tenderly. As my turn came, I kissed her gently on the cheek, took her hand and whispered, "I like you so much, Grandma, and I am very proud of you!"

Now, as I prepare to graduate from college, I often think of my grandmother's words, and hope she would still feel proud of me. I marvel at the kindness and patience with which she helped me emerge from a difficult childhood to a young womanhood filled with peace. I picture her in the springtime, as the tulips in her garden, and we, her offspring, still bloom with an enthusiasm equaled only by her own. And I continue to work to make sure she will never be disappointed.

Lynnette Curtis

Dinner Out

We went to a little cafe
  just off the campus
  to have a quiet dinner together,
the college students there
  eating, discussing deep philosophical issues.

You sat at our table
  looking suave and debonair in jeans and turtleneck,
  your tousled hair shining,
  your eyes sparkling, full of mischief.
And you worked your charms
  on me and everyone around.

The waitress doted on you,
  your cup always filled
"An extra napkin? Certainly!"
"More crackers for your soup? Of course!"
You flirted notoriously with her
  and with the hostess as well,
  flashing seductive grins at them,
  inviting them to talk,
  eating only the fringes of your meal.

Twice you left our table
   to walk around
   and spread your charms elsewhere,
   stopping at a table or two,
   grinning broadly, flirtatiously,
   soliciting conversation.
I watched you captivate their hearts
   and knew you had taken mine,
   as I sat quietly observing.

Finally, folding my dinner napkin patiently
   and placing it beside my finished plate,
I knew it was time to go,
and walking up to you I said,
   "Let's say good-bye."

And picking you up, I placed you
   in your stroller,
   and as we left,
you waved profusely at everyone,
after your first dinner out with Grandma,
   when you were only two.

Maryann Lee Jacob

"Remember! Hugs and kisses come before 'What did you bring us, Grandma?'"

We Need a Rock

The day before my son's birth was definitely one I'll remember. My mother was in the hospital recovering from a stroke that paralyzed her left side and affected her speech. My sister and I had gone every day to encourage her and try to get her to talk. The doctor said she would speak when she had something to say.

That day, Mom tried to tell me something. Her eyes would look at me and then shoot back to the door. She tried forming the words that her mind was screaming, but her mouth would not cooperate. I hugged her and we cried together. I knew she was worried about me and wanted me to go home, but I knew I had a month to go before the baby was due, and I wanted to stay. We really didn't need words to communicate, but one word from Mom would have given us so much hope. "I'll be back tomorrow," I finally said, as I waved and waddled out the door. I could see her shaking her head as if to say, "You stay at home and rest."

Mom was right. I should have rested. Seven hours later, I was rushed to the emergency room of the same hospital. The doctors said it was placenta previa. All I knew was that the baby and I were in trouble.

With the help of God and some good doctors, I lay upstairs from my mother, with a beautiful little boy in my arms. As I gazed at him, I kept trying to think of a name. A name is important. A name must have a history that my child can be proud of. A name must be rooted in something. But I was too emotionally drained and exhausted by the emergency cesarean to come up with the right one.

Our first son was given his father's name, Daniel. Our second son was given his father's middle name, Michael. Unfortunately, Dan had no more names. Our daughter was named after the most beautiful county in Ireland, Kerry. All the other family names were taken two and three times over by many of my nephews. My uncle told us that Finbar was the patron saint of our family, but I knew that a "Finbar Ryan" would have to learn to defend himself before he learned to walk.

Time was running out and the nurses were pressuring me. Suddenly, I had an idea. I called the nurse and asked her to take a note down to my mother on the third floor: *Mom, it's a boy. Will you name him? Love, Kathy.*

I waited most of the day for some response. Every time I held the baby, I rocked him and whispered, "Soon you will have a name." I'd think about Mom and wish I could see her, and my eyes would fill up with tears. All of a sudden, the nurse was standing in the doorway. She had a mischievous look on her face.

She took the baby and whispered, "Shhh." Startled, I asked, "What's happening?" She motioned for me to get in the wheelchair and be quiet. Another nurse took my baby into the nursery. She wheeled me down a darkened hallway. There in front of the nursery were Dan and my mother, smiling the best crooked smile I ever saw.

"Mom," I called, as the tears welled up in my eyes. This was her first time off the third floor. Then there was a long silence as she raised her left hand and pointed to the nursery where the nurses had brought my baby to the window. In very slow and labored speech, she said, "Name . . . him . . . Peter. We . . . need . . . a rock."

Kathy Ryan

10

THANK YOU, MOM

All that I am or hope to be, I owe to my mother.

Abraham Lincoln

Mama and Miss Jordan

There are only two lasting bequests we can hope to give our children. One of these is roots; the other is wings.

Hodding Carter

Mama called to me, grasping my chin in her hand with a firmness that meant she wanted me to pay attention. I started awake, realizing it must be nearly midnight. Her expression was severe. "Mary," she said, "where's your homework?"

Then I remembered. I had not finished my assignments. I had not left my completed papers on the kitchen table where she could see them when she returned home from the last of three jobs that she held. "Oh, Mama, I fell asleep," I told her weakly.

"Well, you better get up now and finish your work. Your studies come first!" she said, releasing my chin at last.

I dragged myself out of bed, found my books and papers, and set out to finish my assignments. As I did so, I could not help feeling a burning injustice had been done. Why me? Why did she always seem to single me out, especially for such harsh treatment?

But with Mama, you didn't argue. You just obeyed. I finished my work and gave it to her to check. By this time she was dozing in the rocker, exhausted by a workday that had begun before sunup.

My mother, Josephine Hatwood, had wanted to be a nurse. But her parents died when she was a child, and she had to leave school in the sixth grade. Mama has worked ever since.

My first memories were of the little house we had in Altavista, Virginia. It was an attractive bungalow with a small garden. My father worked in construction. Those were happy years.

Later, Daddy became ill. We used to ride the train down to Lynchburg with Mama to visit Daddy in the hospital. But he got worse and worse, and we could see Mama fighting off tears on the ride back home.

Then Daddy died, and there was no insurance to pay the mountain of medical bills. We lost the house and moved to Lynchburg, where Mama worked as a domestic for three families, in addition to cleaning churches, to feed and clothe my sister Ann and me.

I remember when Ann and I walked barefoot to school one fine September day because our shoes had worn out and there wasn't enough money for Mama to buy us new ones. The principal looked at us and raised his eyebrows, but didn't say anything. The next day we thought he would speak, but he didn't. The third day he met us at the door.

"Why don't you have shoes on?"

We explained that Mama couldn't afford to buy us shoes. "Well," he said, "you'll have to go home. We can't have you attending school barefoot. You'll have to tell your mother."

Ann took my hand, and we turned to go back home. Being the more mischievous one, I suggested we spend the day in a nearby corn field instead. Just about the time school was over, we went home. There was Mama, waiting for us. That was most unusual, but the gossip line is faster than Western Union in a town like Lynchburg.

Mama was frowning—and standing straight as a tent pole. She asked us where we had been. I made up a story rather than upset her. Then she started crying. "You were not in school today," she said. It was clear she knew everything. She told us how important it was to get an education. She also told us never to be ashamed of being poor. "It's not what you wear, it's who you are," she said. "That's what matters." A few days later, when she got paid, she took money she would have used to pay bills to buy us new shoes.

Mama had so few private moments with us that we cherished each one, especially those times when we read aloud. I'd climb into her bed and wait until it was my time to read. Then I got to be right next to Mama until it was another sister's turn.

But for all the warmth I felt, Mama's toughness with me always left me feeling as if I pleased her less than her other children and that I could never entirely gain her good wishes. My sister Marianne, whom Mama took in as a foster child when her mother died, seemed to have advantages I never enjoyed. I remember how envious I was when Mama got Marianne an extra coat, while I had to make do with my old worn one. I couldn't understand it. But Mama had sensed that Marianne's needs were greater than mine because of her early loss.

Mama had given me one gift, however. I had the habit of happiness, so even if my small world was not entirely sunny, neither was it sad. I also loved to talk, a trait not always appreciated by Miss Jordan, my tenth-grade English teacher.

She was a teacher no one wanted because she was so strict. She stood about five-foot-five, was very thin, and wore her hair pulled back in a way that gave her a horsy look. And she wore those half-circular reading glasses. Whenever she got upset, she lowered her head and peered at you over the tops of her glasses. You could feel the temperature drop when she set her features like that.

One day in her class, I was so busy talking I didn't realize she had stopped teaching and was scowling straight at me. "Young lady, I would like to see you after school."

Later Miss Jordan explained she expected me to listen. "For punishment I want you to write a thousand-word essay on education and its impact on the economy," she said.

I met my deadline. I was confident. It was a good paper. Next day in class, however, she called me forward and returned my paper. "Go back and rewrite it," she said. "Remember, each paragraph is supposed to begin with a topic sentence." When she returned my paper a second time, she corrected the grammar. The third time, the spelling. The fourth time, it was punctuation. The fifth time, it wasn't neat enough. I was sick!

The sixth time, I rewrote the whole paper slowly, in ink, leaving generous margins. When she saw it, she removed her glasses and smiled. She finally accepted the paper.

It must have been two or three months later when, again, I was talking in class. The kids were saying, "Mary, stop! Miss Jordan is staring!" I glanced up, and she had that same look on her face. "Did you hear what I said, Mary?"

"I'm sorry, I didn't."

Miss Jordan continued: "I was talking about an essay contest that was held citywide. They've announced the winners." She paused. "Class, I am happy to inform you that Mary has won third prize in the essay contest—on the impact of education on the economy."

I was amazed and thrilled. It was the first time I had ever won a prize. Later, Miss Jordan said that what was important was the lesson I had learned. When I wrote and rewrote that paper for her, I began to learn how to discipline myself. I was touched. Except for Mama, she was the person I most wanted to please in this world.

At the end of tenth grade, the whole class took a comprehensive achievement test, and I came in number five. Suddenly all the teachers urged me to consider college. But it remained a remote hope. There was no way I could afford to go. I applied anyway and was accepted to Virginia State College.

When graduation night came, Mama was there, especially proud because I was the first member of our family to finish high school (followed a year later by my sister Ann). Mama sat up near the front, and I caught her eye as I got my diploma. She was smiling through the tears.

Even that wasn't the high spot of the evening. To my amazement, they called my name, and they just kept calling. Each time, another announcement of another scholarship for college. I could go to college after all!

They hadn't told me or Mama anything. But I think my favorite teacher, Miss Jordan, knew because she was smiling and nodding her head as if to say, "See, now, what you can do with discipline?"

I kept winning scholarships and also worked summers while I majored in business education. Even at college, I heard remarks about my simple clothing—most of it handed down or sewn by Mama. I just kept remembering her words—"It's not what you wear, it's who you are." Still, when no one could see, I cried a lot. Yet I knew it was nothing compared with the pain and suffering Mama had gone through for me.

Some of my friends in graduate school became incensed when they began to appreciate what generations of discrimination had cost them. But Miss Jordan's admonitions on self-discipline kept me intent on my studies. And Mama's example and words kept me from ever being angry or discouraged. "Mary Alice, if you're unhappy with things, try to change them," she would say. "And if you're knocked down, get up and start over again!"

Since then, the strengths and skills that I acquired from both Mama and Miss Jordan have acted as twin beacons that have guided me, for many years as a classroom teacher in Alexandria, and more recently as president of the National Education Association. I have tried to emulate Mama's fortitude and Miss Jordan's clarity of mind. And in my battles against discrimination and on behalf of teachers, I have come to appreciate the value of Mama's unyielding demands. Still, one question continued to gnaw at me for more than 30 years.

Then Mama came to visit. We were standing side by side, washing up some pots and pans after a family gathering. I drew a deep breath. "Mama, how come you were always so much tougher on me than on any of the others?"

She laid down her dish towel and looked pensive. But she didn't say anything.

The next morning Mama and I sat at the breakfast table, looking out to the garden. We talked about nothing in particular, and then I poured both of us a second cup of coffee. We sat in silence for a moment more, when Mama took my chin in her hand with that calm firmness. She looked me straight in the eye and said, "You asked me a question yesterday, Mary Alice. I've been thinking of an answer. You had strength. But you were very strong-willed. I had to be harder on you because you had more gifts, more to give, and it was important for you to get all the schooling you could because I just knew that many other people would be depending on you to do your best. That's my answer to your question, Mary Alice."

She was still holding my chin, and I could hear the grandfather clock ticking in the den. I nodded, and she relinquished her grip. "I understand, Mama." At last I did.

Mary Hatwood Futrell

When a Mother Blows Out 75 Candles

She secretly hopes a tank of oxygen is one of her gifts.

Through the years she has hollered, said and prayed, "Jesus, Mary and Joseph, grant me patience!" 1,245,187 times.

Her hands have hung diapers on pulley clotheslines, sterilized bottles, carried babies from the third-floor apartment, ironed sunsuits and proudly pushed baby buggies.

She has peeled more potatoes than six marines on K.P. duty.

Her hair has been set in steel curlers, permed, rinsed with Nestle's coloring capsules, and styled in pageboys, the poodle look and the beehive hairdo; been permed again and turned silver.

The "parlor" was where she entertained company, the "pantry" held the groceries, the "icebox" held a pint of ice cream, and the "wringer washing machine" was hers to use on Tuesday.

She has earned her nursing degree through measles, chicken pox, mumps, pneumonia, polio, TB, fevers, stitches, flu, fractured arms and broken hearts.

At one time or another her closet held housedresses, feathered hats, white gloves, skirts with short hemlines and with long hemlines, pants suits, billowy dresses of chiffon, sheath dresses, a Sunday coat and the Christmas toys she ordered from the Sears catalog.

Her heart has known the ecstasy of a man's love, the joy of children, the heartbreak of their mistakes, the warmth of life's friendships, the celebration of weddings, the magnificent blessings of grandchildren and great-grandchildren.

Who can count the floors she scrubbed, the dinners she cooked, the birthday gifts she wrapped, the spelling words she listened to, the bedtime stories she read, the excuses she heard, the prayers she whispered to God each day?

Her arms have rocked generations of babies. Her hands have prepared countless "favorite" dishes. Her knees have knelt in prayer time and time again for those she loved. Her mouth has kissed owwies that hurt. Her back has bent to bathe dirty cowboys, pick up teens' clothes, gather flowers from her garden and grow old.

She has journeyed through life with its tears and laughter, watching yesterday's sunsets become tomorrow's sunrises of hope and promise. Because of her and the man who took her hand, family life and love continue through the generations.

When a mother blows out 75 candles, blessed are they who surround her with their love.

Alice Collins
Submitted by Geraldine Doyle

Six of the Seven Wonders of My World

"This is one of those things I would never be doing if I had not had seven children," my mother turned to tell me, as we rode through the New Mexico desert in a Chevrolet convertible. She had arrived in Tucson two days before, to accompany me on my move to Washington, D.C. When I told her that I was making the trip, she didn't wait for me to ask her to help. She just took time off from work, made the reservations, and flew from Chicago to lend a hand and keep me company.

I have often heard it said that when there are seven children, someone is always left behind, as if there were a mathematical equation (number of hours divided by number of children equals amount of attention per child). This was not my reality. I don't know how my mother did it, but I never felt second—not to my siblings, not to her career or activities, not even to my father.

I remember sitting on her lap as a child, listening to her explain about the eight equal pieces of her heart, one for each of us children and one for my father. I have no idea where my brothers and sisters were when my mother and

I played our game of "Mrs. O'Leary and Mrs. Foley," enjoying tea and cookies while gossiping about the neighbors. Or when she read me to sleep and sang her bedtime song, "Go to sleep, my little pumpkin / to the tips of your toes / If you sleep, my little pumpkin / you'll turn into a rose."

When I started kindergarten, my mother told me that if I ever felt alone, all I had to do was blow her a kiss, and she would receive it and blow it right back. I really believed that she got my kisses and that I felt hers in return, and I still believe so today. Somehow the phone always rings when I most need her.

Wherever I am, whatever is happening in my life, I automatically share everything with her first. That makes me wonder what I'll do someday without her. But I've come to understand that my mother will *always* be here for me. That's because she's put the most enduring parts of herself into the seven of us, so I won't ever feel alone. . . .

When I need her opinion, on anything from raising my children to how to cut my hair, I will call my sister Lisa. From her I'll get mother's well thought-out, fair and honest advice.

When I need help solving a problem, I'll call my brother Bill, for he has Mother's wisdom and creativity. He also has her ability to look at the world and convince me that he should be running it.

When I think I have too much to do and not enough time for it all, when I need my mother's strength and humor, I will call Gay, who raises her four children and works three jobs, but still finds time to talk and listen and share a good laugh.

When the world seems dull and repetitive, I will call Jim for a dose of Mother's magic. Like her, Jim sees the wonder in things. Whether he's talking to a child or an adult, he will swear at Christmas time that he saw an elf at work.

For Mother's compassion, when I need somebody to listen and accept me without qualifications, I'll call Mary, who will make the tea and let me cry, knowing when to be silent.

And when I need my mother's courage, when I can't get myself to do something I know I should do, I will call my sister Doyle, who, although she is the youngest, has always had an instinct for what is right and the self-confidence to do it.

So here we were, driving through the desert, with my mother talking about certain things she would not be doing had she not had seven children. Well, there are *many* wonderful things the seven of us wouldn't have if she had not had seven children—because *we* are my mother's greatest gift to us.

Jane Harless Woodward

"How do you divide your love among four children?"
"I don't divide it. I multiply it."

Mailboxes

The family mailbox stood at the end of the half-mile-long lane. In tall, proud white capital letters it announced to all who passed by: BURRES. To us children, that metal container on a post was a source of endless anticipation and independence, and a promise of unconditional love.

Our mother created this sense of adventure for us, probably not inadvertently. She believed children needed to learn things. To Mom, everything was a teachable moment, and she was a master teacher.

Each day around noontime, my mother would walk down the lane to get the mail. When we children saw her head for the lane on Saturdays, we would drop our activities and scurry to join her, as would the dog member of the family. Mom found great pleasure in her children's company, happily and playfully greeting us as we joined her. The half-mile trek to and from the mailbox was a long way for short legs, but well worth it. During these trips, her mood was reliably joyous. This was an opportunity for us to bask in our mother's love.

Once we arrived at the mailbox, Mom would pick out the mail and, while sorting through it, announce if mail had arrived for any of the children—though she wouldn't give out the names of just who among us had received mail. By doing it this way, she kept all of us children in suspense until we reached the house, at which time she would give us our individual mail. Mother taught us to respect each other's privacy, and to be very good sports about who did and did not receive mail on any given day. "Here," she would say, "this belongs to you." We were all allowed to open the mail that came in our names without Mom looking over our shoulders.

Surprisingly, each child received mail from time to time. Even more surprisingly, each child received mail in fairly equal quantities. Sometimes a magazine arrived in a child's name; sometimes a note from an aunt, uncle, grandma, grandpa or Sunday School teacher (who was also our neighbor and Mom's good friend). No child was left wanting. Even junk mail arrived on cue. It didn't matter whether it was written by a person or by a machine, getting mail with your name on it was exciting and esteeming.

The practice of us children getting to open our own mail was followed from the day I was old enough to know what mail was, until the day I left home. I didn't understand until I was much older that while we children were caught up in the fun of receiving mail, Mother had a bigger agenda.

On those brief strolls, Mom would sometimes tell us a story made up to fit the moment. At other times, she used the walk to teach us about God. Sometimes these were the same. Mom used every opportunity to help us become aware of the obvious miracles of creation. There wasn't a bird or bee, or any flora or fauna that went unnoticed. The fascinating habits of animals on the ground or in the air; the intricacy and beauty in the colors and shapes and fragrances of flowers; how the bees fly to these flowers to gather their pollen; the sun with its endless power to warm and give brilliant light; all were pointed out to us for appreciation.

We adored her. She was our everything. This was a joyous woman, an eternal optimist, always smiling, always humming, her words punctuated with an easy flowing laughter that caused her to toss her long, soft brown hair over her shoulders.

And so it is that the sight of mailboxes, especially those at the end of long lanes, retains special meaning for me. They remind me of my mother's love and the values and beliefs she so lovingly conveyed. She embodied joy, love and respect, and taught these lessons every day.

Bettie B. Youngs

My Mother's Riches

There must be something pretty special about a mother who can raise a daughter oblivious to the poverty she lived in. I didn't even know I was poor until I was in the second grade. I had everything I needed; nine brothers and sisters to play with, books to read, a friend in a handmade Raggedy Ann, and clean clothing my mother skillfully mended or often made herself. My hair was washed and braided by my mother each evening for school the next day, my brown shoes polished and shined. I was blissfully happy at school, loving the smell of the new crayons and the thick art paper the teacher handed out for projects. I soaked up knowledge like a sponge, earning the coveted privilege of taking messages to the principal's office one week.

I still remember the feeling of pride as I went by myself up the stairs of the school to deliver that day's lunch count. As I returned to my classroom, I met two older girls going back up the stairway. "Look, it's the poor girl," one whispered to the other, and they giggled. Face flaming red and choking back tears, the rest of the day was a blur.

Walking home that day, I tried to sort out the conflicting feelings that the girl's comments had wrought. I wondered why the girls thought I was poor. I looked down critically at my dress and for the first time noticed how faded it was, a crease at the hem visibly announcing that the dress was a hand-me-down. Despite the fact that the heavy boy's shoes were the only kind with enough support to keep me from walking on the sides of my feet, I was suddenly embarrassed that I wore ugly brown shoes.

By the time I got home, I felt sorry for myself. I felt as if I were entering a stranger's house, looking critically at everything. I saw the torn linoleum in the kitchen, smudged fingerprints on the old paint in the doorways. Dejected, I didn't respond to my mother's cheery greeting in the kitchen, where she prepared oatmeal cookies and powdered milk for a snack. I was sure the other girls in school didn't have to have powdered milk. I brooded in my room until suppertime, wondering how to approach the topic of poverty with my mother. Why hadn't she told me, I wondered. Why did I have to find out from someone else?

When I had worked up enough courage, I went out to the kitchen. "Are we poor?" I blurted out, somewhat defiantly. I expected her to deny it, defend it, or at least explain it away, so I wouldn't feel so bad about it. My mother looked at me contemplatively, not saying anything for a minute. "Poor?" she repeated, as she set down the paring knife she'd been peeling potatoes with. "No, we're not poor. Just look at all we have," she said, as she gestured toward my brothers and sisters playing in the next room.

Through her eyes I saw the wood stove that filled the house with warmth, the colorful curtains and homemade rag rugs that decorated the house, the plate full of oatmeal cookies on the counter. Outside the kitchen window I could see the wide open space of country that offered so much fun and adventure for 10 children. She continued, "Maybe some people would think we are poor in terms of money, but we have so much." And with a smile of contentment, my mother turned back to preparing a meal for her family, not realizing she had fed far more than an empty stomach that evening. She had fed my heart and soul.

Mary Kenyon

Just Plain Wrong

To say my mother was plain is neither criticism nor complaint. She was, in fact, simply one of those women whom people didn't notice. The world is full of the proverbial "plain Jane" types.

Born into a painfully long line of alcoholics, my mother decided at the age of 17 to leave St. Louis because, as she put it, "I couldn't take another minute of the fighting and drinking and craziness." She moved in with her California cousin and his family to begin a new life. That was in 1959.

In 1960, she married my father—a Navy man—and over the next four years they had Tammy, Tina and me, Jerry. My parents bought a small, plain house in Orange County in 1967. In 1975, having both given it their best, my parents divorced. I was 12.

Maybe it was because of the enormous change a divorce brings, I don't know—but I suddenly noticed my mother more as a person than a parent. I started noticing her face with its unstartling features. Her eyes had great dark circles about them, and her shape had suffered the fate of the birthing process and its aftermath. Men did not notice my single mother. They never seemed to notice those flaming eyes that I'd begun to take note of as time passed.

As single mothers often have to do, mine took a second job at night delivering racing forms to liquor stores. She used to promise me a chocolate-dipped cone from Foster's Freeze if I'd just ride along with her, saying it was the only time she got to see me anymore. She would take stacks of forms into the liquor stores, barely getting a grunt out of the men behind the counters. My mother seemed invisible to men.

As I grew into a young man, I became silently bitter about people's general disinterest in my mother. I knew the lethal wit she wielded and the immense knowledge she'd acquired from having been an insatiable reader. It was all right there in those eyes. It wasn't a critical observation typical of teenagers when it comes to their parents. I simply noticed that my mother's silently heroic life was passing by unmarked, unappreciated. It pained me.

On February 19th, 1986, I got a phone call in the middle of my shift at a wholesale warehouse. It was my mother, with the news that the cold she'd been trying to shake for two months was due to a tumor in her left lung that had "trapped" the cold inside. A week later a surgeon opened her up, noticed that the tumor had wrapped around her aorta in an upward spiral toward her heart, and promptly closed her chest back up. He spoke at length of chemotherapy and radiation, but his eyes gave us the truth.

My plain mother fought that tumor like a warrior, and no one seemed to notice. She withstood the effects of radiation on her voice box and on her abilities to swallow and even breathe. In no plain fashion, she faced the nightmare of chemotherapy, even buying a screaming red wig to try to lighten the family up about the whole thing. It didn't work. She vowed to "beat this beast," until she lost consciousness on February 2, 1987, and passed away with her three children holding both hands and stroking those plain, unstartling cheeks. It angered me.

I was enraged at the world for not having noticed her. *I* noticed her. I watched the struggle and the loneliness take their toll on her. How could they fail to see that this physically uninspiring woman was, in fact, a gorgeous human being? I was furious until the funeral.

People I didn't know began pouring into the plain, little chapel where my mother was to be noticed for the last time. Coworkers from jobs two decades before came in, telling me that the last time they saw me I was in diapers. Friends I never knew about from the job she'd had until she was too sick to work flooded in, hugging my sisters and me. Even her racing form boss from eight years earlier came, shook my hand, and told me that my plain mother was "just about the kindest woman I ever knew."

I'd started noticing my mother as a person at 12, and I felt her life plain. I looked out at the standing-room-only chapel filled with good people who *had* noticed my mother, and who had judged her as anything but plain. She had made her mark on their lives, and *I'd* never noticed. It never felt so good to be so wrong. They'd noticed all along, and I wasn't angry anymore.

Gerald E. Thurston Jr.

Great Lady

It seems to me that my mother was the most splendid woman I ever knew. . . . I have met a lot of people knocking around the world since, but I have never met a more thoroughly refined woman than my mother. If I have amounted to anything, it will be due to her.

Charles Chaplin

I remember when I was in fourth grade and you used to do things like stay up half the night just to make me a Zorro outfit for Halloween. I knew you were a good mom, but I didn't realize what a great lady you were.

I can remember your working two jobs sometimes and running the beauty shop in the front of our home so that our family would be able to make ends meet. You worked long, long hours and somehow managed to smile all the way through it. I knew you were a hard worker, but I didn't realize what a great lady you were.

I remember the night that I came to you late—in fact, it was near midnight or perhaps beyond—and told you that I was supposed to be a king in a play at school the next day. Somehow you rose to the occasion and created a king's purple robe with ermine on it (made of cotton and black markers). After all that work I still forgot to turn around in the play, so that no one really saw the completion of all your work. Still, you were able to laugh and love and enjoy even those kinds of moments. I knew then that you were a mother like no other, who could rise to any occasion. But I didn't realize what a great lady you were.

I remember when I split my head open for the sixth time in a row and you told the school, "He will be okay. Just give him a little rest. I'll come and check on him later." They knew and I knew that you were tough, but I didn't realize what a great lady you were.

I can remember in junior high and high school you helping me muddle through my homework—you making costumes for special events at school, you attending all my games. I knew at the time that you would try almost anything if it would help one of your children, but I didn't realize what a great lady you were.

I remember bringing 43 kids home at 3:30 one morning when I worked for Young Life, and asking if it would be okay if they stayed over for the night and had breakfast. I remember you getting up at 4:30 to pull off this heroic feat. I knew at the time that you were a joyous and generous giver, but I didn't realize what a great lady you were.

I can remember you attending all my football and basketball games in high school and getting so excited that you hit the person in front of you with your pompoms. I could even hear you rooting for me way out in the middle of the field. I knew then that you were one of the classic cheerleaders of all time, but I didn't realize what a great lady you were.

I remember all the sacrifices you made so I could go to Stanford—the extra work you took on, the care packages you sent so regularly, the mail that reminded me that I wasn't in this all alone. I knew you were a great friend, but I didn't realize what a great lady you were.

I remember graduating from Stanford and deciding to work for $200 a month, loving kids through Young Life. Although you and Dad thought I had fallen off the end of the ladder, you still encouraged me. In fact, I remember when you came down to help me fix up my little one-room abode. You added your special, loving touch to what would have been very simple quarters. I realized then—and time and time again—what a creative genius you were, but I didn't realize what a great lady you were.

Time wore on, I grew older and got married and started a family. You became "NaNa" and cherished your new role, yet you never seemed to grow older. I realized then that God had carved out a special place in life when he made you, but I didn't realize what a great, great lady you were.

I got slowed down by an accident. Things got a little tougher for me. But you stood alongside as you always had. Some things, I thought, never change—and I was deeply grateful. I realized then what I had known for a long time—what a great nurse you can be—but I didn't realize what a great, great lady you were.

I wrote some books, and people seemed to like them. You and Dad were so proud that sometimes you gave people copies of the books just to show what one of your kids had done. I realized then what a great promoter you were, but I didn't realize what a great, great lady you were.

Times have changed . . . seasons have passed, and one of the greatest men I have ever known has passed along as well. I can still remember you at the memorial service, standing tall and proud in a brilliant purple dress, reminding people, "How blessed we have been, and how thankful we are for a life well lived." In those moments I saw a woman who could stand tall and grateful amidst the most difficult of circumstances. I was beginning to discover what a great, great lady you are.

In the last year, when you have had to stand alone as never before, all of what I have observed and experienced all those years has come together in a brand new way. In spite of it all, now your laughter is richer, your strength is stronger, your love is deeper, and I am discovering in truth what a great, great lady you are.

Tim Hansel

Afterword

Prayer for My Mother

Dear God,

Now that I am no longer young, I have friends whose mothers have passed away. I have heard these sons and daughters say they never fully appreciated their mothers until it was too late to tell them.

I am blessed with a dear mother who is still alive. I appreciate her more each day. My mother does not change, but I do. As I grow older and wiser, I realize what an extraordinary person she is. How sad that I am unable to speak these words in her presence, but they flow easily from my pen.

How does a daughter begin to thank her mother for life itself? For the love, patience and just plain hard work that go into raising a child? For running after a toddler, for understanding a moody teenager, for tolerating a college student who knows everything? For waiting for the day when a daughter realizes how wise her mother really is?

How does a grown woman thank a mother for continuing to be a mother? For being ready with advice (when asked) or remaining silent when it is most appreciated?

For not saying, "I told you so," when she could have uttered those words dozens of times? For being essentially herself—loving, thoughtful, patient and forgiving?

I don't know how, dear God, except to ask you to bless her as richly as she deserves and to help me live up to the example she has set. I pray that I will look as good in the eyes of my children as my mother looks in mine.

—A Daughter

Ann Landers
Submitted by Lynn Kalinowski

More Chicken Soup?

Many of the stories and poems you have read in this book were submitted by readers like you who had read earlier *Chicken Soup for the Soul* books. We are planning to publish five or six *Chicken Soup for the Soul* books every year. We invite you to contribute a story to one of these future volumes.

Stories may be up to 1,200 words and must uplift or inspire. You may submit an original piece or something you clip out of the local newspaper, a magazine, a church bulletin or a company newsletter. It could also be your favorite quotation you've put on your refrigerator door or a personal experience that has touched you deeply.

In addition to future *Servings of Chicken Soup for the Soul,* some of the future books we have planned are *A 2nd Helping of Chicken Soup for the Woman's Soul, Christian Soul* and *Teenage Soul* as well as *Chicken Soup for the . . . Teacher's Soul, Jewish Soul, Pet Lover's Soul, Kid's Soul, Country Soul, Laughing Soul, Grieving Soul, Unsinkable Soul, Divorced Soul* and *Loving Couple's Soul.*

Just send a copy of your stories and other pieces, indicating which edition they are for, to the following address:

Chicken Soup for the ***(Specify Which Edition)*** **Soul**
P.O. Box 30880 • Santa Barbara, CA 93130
phone: 805-563-2935 • fax: 805-563-2945
e-mail: soup4soul@aol.com
Web site: http://www.chickensoup.com

We will be sure that both you and the author are credited for your submission.

For information about speaking engagements, other books, audiotapes, workshops and training programs, please contact any of the authors directly.

Supporting Mothers and Children of the World

In the spirit of supporting mothers and children everywhere, the publisher and coauthors of *Chicken Soup for the Mother's Soul* will make a donation to:

Save the Children Federation, Inc.
54 Wilton Road
P.O. Box 950
Westport, CT 06880

Save the Children, a not-for-profit organization, is dedicated to making lasting, positive changes in the lives of disadvantaged children in the United States and throughout the world. For 65 years, Save the Children has been working with families and communities in 40 nations, developing and managing programs in health, education, economic opportunity and emergency relief. Its programs reach more than 1.5 million children and their families in Africa, Asia, Europe, Latin America, the Middle East and the United States.

In 1997, Save the Children launched a new initiative in the United States: *Save the Children U.S.* will focus on the issue of keeping kids safe and maximizing their potential during out-of-school time. *Save the Children U.S.* will provide children with access to caring adults, secure places and structured activities during their after school hours, when 44 percent of American children are unsupervised.

Information concerning Save the Children Federation, Inc., including financial, licensing or charitable purposes, may be obtained, without cost, by writing: Save the Children Federation, Inc., Assistant Corporate Secretary, at the above address, telephone (800) 243-5075.

Who Is Jack Canfield?

Jack Canfield is one of America's leading experts in the development of human potential and personal effectiveness. He is both a dynamic, entertaining speaker and a highly sought-after trainer. Jack has a wonderful ability to inform and inspire audiences toward increased levels of self-esteem and peak performance.

He is the author and narrator of several bestselling audio- and videocassette programs, including *Self-Esteem and Peak Performance, How to Build High Self-Esteem, Self-Esteem in the Classroom* and *Chicken Soup for the Soul—Live.* He is regularly seen on television shows such as *Good Morning America, 20/20* and *NBC Nightly News.* Jack has coauthored numerous books, including the *Chicken Soup for the Soul* series, *Dare to Win* and *The Aladdin Factor* (all with Mark Victor Hansen), *100 Ways to Build Self-Concept in the Classroom* (with Harold C. Wells) and *Heart at Work* (with Jacqueline Miller).

Jack is a regularly featured speaker for professional associations, school districts, government agencies, churches, hospitals, sales organizations and corporations. His clients have included the American Dental Association, the American Management Association, AT&T, Campbell Soup, Clairol, Domino's Pizza, GE, ITT, Hartford Insurance, Johnson & Johnson, the Million Dollar Roundtable, NCR, New England Telephone, Re/Max, Scott Paper, TRW and Virgin Records. Jack is also on the faculty of Income Builders International, a school for entrepreneurs.

Jack conducts an annual eight-day Training of Trainers program in the areas of self-esteem and peak performance. It attracts educators, counselors, parenting trainers, corporate trainers, professional speakers, ministers and others interested in developing their speaking and seminar-leading skills.

For further information about Jack's books, tapes and training programs, or to schedule him for a presentation, please contact:

The Canfield Training Group
P.O. Box 30880 • Santa Barbara , CA 93130
phone: 800-237-8336 • fax: 805-563-2945
Web site: http://www.chickensoup.com
to send e-mail: soup4soul@aol.com
to receive information via e-mail: chickensoup@zoom.com

Who Is Mark Victor Hansen?

Mark Victor Hansen is a professional speaker who, in the last 20 years, has made over 4,000 presentations to more than 2 million people in 32 countries. His presentations cover sales excellence and strategies; personal empowerment and development; and how to triple your income and double your time off.

Mark has spent a lifetime dedicated to his mission to make a profound and positive difference in people's lives. Throughout his career, he has inspired hundreds of thousands of people to create a more powerful and purposeful future for themselves while stimulating the sale of billions of dollars worth of goods and services.

Mark is a prolific writer and has authored *Future Diary, How to Achieve Total Prosperity* and *The Miracle of Tithing.* He is coauthor of the *Chicken Soup for the Soul* series, *Dare to Win* and *The Aladdin Factor* (all with Jack Canfield) and *The Master Motivator* (with Joe Batten).

Mark has also produced a complete library of personal empowerment audio- and videocassette programs that have enabled his listeners to recognize and use their innate abilities in their business and personal lives. His message has made him a popular television and radio personality, with appearances on ABC, NBC, CBS, HBO, PBS and CNN. He has also appeared on the cover of numerous magazines, including *Success, Entrepreneur* and *Changes.*

Mark is a big man with a heart and spirit to match—an inspiration to all who seek to better themselves.

For further information about Mark write:

P.O. Box 7665
Newport Beach, CA 92658
phone: 714-759-9304 or 800-433-2314
fax: 714-722-6912
Web site: http://www.chickensoup.com

Who Is Jennifer Read Hawthorne?

Jennifer Read Hawthorne is coauthor of the #1 *New York Times* bestseller *Chicken Soup for the Woman's Soul: 101 Stories to Open the Hearts and Rekindle the Spirits of Women.* Currently at work on future *Chicken Soup for the Soul* books, she also delivers *Chicken Soup for the Soul* presentations nationwide, sharing inspirational stories of love and hope, courage and dreams.

Jennifer is known as a dynamic and insightful speaker, with a great sense of humor and a gift for telling stories. From an early age she developed a deep appreciation for language, cultivated by her parents. She attributes her love of storytelling to the legacy of her late father, Brooks Read, a renowned Master Storyteller whose original Brer Rabbit stories filled her childhood with magic and a sense of the power of words.

As a Peace Corps volunteer in West Africa teaching English as a foreign language, Jennifer discovered the universality of stories to teach, move, uplift and connect people. Her *Chicken Soup for the Soul* presentations make audiences laugh and cry; many people say their lives are changed for the better as a result of hearing her speak.

Jennifer is cofounder of The Esteem Group, a company specializing in self-esteem and inspirational programs for women. A professional speaker since 1975, she has spoken to thousands of people around the world about personal growth, self-development and professional success. Her clients have included professional associations, Fortune 500 companies, and government and educational organizations such as AT&T, Delta Airlines, Hallmark Cards, The American Legion, Norand, Cargill, the State of Iowa and Clemson University.

Jennifer is a native of Baton Rouge, Louisiana, where she graduated from Louisiana State University with a degree in journalism. She lives in Fairfield, Iowa, with her husband, Dan, and two stepchildren, Amy and William.

If you would like to schedule Jennifer for a *Chicken Soup for the Soul* keynote address or seminar, you may contact her at:

Jennifer Hawthorne Inc.
1105 South D Street
Fairfield, IA 52556
phone: 515-472-7136 • fax: 515-469-6908

Who Is Marci Shimoff?

Marci Shimoff is coauthor of the #1 *New York Times* bestseller *Chicken Soup for the Woman's Soul.* She is also a professional speaker and trainer who, for the last 17 years, has inspired thousands of people with her message of personal and professional growth. She gives seminars and keynote addresses on self-esteem, stress management, communication skills and peak performance. In the last few years, she has specialized in delivering *Chicken Soup for the Soul* keynote addresses to audiences around the world.

Marci is cofounder and president of The Esteem Group, a company that offers self-esteem and inspirational programs for women. As a top-rated speaker for Fortune 500 companies, Marci's clients have included AT&T, General Motors, Sears, Amoco, American Airlines and Bristol-Myers Squibb. She has also been a featured speaker for numerous professional organizations, universities and women's associations, where she is known for her lively humor and her dynamic delivery.

Marci combines her energetic style with a strong knowledge base. She earned her MBA from UCLA; she also studied for one year in the U.S. and Europe to earn an advanced certificate as a stress-management consultant. Since 1989, Marci has studied self-esteem with Jack Canfield, and has assisted in his annual Training of Trainers program for professionals.

In 1983, Marci coauthored a highly acclaimed study of the 50 top business women in America. Since that time, she has specialized in addressing women's audiences, focusing on helping women discover the extraordinary within themselves.

Of all the projects Marci has worked on in her career, none have been as fulfilling as creating *Chicken Soup for the Soul* books. Currently at work on future editions of *Chicken Soup for the Soul,* she is thrilled at the opportunity to help touch the hearts and rekindle the spirits of millions of people throughout the world.

If you would like to schedule Marci for a *Chicken Soup for the Soul* keynote address or seminar, you can reach her at:

The Esteem Group
1105 South D Street
Fairfield, IA 52556
phone: 515-472-9394 • fax: 515-472-5065

Contributors

Joan Wester Anderson is a bestselling author and is recognized around the world as an authority on angelic and miraculous intervention in everyday life. Over 2 million copies of her books have been sold. She can be reached at PO Box 1694, Arlington Heights, IL 60006.

Marsha Arons is a writer and speaker. Her areas of interest include women's issues, child-parent relationships, Christian-Jewish relations, and focusing on the positive aspects of life. She is delighted to be a contributor to the *Chicken Soup* books including *Chicken Soup for the Woman's Soul.* In addition, Marsha's stories, essays and articles have appeared in *Good Housekeeping, Redbook, Woman's Day, Woman's World* and *Reader's Digest.* She is currently at work on a collection of stories having to do with parenting and a novel for young adults. She can be reached for writing and speaking assignments at her e-mail address: ra8737@aol.com. or by calling 847-329-0280.

Aaron Bacall is a New York cartoonist whose work appears in magazines, books and advertisements. He worked as a pharmaceutical research chemist and a university educator before turning to full-time cartooning. He can be reached somewhere in cyberspace at abcartoon@juno.com or via fax at 718-370-2629.

Sandra Julian Barker is a freelance writer with short stories and articles in a number of newspapers and magazines. She hopes to one day be a published novelist. She and her husband have three children and live in Chesapeake, Virginia.

Deborah Bebb is a freelance writer and editor. Most of her articles are about real people and the miracles that touch their lives. She lives in Phoenix, Arizona, with her husband, Michael, and her 13-year-old son, Douglas. She can be reached at 602-581-3751.

Bits & Pieces, the magazine that inspires the world, has motivated and amused millions for almost 30 years. For your free issue, call 800-526-2554. Available in English, Spanish and Japanese.

Judy Bodmer watched her sons, who are now in college, play sports for over 10 years in Kirkland, Washington. She works as a library assistant at Lake Forest Park and teaches creative writing at Lake Washington Technical College. Along with her husband, Larry, she volunteers her time working with engaged and married couples through her church.

Carolyn Campbell has published more than 200 articles in national magazines such as *Ladies' Home Journal, Family Circle, First for Women, Woman's World* and *Guideposts.* She is also a monthly columnist for *Business Startups.* Her articles have been published internationally in Hong Kong, Germany, Denmark and Australia. Her areas of specialty include informational topics, relationships and lifestyle issues, and articles about women, particularly those who overcome obstacles to achieve success. She lives in Salt Lake City, Utah, with her husband and four children who range in age from 21 to 7. She can be reached at 801-943-6571.

Bill Canty's cartoons have appeared in many national magazines, including the *Saturday Evening Post, Good Housekeeping, Better Homes and Gardens, Woman's World, National Review* and *Medical Economics.* His syndicated feature *All About Town* runs in 40 newspapers. Bill can be reached at PO Box 1053, S. Wellfleet, MA 02663 or call 508-349-7549.

Dave Carpenter has been a full-time cartoonist and humorous illustrator since 1981. His cartoons have appeared in *Barrons,* the *Wall Street Journal, Forbes, Better Homes and Gardens, Good Housekeeping, Woman's World, First,* the *Saturday Evening Post* and numerous other publications. Dave can be reached at PO Box 520, Emmetsburg, IA 50536 or by calling 712-852-3725.

Mary Chambers' cartoons come straight from her experiences as a mother of seven. She is the author of the cartoon books *Motherhood Is Stranger Than Fiction* and *Church Is Stranger Than Fiction.* She coauthored *Faith in Orbit* with four cartoonists. She and her family live in Carthage, Missouri.

Liane Kupferberg Carter is a freelance writer whose work has appeared in the *New York Times, McCall's, Child, Glamour, Cosmopolitan* and *Newsday.* She lives with her family in Westchester, New York, and is a community activist on behalf of children with special needs. She can be reached at lcarter@cloud9.net.

Diana L. Chapman has been a newspaper journalist for more than 11 years, having worked at such newspapers as the *Los Angeles Times,* the *San Diego Union* and *Los Angeles Copley Newspapers.* She specializes in touching human interest stories and is currently working on a book involving health issues, since she was diagnosed with multiple sclerosis in 1993. She has been married for seven years and has one son, Herbert "Ryan" Hart. She can be reached at 837 Elberon #3A, San Pedro, CA 90731 or call 310-548-1192.

Billie B. Chesney is a native of Kansas. She is a grandmother of five, a Bible study leader and a freelance writer. Her essays, short stories and reminiscences have won several awards and have been published in *Good Old Days, Cappers* and *One of a Kind* magazines. A theme book soon to be published by *Reminisce* magazine will include some of her work. Billie and her husband, Dale, live in Kingsport, Tennessee.

Rebecca Christian is the mother of three and is a humorous and inspirational speaker/writer who has spoken at many annual meetings and women's conferences. Her work has appeared in over 100 magazines and newspapers. She can be reached at 641 Alta Vista St., Dubuque, IA 52001. Phone/fax 319-582-9193.

Dan Clark is the international ambassador of the "Art of Being Alive." He has spoken to over 2 million people worldwide. Dan is an actor, songwriter, recording artist, video producer and award-winning athlete. He is the well-known author of seven books, including *Getting High—How to Really Do It, One*

Minute Messages, The Art of Being Alive and *Puppies for Sale and Other Inspirational Tales.* He can be reached at PO Box 8689, Salt Lake City, UT 84108 or call 801-485-5755.

Margie Coburn retired recently from her local hospital after 25 years. Her freelance writings are mostly inspirational or reflective of her interesting, happy life experiences. She enjoys church work, public speaking and being a volunteer historical site tour guide. She lives at 106 Azalea St., Greenville, NC 27834 or call 919-752-3219.

Muriel Cochrane and her husband are in their 80s. They lost their son, John in 1966 during the Vietnam War. They have four lovely daughters, 14 grandchildren and 25 great-grandchildren. Muriel has written several poems over the years dealing with home, family and friendships.

Shari Cohen is the author of eight books for children. She also writes articles for magazines and newspapers about family life. Shari lives in Woodland Hills, California, with her husband, Paul, and their three teenagers. She can be reached at PO Box 6593, Woodland Hills, CA 91365.

Alice Collins, wife, mother, and grandmother defrosts chicken, has hot flashes, misplaces her glasses and celebrates family life in her columns and books, or when speaking in front of audiences. She can be reached next to the overflowing hamper in Oak Lawn, Illinois, at 708-422-7568.

Lynnette Curtis is a senior English major at the University of Nevada, Las Vegas. She also works as an editorial assistant at the *Las Vegas Review-Journal.* She can be reached via e-mail at msnettiel@aol.com.

Edith M. Dean is a freelance author of three (coauthor with George Andersen of one) and more than 250 articles. Her work is inspirational. She lives with her husband, Jim, in Conway, Arkansas.

Benita Epstein is a freelance cartoonist whose work has appeared in over 150 books and magazines such as *Punch, Barron's* and the *Saturday Evening Post.* She also has dozens of greeting cards published by Marcel Shurman and Silver Dog. You can reach her at (fax) 760-634-3705 or benitaE@aol.com.

Judy Farris is the mother of two teenage daughters. For the past several years, she has devoted all her free time to writing poetry and short prose and is involved in community college theater in Palm Desert, California, where she lives with her husband, Karl.

Donna Getzinger writes stories, novels and plays for children. She also writes fantasy novels for adults. Her work has appeared in such publications as *Children's Digest, Funny Times, Listen* and *What's Love? Love Prints Novellettes.* Also a professional singer, Donna invites you to inquire about her music or fiction. She can be reached at 213-718-0036.

Randee Goldsmith is the product manager for *Chicken Soup for the Soul* at Health Communications, Inc. She is the mother of one son, Alan. Originally from Southfield, Michigan, Randee is a graduate of Michigan State University. Currently living in Boca Raton, Florida, Randee can be reached at Health Communications, Inc., 3201 SW 15th St., Deerfield Beach, FL 33442.

Linda Goodman has shared her stories with audiences throughout the country. She was the 1995 recipient of the *Excellency in Storytelling Award* presented by Connecticut's Storytelling Institute. Her tape, *Jesse and Other Stories,* and her short-story collection, *Daughters of the Appalachians,* have received glowing reviews. You can reach Linda at 508-562-9575.

Jennifer Graham lives in Naperville, Illinois, with her husband, Bob, and their two children, Charley and Katherine. Jennifer's colorful family provides endless material for her freelance writing. She can be reached at 630-717-6788.

Loretta Hall is the mother of three girls and the grandmother of two. To maintain a family-oriented schedule while contributing to the family income, she works as a freelance writer. Her articles deal with family issues, business topics and technological developments. She can be reached at 505-293-2337.

Jean Harper is a wife, mother of two, writer, public speaker and pilot for United Airlines, currently a captain on the Boeing 757. She considers her finest talent to be storytelling and uses her varied and unusual background in public speaking to address the subjects of aviation, Christianity and career guidance as well as inspirational topics.

Amy Hilliard-Jones is president of the Hilliard-Jones Marketing Group, a consulting firm in Chicago specializing in multicultural marketing. She enjoys being the mother of Angelica and Nicholas, and looks forward to writing and speaking more about her search for success, sanity and spiritual fulfillment.

Colleen Derrick Horning is a segment producer for WFAA-TV's *Good Morning Texas,* which airs live daily on ABC in Dallas, Texas. She especially enjoys producing the "Mom" segments. Her husband, Rob, also works at WFAA-TV. They've been married for six years and their combined family includes Nicholas, 16, and Sterling, 4. Colleen, as any writing mother would do, logs Sterling's amazing daily quotes. His latest: "Lucy, I'm home!"

Maryann Lee Jacob is a psychology teacher at Stevens High School in Rapid City, South Dakota. She has several poems published in South Dakota's *Prairie Winds.* She also has a college grammar book published entitled *Fundamentals of English.* She has five children and can be reached at 3304 Idlewild Court, Rapid City, SD or call 605-341-2843.

Jane Jayroe, Miss America 1967, has had a distinguished career as a television news anchor in the Oklahoma City and Dallas/Ft. Worth markets. She currently writes and produces inspirational and/or health messages for the broadcast and print markets. She has been published in *McCall's, Out of the Blue Delight Comes into Your Life* and *The Daily Oklahoman.* She is working on her first book. For information about her audiocassette tapes *Daily Devotionals,* write to her at PO Box 21537, Oklahoma City, OK 73156.

Sandy Jones wrote for the *Manson Journal* an Iowa newspaper, before moving to Santa Ana, California. She has written programs for church and children's theatre, and articles on marriage enrichment, wedding planning and family. Sandy and her husband, Steve, just completed their first book, a light-hearted story about becoming new grandparents.

Anne Jordan, R.N., is a mother of three and president of Children and Families, Inc. with her husband, Tim Jordan, M.D. They provide counseling for families, parenting and couples classes, and self-esteem summer camps for kids and teens. For information call 314-530-1883 or write 444 Chesterfield Center, Suite 205, Chesterfield, MO 63017.

Sherwin Kaufman is the grandson of the noted humorist Sholom Aleichem. He is a retired physician with a new career as a composer, lyricist and poet. *A Child's Vision* is one of a group of his poems and lyrics about children. He can be reached at 212-744-5788.

Christina Keenan is a freelance writer and poet who is also a registered nurse. She is a winner of several writing awards and is a published poet. Her work explores women's issues and motherhood. She specializes in creating custom gift poetry for occasions close to her heart. Christina resides in Frankfort, Illinois. She may be reached at 815-464-6843.

Mary Kenyon is the mother of six homeschooled children and author of *Homeschooling from Scratch.* She helps her husband, David, with the mail-order aspect of their bookstore, Once Upon a Time Family Books, in Manchester, Iowa. She can be reached at 319-927-6616.

Emily Perl Kingsley is a mother, lecturer and professional writer who has received 11 Emmy awards for her work writing scripts and songs for *Sesame Street.* A frequent speaker on the subject of disability rights, she serves on a committee to improve the way disabled people are portrayed in the media. She and her son, Jason, who has Down's syndrome, have appeared on *Oprah, Good Morning America* and *All My Children.*

Jane Kirby is a full-time mother and part-time nutrition writer. She is active in many woman's organizations including The Vermont Woman's Fund and Planned Parenthood. She lives with her son, Jacob, in Charlotte, Vermont.

Evelyn S. Kraut is a retired mathematics teacher and holds a Ph.D in Educational Theory. She is a full-time volunteer for Jewish Federation of Broward County, Florida. Her articles, stories and letters are published in local papers. She also raises scholarship funds for Hunter College, New York City.

Antoinette Kuritz is a career mom who has also taught at both the high school and elementary levels. Currently, she is a community relations coordinator for Barnes & Noble. She also writes a family focus column for a local newspaper. She can be reached at PO Box 67, Del Mar, CA 92014.

Cindy Ladage is a farmer's wife and mother of three children. She helps her husband on the farm and works part-time at the Illinois Department of Nuclear Safety. She also works as a freelance writer, writing both fiction and non-fiction material. She can be contacted at 35216 E. 5th Rd., Virden, IL 62690.

Victoria Lapikas is a full-time mother of four children. She works for a home medical equipment company and is a part-time student at Penn State University. She and her husband, Tom, live in Sharon, Pennsylvania.

Rosemary Laurey is a writer and special education teacher who considers the raising of three wonderful men her greatest oeuvre. A native of England, Rosemary lives in Columbus, Ohio, with her husband, George.

Kathryn Lay is a freelance writer and author living in Bedord, Texas, with her husband, Richard, and their daughter. Her writing includes personal experiences and inspirational pieces as well as children's fiction. She can be reached at 817-285-0166.

Jacklyn Lee Lindstrom recently retired and is at last devoting full time to her two passions—writing and painting. Her belief that "a smile lifts the spirit and makes fewer wrinkles" is reflected in her writings about the lighter side of life. You can contact her at 13533 Lynn Ave. S., Savage, MN 55378 or call 612-890-9333.

Michael Lindvall is a writer and minister and serves the First Presbyterian Church in Ann Arbor, Michigan, as pastor. He grew up in Minnesota and the Upper Peninsula of Michigan and is married to Terri, an artist. They have three children, Madeline, Benjamin and Grace. The story included is from *The Good News from North Haven,* available from Pocket Books. He is currently at work on a second book, also a collection of stories about life in community.

Sharon Linnéa has been a book editor and a staff writer for four national magazines. She and her husband have a son, Jonathan, and daughter, Linnéa. She speaks often at writers' conferences, as well as to schools on kids' needs for heroes. Autographed copies of either of her two latest books, the young-adult biographies *Raoul Wallenberg: The Man Who Stopped Death* (JPS) and *Princess Ka'iulani, Hope of a Nation, Heart of a People* (Eerdmans) can be purchased by sending $15.00 payable to Sharon Linnéa, c/o Shimersbrook, 290 River Road, Montague, NJ 07827.

Mike Lipstock is a 73-year-old optician who started writing after retirement. His work has appeared in close to 100 magazines and four anthologies. He is listed in *The Directory of American Poets and Fiction Writers.*

Jeanette Lisefski is the proud mother of three fantastic children and the founder of At-Home Mothers' Resource Center and the National Association of At-Home Mothers. These organizations provide mothers-at-home and those who want to be—with a wide array of information, services, support and encouragement to help make at-home motherhood work for them. You can reach Jeanette at At-Home Mothers' Resource Center, 406 E. Buchanan, Fairfield, IA 52556 or fax her at 515-469-3068; e-mail: ahmrc@lisco.com.

Mary Marcdante is an insightful, warm, down-to-earth professional speaker, trainer and writer whose programs on personal change, stress management and communication bring solutions and fun to conventions, businesses, communities and health-care conferences around the world. She helps people make healthier choices, push personal boundaries and live more creative, inspired and fulfilling lives. She is the author of *Inspiring Words for Inspiring People* and the upcoming *Questions for My Mother.* She can be reached at 619-792-6786 or write to PO Box 2417, Del Mar, CA 92014 or e-mail at mmarcdante@aol.com.

Terry Marotta is a syndicated columnist and author of *I Thought He Was a Speed Bump, and Other Excuses from Life in the Fast Line,* which is a collection of reader-favorite pieces. She lives with her husband, David, and six or seven other various life forms in Winchester, Massachusetts.

Janet Meyer is a writer and therapist in La Crosse, Wisconsin. She lives with her husband, Gerry, daughter, Melissa, and keeshond, Kudos. Her passions include parenting, pets and travel. Motherhood continues to amaze and inspire her.

Amsheva Miller lived in India where she and her husband adopted three Indian children and then returned to the United States. She is the developer and teacher of Cellular Repatterning™, a healing modality derived from an ancient Indian tradition of vibrational healing.

John Morris is a motivational speaker and writer who uses his major league baseball experiences—including playing in the World Series—as metaphors to illustrate techniques and attitudes needed for business and personal success. John lives with his wife, Linda, and two cats in St. Petersburg, Florida. You can reach him at 813-345-2722.

Sue Moustakas, mother of five, designed her career to combine raising the children with the love of teaching. She owns and operates SANDBOX Pre-Schools in the southwest suburbs of Chicago. She teaches early childhood classes and is a firm believer that young children are wizards.

Tom Mulligan is a freelance writer living in North Michigan. He writes articles, essays and fiction. He can be contacted for writing assignments at 8427 E. Au Sable Rd., St. Helen, MI 48656.

Sheryl Nicholson is an international professional speaker and mother of five. She speaks on leadership, sales and balancing life. Sheryl presents over 100 seminars a year to men and women. She is often seen on television and heard on radio. She can be contacted at 800-245-3735 or at her web site, sheryl.com.

Linda O'Camb is a registered nurse and proud mother of four children: Steve, George, Cheryl and Jennifer. She has three grandchildren: Bryanna, Landon and Kaela. Linda believes the bond between mother and child is like no other. She really enjoys her newfound family. Linda and her family live in Fillmore, Utah.

Rochelle Pennington is a freelance writer currently finishing her first book, *A Turning.* As a stay-at-home mother and wife, she is actively involved in Christian education and volunteer care for the terminally ill through Hospice Hope. She can be reached at N1911 Double D Road, Campbellsport, WI 53010 or call 414-533-5880.

Christine Beyer Perez grew up in Michigan but now lives in Kansas with her husband, Rudy, and their children, Valentina, Francesca and Jordan. She has written for *Cosmopolitan* and other national magazines and is currently managing editor of *Kansas City Persona.* Write to her at 14944 Glenwood, Overland Park, KS 66223.

Sarah A. Rivers is a Salem College graduate and a non-resident member of the Junior League of Charlotte, North Carolina. Her interests lie in writing inspirational poetry and nonfiction articles for publication. She and her husband, Ralph, live in Dallas, Texas. Sarah can be reached at 214-503-0195.

Dan Rosandich draws for publications nationwide including magazines, book publishers and newsletters and will tackle any assignments. His work has appeared in *Saturday Evening Post* and *National Review.* Rosandich can be reached anytime, voice or fax at 906-482-6234.

Joseph C. Rosenbaum is a retired accountant, living in Pembroke Pines, Florida, with his lovely wife, Christine. His son, Philip, is a business news producer for CNN in New York. Joseph survived the holocaust in Poland. After the war, he moved to the United States. His hobbies are writing, reading, walking, exercising and traveling.

Kathy Ryan is a widowed mother of four children. She is the director of social ministries and family life in a parish on Long Island. Kathy's work includes a ministry to young moms, bereaved people, and those divorced and separated. She uses storytelling as a vehicle for growth and healing in all her Family Life Programs.

Harley Schwadron is a self-taught cartoonist living in Ann Arbor, Michigan. He worked as a journalist and public relations writer before switching to cartooning full-time in 1984. His cartoons appear in *Barron's, Harvard Business Review, Wall Street Journal, National Law Journal* and many others. He can be reached at PO Box 1347, Ann Arbor, MI 48106 or call 313-426-8433.

Niki Sepsas is a freelance writer and tour guide living in Birmingham, Alabama. In addition to articles for travel and adventure magazines, he writes company and personality profiles, advertising copy, corporate newsletters, and marketing brochures. He can be reached at 205-942-5335.

Deborah Shouse is a writer whose work has appeared in *Newsweek, Redbook, Family Circle* and *Ms.* She is the author of several business handbooks, including *Name Tags Plus* and *Breaking the Ice,* and she coauthored *Working Woman's Communications Survival Guide.* Deborah also loves teaching, creative thinking and writing. You can reach Deborah at 913-671-7195.

Jeannie Ecke Sowell is a wife of 32 years, mother of two, grandmother of four and great-grandmother of one. She and her husband, Pickalleo, live in Camp Wood, Texas, where they work side by side in their own taxidermy studio. She can be reached at 210-597-3264.

Michael L. Staver is a motivational speaker/consultant and personal coach. He is passionately committed to encouraging people to pursue their dreams. When he is not on the road, he lives in California. He can be reached at 714-741-3012.

LeAnn Thieman is an author and speaker. Her presentations inspire us to live our priorities and balance our lives physically, mentally and spiritually while making a difference in the world. Contact her or order a copy of her book at 112 North College, Fort Collins, CO 80524 or call 970-223-1574.

Gerald E. Thurston Jr. is the drug prevention coordinator for a school district in Visalia, California. He is also pursuing a master's degree in interpersonal communication. He writes creatively as a hobby and is available to present workshops on organizational and interpersonal communication. He can be reached at 209-625-8805.

Judith Towse-Roberts is head of the creative writing department of Paseo Academy Arts High School in Kansas City, Missouri. She holds two master's degrees in counseling and secondary English. Judith is also an adjunct professor at Avila College. She is the mother of Tommy, Lisa and Jenni, her greatest loves.

Daryl Ott Underhill is president of In Any Event, Inc., specializing in motivational marketing programs and special interest publications. Her latest book project is *Writes of Passage . . . Every Woman Has a Story*. She can be reached at 4236 Rancho Dr., Phoenix, AZ 85018 or call 602-952-9472.

Glenn Van Ekeren is a dynamic speaker and trainer who is dedicated to assisting people and organizations in maximizing their potential. Glenn is the author of *The Speaker's Sourcebook, The Speaker's Sourcebook II* and the popular *Potential* newsletter. Glenn has a wide variety of written publications and audio and video presentations available. He can be reached at People Building Institute, 330 Village Circle, Sheldon, IA 51201 or call 800-899-4878.

Phyllis Volkens, an Iowa native, had a unique talent for transcribing life experiences from her heart to the printed page. When asked what she wrote about, she would say, "I write about people, what makes them laugh and cry." Her writing appeared in various newspapers and magazines including the *Denver Post, Reader's Digest* and *Chicken Soup for the Woman's Soul.* Phyllis passed away May 3, 1996. We all miss her.

Barbara L. Warner lives with her husband, Brian, and two sons outside of Dallas, Texas. She is a high school English teacher and freelance writer who is working to promote the fostering and adoption of our country's waiting children.

David Weatherford, Ph.D., is a child psychologist who has published numerous academic works as well as humorous, romantic and inspirational poems. He self-published *Love Is,* a book of aphorisms. His writing is influenced by coping with long-term kidney dialysis and surviving cancer. "Tribute to Mothers" is based on a poem written for his mother on Mother's Day. Contact David at 1658 Doubletree Lane, Nashville, TN 37217.

Beatrice Weeks is a wife, mother and registered nurse. She returned to the University of Michigan at age 50, earned a B.A. and subsequently wrote *The Secret of the Tenth Planet.* She presently enjoys her winters in New Port Richey, Florida, and summers near Manistee, Michigan.

Sue West is a publisher, educator, writer and meditation instructor. She has lived on four continents and feels at home just about everywhere. She can be reached at 5540 Fremont St., Oakland, CA 94608.

Jeanne White is the founder and president of *The Ryan White Foundation,* a national educational organization dedicated to preventing the further spread of HIV among youth. She speaks throughout the United States about her son, Ryan, and her work in AIDS prevention. She has written, with Susan Dworkin, *Weeding Out the Tears: A Mother's Story of Love, Loss and Renewal.* Published April, 1997 by Avon Books. Jeanne can be reached through the foundation at 1717 W. 86th St., Suite 220, Indianapolis, IN 46260 or call 800-444-7926.

Robert F. Whittle Jr. is an officer, an engineer and a farmer from Mystic, Connecticut. After graduating from West Point in 1990, Captain Whittle soldiered for five years in Germany and Korea, then earned an M.S. in Environmental Engineering at the University of Texas. He loves skiing, traveling and writing.

Jane Harless Woodward is an attorney and college professor. She and her husband, Larry, live in Virginia Beach, Virginia.

Peggy Andy Wyatt has appeared in national publications as well as those in countries around the world. She is presently the editorial cartoonist for a newspaper in Destin, Florida, having won several Florida Press Association Awards. She studied at Boston University and the Art Students League in New York City, completing her bachelor's degree at the University of Miami, Florida. She can be reached at PO Box 427, Destin, FL 32540.

Bettie B. Youngs, Ph.D., Ed.D., is an international lecturer and consultant living in Del Mar, California. She is the author of 14 books published in 28 languages including the bestseller *Values from the Heartland* and *Gifts of the Heart.* Her story is reprinted from *Values from the Heartland* (Health Communications, Inc.). You can contact Bettie by writing to 3060 Racetrack View Dr., Del Mar, CA 92014.

Permissions *(continued from page iv)*

A Tribute to Mothers. Reprinted with permission of David Weatherford. ©1997 David Weatherford.

The Choice. Reprinted with permission from *Guideposts Magazine.* ©1985 by Guideposts, Carmel, NY 10512.

Baby-Lift. Reprinted by permission of Sharon Linnéa and LeAnn Thieman. ©1997 Sharon Linnéa and LeAnn Thieman.

A Surprise Gift for Mother. Reprinted by permission of Sarah A. Rivers. ©1997 Sarah A. Rivers.

Mother's Day. Reprinted by permission of Niki Sepsas. ©1997 Niki Sepsas.

All Those Years. Reprinted by permission of Alice Collins. ©1997 Alice Collins.

The Bobby Pins. Reprinted by permission of Linda Goodman. ©1997 Linda Goodman.

Squeeze My Hand and I'll Tell You That I Love You. Reprinted by permission of Mary Marcdante. ©1997 Mary Marcdante.

In the Genes. Reprinted by permission of The Economics Press. Excerpted from *The Best of Bits & Pieces.* ©1995 The Economics Press.

A Child Is Born. Reprinted by permission of Reverend Michael Lindvall. ©1997 Reverend Michael Lindvall.

A Perfect Child. Reprinted with permission from *Guideposts Magazine.* ©1994 by Guideposts, Carmel, NY 10512.

Most Kids Are Born Only Once. Reprinted by permission of Joseph C. Rosenbaum. ©1997 Joseph C. Rosenbaum.

Room for Another. Reprinted with permission from *Guideposts Magazine.* ©1994 by Guideposts, Carmel, NY 10512.

The Unlocked Door. Reprinted by permission of New Leaf Press. Excerpted from *Moments for Mothers* by Robert Strand. ©1997 New Leaf Press.

Mom for a Day. Reprinted by permission of Anne Jordan. ©1997 Anne Jordan.

Daddy's Little Girl. Reprinted by permission from the January 1990 *Reader's Digest.* ©1990 by The *Reader's Digest* Association, Inc.

To Read When You're Alone. Reprinted by permission of Mike Staver. ©1997 Mike Staver.

With a Little Help from Mama. Reprinted with permission from *Guideposts Magazine.* ©1994 by Guideposts, Carmel, NY 10512.

My Mother Says . . . Reprinted by permission of Robert F. Whittle Jr. ©1997 Robert F. Whittle Jr.

The Inspection. Reprinted by permission of Glenn Van Ekeren. ©1997 Glenn Van Ekeren.

What Color Is a Hug? Reprinted by permission of Loretta Hall. ©1997 Loretta Hall.

Garlic Tales. Reprinted by permission of Mike Lipstock. ©1997 Mike Lipstock.

The Tooth Fairy. Reprinted by permission of Suzanne Moustakas. ©1997 Suzanne Moustakas.

Love Notes. Reprinted by permission of Antoinette Kuritz. ©1997 Antoinette Kuritz.

Saved by the Belt. Reprinted by permission of Randee Goldsmith. ©1997 Randee Goldsmith.

Red-Letter Failure Day. Reprinted by permission of Judith Towse-Roberts. ©1997 Judith Towse-Roberts.

The Midnight Caller. Reprinted by permission of Edith Dean. ©1997 Edith Dean.

My Son, Ryan. Reprinted by permission of Jeanne White. ©1997 Jeanne White.

Awright, Mom? Reprinted by permission of Christine Perez. ©1997 Christine Perez.

Moving Mountains. Reprinted by permission of Thomas Nelson Publishers. ©1997 Jim Stovall. Excerpted from *You Don't Have to Be Blind to See.* All rights reserved.

Hearts Across the World. Reprinted by permission of Amsheva Miller. ©1997 Amsheva Miller.

Real Vision. Reprinted by permission of Marsha Arons. ©1997 Marsha Arons.

Every Morning Is a Gift. Reprinted by permission of Deborah Bebb. ©1997 Deborah Bebb. Excerpted from *Woman's World* Magazine.

A Love Without Limits. Reprinted by permission of Chet Dembeck. ©1997 Chet Dembeck. Excerpted from *Woman's World* Magazine.

A Mother's Fight for a Special Child. Reprinted by permission of Tom Mulligan. ©1997 Tom Mulligan.

Welcome to Holland. Reprinted by permission of Emily Perl Kingsley. ©1987 Emily Perl Kingsley.

Mom's the Word. Reprinted by permission of Deborah Shouse. ©1997 Deborah Shouse.

Art 101. Reprinted by permission from the December 1995 *Reader's Digest.* ©1995 by The *Reader's Digest* Association, Inc.

Motherhood—A Trivial Pursuit? Reprinted by permission of Jacklyn Lee Lindstrom. ©1997 Jacklyn Lee Lindstrom.

A Mother's Letter to a Son Starting Kindergarten. Reprinted by permission of Rebecca Christian. ©1997 Rebecca Christian.

Tale of a Sports Mom. Reprinted by permission of Judy Bodmer. ©1997 Judy Bodmer.

No More Oatmeal Kisses. Reprinted by permission, ©Newsday, Inc., 1969.

The Signs of Advanced Momhood. Reprinted by permission of Liane Kupferberg Carter. ©1997 Liane Kupferberg Carter.

Forever, For Always, and No Matter What! Reprinted by permission of Jeanette Lisefski. ©1997 Jeanette Lisefski.

Breaking In Baby. Excerpted from *Babies and other Hazards of Sex* by Dave Barry. ©1984, Rodale Press. Reprinted with permission. All rights reserved. Reprinted with permission from the *Reader's Digest* Association, Inc.

When a Child Goes off to College. Reprinted by permission of Stanley Volkens, executor for Phyllis Volkens.

Mother's Helper. Reprinted by permission of Jane Jayroe. ©1997 Jane Jayroe.

The Stepmother. Reprinted by permission of Jennifer Graham. ©1997 Jennifer Graham.

An Indescribable Gift. Reprinted by permission of Jeanette Lisefski. ©1997 Jeanette Lisefski.

Motherwit. Reprinted by permission of Amy Hilliard-Jones. ©1997 Amy Hilliard-Jones.

She Looks Like Us. Reprinted by permission of Judy Farris. ©1997 Judy Farris.

Mom. Reprinted by permission of Barbara L. Warner. ©1997 Barbara L. Warner.

I Don't Want a New Baby. Reprinted by permission of Rosemary Laurey. ©1997 Rosemary Laurey.

Out of Our Hands. Reprinted by permission of Colleen Derrick Horning. ©1997 Colleen Derrick Horning.

A Treasure Without Price. Reprinted by permission of Sandra Julian Barker. ©1997 Sandra Julian Barker.

The Chosen One. Reprinted by permission of Sue West. ©1997 Sue West.

Dance with Me. Reprinted by permission of Jean Harper. ©1997 Jean Harper.

The Prognosis. Reprinted by permission of Rochelle M. Pennington. ©1997 Rochelle M. Pennington.

The Family Dinner. Reprinted by permission of Shari Cohen. ©1997 Shari Cohen.

Bouncing Back. Reprinted by permission of Harper Collins Publishers Inc. ©1997 by Joan Rivers. Excerpt from *Bouncing Back* by Joan Rivers.

My Daughter, My Teacher. Reprinted by permission of Janet S. Meyer. ©1997 Janet S. Meyer.

The Broken Doll. Reprinted by permission of Dan Clark. ©1997 Dan Clark.

A Child's Vision. Reprinted by permission of Sherwin Kaufman. ©1997 Sherwin Kaufman.

May Day. Reprinted by permission of Donna Getzinger. ©1997 Donna Getzinger.

The Day I Was Too Busy. Reprinted by permission of Cindy Ladage. ©1997 Cindy Ladage.

The Play's the Thing. Reprinted by permission of Pocket Books, a division of Simon & Schuster from *I Am a Mother of Sons* by Jayne Jaudon Ferrer. ©1996 by Jayne Jaudon Ferrer.

Swift Second. Reprinted by permission of Daryl Ott Underhill. ©1997 Daryl Ott Underhill.

When Mother Came to Tea. Reprinted by permission of Margie M. Coburn. ©1997 Margie M. Coburn.

Finding Her There. Reprinted by permission of Christina Keenan. ©1997 Christina Keenan.

Angel in Uniform. Reprinted by permission of Jeannie Ecke Sowell. ©1997 Jeannie Ecke Sowell.

The Healing. Reprinted by permission of Sandy Jones. ©1997 Sandy Jones.

Adopting a Dream. Reprinted by permission of Kathryn Lay. ©1997 Kathryn Lay.

Honey, You'd Better Sit Down. Reprinted by permission of Sheryl Nicholson. ©1997 Sheryl Nicholson.

A Promise on Mother's Day. From the book *Where Miracles Happen: True Stories of Heavenly Encounters* by Joan Wester Anderson. ©1995 by Joan Wester Anderson. Published by Brett Books, Inc. Reprinted by permission.

Mother and Child Reunion. Reprinted by permission of Carolyn Campbell. ©1997 Carolyn Campbell.

After 40 Years. Reprinted by permission of Linda O'Camb. ©1997 Linda O'Camb.

Four Angels. From *Angel Letters* by Sophy Burnham. ©1991 by Sophy Burnham.

Reprinted by permission of Ballantine Books, a division of Random House, Inc.

Home Run for Mom. Reprinted by permission of John Morris. ©1997 John Morris.

Remembering Will Have to Do. Reprinted by permission of Victoria A. Lapikas. ©1997 Victoria A. Lapikas.

Celebrating My Mother. Reprinted by permission of Terry Marotta. ©1992 Terry Marotta.

A Motherless Child. Reprinted by permission of Jane Kirby. ©1997 Jane Kirby.

Robin. Excerpted from *Barbara Bush: A Memoir.* Reprinted with special permission from Simon & Schuster ©1994. All rights reserved.

When the Telephone Rang. Excerpt from *Lessons of Love* by Melody Beattie. ©1994 by Melody Beattie. Reprinted by permission of Harper Collins Publishers, Inc.

John. Reprinted by permission of Muriel Cochrane. ©1997 Muriel Cochrane.

To Captain Candy and the Women Who Took to the Skies. Reprinted by permission of Diana L. Chapman. ©1997 Diana L. Chapman.

I Was Born for This Job. Reprinted by permission of Billie B. Chesney. ©1997 Billie B. Chesney.

Grandma's Garden. Reprinted by permission of Lynnette Curtis. ©1997 Lynnette Curtis.

Dinner Out. Reprinted by permission of Maryann Lee Jacobs. ©1997 Maryann Lee Jacobs.

We Need a Rock. Reprinted by permission of Kathy Ryan. ©1997 Kathy Ryan.

Mama and Miss Jordan. Reprinted by permission from the July 1989 *Reader's Digest.* ©1989 by The *Reader's Digest* Association, Inc.

When a Mother Blows Out 75 Candles. Reprinted by permission of Alice Collins. ©1997 Alice Collins.

Six of the Seven Wonders of My World. Reprinted by permission of Jane Harless Woodward. ©1997 Jane Harless Woodward.

Mailboxes. Reprinted with permission by publisher Health Communications, Inc., Deerfield Beach, Florida, from *Values from the Heartland* by Bettie B. Youngs. ©1995 Bettie B. Youngs.

My Mother's Riches. Reprinted by permission of Mary Kenyon. ©1997 Mary Kenyon.

Just Plain Wrong. Reprinted by permission of Gerald E. Thurston Jr. ©1997 Gerald E. Thurston Jr.

Great Lady. Excerpted from *Holy Sweat* by Tim Hansel. ©1989, Word, Inc., Dallas, Texas. Reprinted with permission. All rights reserved.

Prayer for My Mother. Permission granted by Ann Landers and Creators Syndicate.

Books to Nurture Your Body & Soul!

Chicken Soup for the Surviving Soul

Heartwarming accounts of courageous people who found the power to battle cancer in their endless hope, unwavering faith and steadfast determination will inspire you to adopt a positive attitude, discover your faith and cherish every moment. Just what the doctor ordered for healing body, mind and soul. #4029—$12.95

Chicken Soup for the Soul® Cookbook

In the spirit of *Chicken Soup for the Soul*, these inspiring stories revisit time-honored values such as love, loyalty and courage. Each story is paired with a kitchen-tested recipe providing nourishment for both body and soul. # 3545—$16.95

Chicken Soup for the Soul® at Work

This *New York Times* business bestseller is a timely addition to the ever-popular *Chicken Soup for the Soul* collection. This volume provides a much-needed spiritual boost for readers living in an age of global markets, corporate downsizing and unstable economies. #424X—$12.95

Selected books are also available in hardcover, large print, audiocassette and compact disc.

Available in bookstores everywhere or call **1-800-441-5569** for Visa or MasterCard orders. Prices do not include shipping and handling. Your response code is **CSM**.

Hear the Heartwarming Goodness of Chicken Soup for the Soul® on Audio

Health Communications, Inc. proudly presents its audio collection of the *Chicken Soup for the Soul* series. Each book is available on tape or CD for your convenience. Brighten your life by listening to these words of inspiration.

The Best of the Original Chicken Soup for the Soul® Audio
Code 3723 one 90-minute cassette **$9.95**
Code 4339 one 70-minute CD **$11.95**

The Best of A 2nd Helping of Chicken Soup for the Soul® Audio
Code 3766 two 90-minute cassettes....**$14.95**
Code 4347 one 70-minute CD **$11.95**

The Best of A 3rd Serving of Chicken Soup for the Soul® Audio
Code 4045 one 90-minute cassette **$9.95**
Code 4355 one 70-minute CD **$11.95**

The Best of a 4th Course of Chicken Soup for the Soul® Audio
Code 4711 one 90-minute cassette **$9.95**
Code 472X one 70-minute CD.............**$11.95**

Chicken Soup for the Soul® Audio Gift Set
Code 3103 6 cassettes, 7 hours...........**$29.95**

Available at your favorite bookstore or call 1-800-441-5569 for Visa or MasterCard orders. Prices do not include shipping and handling. Your response code is **CSM.**

Despite the fact that one in every six people in the United States is a grandparent, there is no ritual of celebration for such a big life-passage and no instruction manual for being a grandparent...until now! This comprehensive practical guide uses anecdotes, quotes and exercises to help readers develop their own grandparenting strategy and make the most of this rewarding stage of life.

1-55874-397-9, 200 pp., 6 ½ x 9, trade paper..................................$10.95

Available at your favorite bookstore or call 1-800-5569 for Visa or MasterCard orders. Prices do not include shipping and handling. Your response code is CSM.